Yeshiva University Museum

JOSÉ
GURVICH
AND THE JEWISH IDENTITY

museogurvich

general coordination
Prof. Alicia Haber

monograph
Alicia Haber

texts
Felipe Arocena
Nisso Acher
Joséphine Balken
Martín Gurvich
Isaac Margulies
Manuel Tenenbaum

graphic design
Taller de Comunicación

correction
Lic. Aída R. Altieri

translation
Richard Manning
Mariana Méndez
Matías Lasarte

photography
Carly Angenscheidt
Alfredo Rowinski
Testoni Estudios
Eduardo Baldisan
Foto Síntesis
Arturo Sánchez
Marcel Lousteau

printing
Ronor
Buenos Aires, Argentina

ISBN: 978-9974-7778-4-2

Museo Gurvich
Ituzaingó 1377 - phone + (598) 2915 7826
11000 Montevideo – Uruguay

Acknowledgements

Alicia Haber would like to thank Julia Añorga de Gurvich (Totó), who provided her with invaluable information on the artist in numerous interviews; Martín Gurvich and the Fundación Gurvich for their constant support during the research and for making it possible to access pieces of the collection yet unknown, and with many varied documents; the collectors who let her access their cultural wealth; Vera Jordan, Pinjas "Pancho" Goetz, and Boris and Maia Blinde for all the information they gave her on Gurvich's life and work in Ramot Menashé.

She also thanks all those who warmly collaborated, in the most diverse ways, with the research and production of this book: Fundación Alon; Joséphine Balken; Mr. And Mrs. Yoel Barnea; Perla Bawnik; Mr. And Mrs. Marcelo Bernat; Bernardo Bernstein; Naftali Bezem; Mr. And Mrs. León Biriotti; Mr. And Mrs. Carlos Bister; Mr. And Mrs. Enrique Cadenas; Castells - Rematadores; Jorge y Martín Castillo; Cecilia De Torres; Mr. And Mrs. Eduardo Elsztain; Ricardo Esteves; Galería Ciudadela; Galería de las Misiones; Galería Oscar Prato; Galería Palatina; Galería Sur; Mr. And Mrs. Ernesto Galperín; Mr. And Mrs. Nicolás Galperín; Mr. And Mrs. Víctor Ganón; Mr. And Mrs. Bernardo Graiver; Mr. And Mrs. Gruneisen; Rafael and Cynthia Karel; Eva and Osías Kaufman; Mr. And Mrs. Israel Lublinerman; Enrique and Eduardo Maiorano; Mr. And Mrs. Enrique Manhard; Tova Medin Malevska; Aida Melman; Mr. And Mrs. Hugo Mosca; Javier Mosca; Juan Lucas Pezzino; Susana Poch; Norberto Ratner; Mr. And Mrs. Alegre Sassón; Edith, Emilia and Nathan Sassón; Esther Shahar; León Shimmel; Mr. And Mrs. Jorge Stainfeld; Mariane Trier; Mr. And Mrs. Darío Werthein; Mr. And Mrs. Marcos Zimet.

She is especially grateful to the chaverim of the Ramot Menashé kibbutz, for their warm and generous help: Ami, Bat, Blinde, Boris and Maia; Diamant, Abraham and Manya; Pinjas "Pancho" Goetz; Ari Goldstein; Vera Jordan; Moshe Landecker; Irit Landecker; Lía Malinoff; Eugenio Rosen; Nitza Shapira.

JOSÉ
GURVICH
AND THE JEWISH IDENTITY

Alicia Haber

To his wife Julia and all those who love Gurvich's work with passion

Universe
1970
oil on canvas
54 x 38 cm

Index

I have trodden
the world
extensively;
the only two
countries
I could live in
are Uruguay and
Israel.

José Gurvich, chats with Totó

Israel is the Land of ancestors; people work there and build for the future and I feel part of it.

José Gurvich, chats with Totó

There is nothing like Uruguay for me; I came from a country with discrimination to one that does not discriminate and I have to acknowledge it for that.

José Gurvich, chats with Totó

Kibbutz composition
c. 1964
oil on wood
79 x 35 cm

Preface

It is a great pleasure and honour for me to write a few lines for the prologue of this beautiful book about José Gurvich and the Jewish identity.

First, because I am delighted that my father's work is increasingly appreciated and studied. He strongly believed that many people should in a sense be part of his work, which is a symbol of optimism and of joy of life, with all its complexities. He was a very warm person and he had a very positive vision of human beings; he had friends wherever he went, Jewish and Christian, black and white, Uruguayan, European, Israeli and American. I am convinced that because his work is so warm, visually rich and creative, and because its message is so optimistic, it will continue to be discovered by more and more people and will be increasingly appreciated as time goes by.

Second, because the Gurvich Museum in Montevideo is going to great lengths to offer the public an exemplary cultural space with top level international exhibitions, activities and publications. In a country like Uruguay that has limited resources, a small population and where cultural activities are not supported by companies, it is a big challenge for the Gurvich Museum to mount important exhibitions and launch publications such as this book.

The Gurvich Museum, building on the efforts of the José Gurvich Foundation, has produced numerous books and catalogues, but this one is undoubtedly unique as it is an in-depth and rigorous study of one of the themes my father was most concerned with, which was his Jewishness and his connection to Israel, where his parents and his sister are laid to rest. The author, Professor Alicia Haber, dedicated more than a year to researching and writing the text, and she also went on a voyage of discovery to the Gurvich Kibbutz in Israel.

In this book we have included almost all the artist's work in which the Jewish or Israeli theme is explicit, and also pieces that feature this element in more subtle ways. Gurvich was not a "religious" man but he was undeniably fascinated with his Jewish roots and the kibbutz, and he was very open spiritually, which led him to his biblical and religious heritage. At a time when religious and sacred images have almost disappeared from Western art, Gurvich was taking a risk when he ventured into explicit religious subjects and scenes from Bible stories. But he succeeded because he did not sacrifice his artistic integrity, and although he was not religious he has left behind a rich religious oeuvre. Gurvich was a universal man, he did not belong to any sect, but that was no obstacle when it came to recognizing and appreciating his roots. A person can be secular and Jewish, universal and Jewish, Uruguayan and Jewish.

My third reason for being delighted is that I am very interested in "religious" or spiritual art. In other words, art that connects with a theological or spiritual tradition, art that presents us with a world of images, characters and situations that take us to a higher plane. Obviously in different traditions this is evoked in different ways. I believe art should help to raise human consciousness, not only "religious" art but also "profane" art; it should help lift us to a higher level. The aim of "religious" art is to lead us towards some kind of transcendence, but obviously not all "religious" art is good art since the visual aspect plays a key role. This means that to succeed, there must be some expression of a religious theme that is also visually beautiful, rich and in some way original.

I am a follower of the Hindu spiritual tradition called Vaishnavism, which is a monotheist current and I have seen in India how religious or spiritual arts (as I prefer to call them) are still very important and present in different schools of dance, music, painting, sculpture, theatre, etc. And I have come to the conclusion that there are great artists and great art in all cultures and in all times in history.

I hope that reading this book and viewing these works of art will help to open up a path to elevation, enrichment and happiness.

Martín Gurvich
Director Museo Gurvich

It is hard to be a Jew
1974
oil on canvas
50 x 40 cm

The Endurance of the Jews

Felipe Arocena

The main aim of Alicia Haber's book on José Gurvich is to recognise his Jewish identity and analyse how it emerged in his work throughout his life. This is the overall objective, but the way this theme is developed, the sources used to nourish it and the conceptual framework that holds it together, all combine to make this an essay on Jewish culture in general and its regeneration in Uruguay in particular.

The artist's original name was Zusmanas Gurvicius. He was born in Lithuania in 1927 into a family of Ashkenazi Jewish origin but he could not be given a Jewish name because anti-Semitism was rife, and one of the many forms it took was that ethnic names were forbidden. To escape from oppression and from the looming threat of genocide, the family emigrated to Montevideo, Uruguay, in 1932.

The family consisted of the parents, Jaie and Jacobo, and two children, Gurvich and his sister. He was five years old and he had never heard so much as one syllable of Spanish spoken. When he was registered at the "Chile" State primary school in the Barrio Sur neighbourhood, he became José Gurvich overnight. The first time someone said, "Hey kid, what's your name?" his mother must have yelled "Yoshale" (the short form of Joseph). He quickly adapted to Uruguayan culture on the streets near the Rambla down by the river, amid the small shops run by austere Jews and at the simple house parties on Saturdays. Years later, during his stay on a kibbutz in Israel, where reviving the Hebrew language was a national crusade, his friends and companions came to know him as Yuski, the shepherd that painted in his spare time.

Each of these names marked a key cultural influence in his life. His early years were lived in fear, poverty, segregation and submission in Lithuania, where a few years later the savage genocide of Jews was fiercer and crueller than anywhere else in Europe. The world of his first five years of life emerged in many of his artistic works, for example in *Boceto para cuadro de Hombre Judío en Lituania* (1973) (*Sketch for the painting of a Jewish man in Lithuania*). The main figure has an expression of terror on his face, his eyes seem reluctant to look at something but he cannot look away, his mouth is no more than a line but it shows disgust, revulsion and disbelief all at once. He is a witness in hell, which is not shown. And there is a man seated with a glass of wine in his hand whose posture suggests impotence in the face of the tragedy at his neighbour's house, a tragedy that will soon engulf him as he sits in the bosom of his family.

For a time, when Gurvich was a boy, Uruguay was under the Terra dictatorship[1] and there were certain anti-immigration policies and some

It is hard to be a Jew
c. 1969
ink on paper
13 x 10 cm

minority feeling in favour of National Socialism, but this was not the dominant mood of the country. The immigrants were free, and they felt that with hard work and perseverance they could achieve a better life. The Jewish community was able to express itself publicly, not only in secular institutions but also in religious ones, and the stigma of being an immigrant gradually faded. At home they continued to speak Yiddish and celebrate Jewish traditions, and Gurvich's mother was free to run the household in line with their Jewish culture.

To the outside world, José was just another Uruguayan kid who learned the national anthem, wore his white uniform to school and did not stand out among the many children of other immigrants including Lebanese, Armenians and Italians. Nonetheless, to his mother he continued to be Yoshale. That was a time when immigrants adapted quickly to Uruguay, a time when the ideal was to build an integrated, secular, homogenous, middle class, Westernised country. The fact that someone was Jewish was irrelevant because what mattered was the model of a country composed of citizens with universal rights, one culture and one language.

In 1955 Gurvich made his first trip to Israel, and there were to be two more visits, in 1965 and 1969. Many people who knew him have said that the first visit wrought a great change in him, and that living in the socialist, communal utopia of a kibbutz and working to help build the State of Israel led him to discover a new way of being Jewish. The Israelis were transforming a barren, stony desert into a garden, they were turning a poor and sparsely populated land into a rich and densely populated country that was to surprise the world with its universities, its technological innovations and its ability to overcome apparently any difficulty. The people there spoke Hebrew and there were Jewish symbols everywhere, in public institutions, on the kibbutz, in private homes, in the press, on street names, even on the postage stamps. And when José Gurvich was there he was known as Yuski.

Gurvich had three first names one after the other, Zusmanus, José and Yuski, and each not only marks a stage in his own life but also represents one of the main characteristics of being Jewish in the last century. Zusmanas Gurvicius relates to the image of the ghetto Jew who was persecuted, discriminated against, treated as a criminal, tortured, attacked in pogroms and has his family, friends and neighbours killed. Gurvich was fortunate enough to be taken away from that, but he would never forget that life experience. José (and Yoshale) personify the exiled Jew, the Wandering Jew who finds a new homeland, the man with a double identity who begins to develop two parallel senses of belonging. In public he is a citizen of the country that takes him in, accepts him and opens the doors to life's opportunities, but at home and in his dreams and in what he eats he is Jewish and he speaks Yiddish. And lastly there is Yuski, the Jew that witnesses the founding of the State of Israel and sees it as an event that heralds the Messiah, as the utopia at the end of the persecution of his culture; that is to say as his personal redemption.[1]

This book is about all three aspects of Gurvich, the child that was born in a small Jewish town in Lithuania, the youngster that grew up in a Jewish immigrant neighbourhood in Montevideo and absorbed Jewish mythology from his mother, and the man that matured and dedicated part of his life to the building of Israel. But the main focus of this book is the Jewish Gurvich; this aspect is given far more weight than the Gurvich in Cerro[2] in Montevideo, the one from the Torres García Workshop or the one that travelled to Greece, New York and Europe, which are perhaps better-known aspects of the painter's life.

When the author leaves Gurvich's Torres García phase aside and focuses on his Jewish dimension she is delving into an area of his life that is not so well known and has not been analysed so much. Needless to say, if it had not been for the crucial influence of Torres García, Gurvich would not have been who he was, but that master shone so bright he ended up eclipsing the unique, individual qualities of many of his disciples, so we can reasonably surmise that Gurvich became what he became by pursuing his Jewish leanings and distancing himself from the Constructive Universalism of his teacher.

The author builds up Gurvich's character using a whole range of research material including scores of interviews with many people including the painter's wife, Julia Añorga (Totó), friends from different circles like Eva Kaufman and Vera Jordan, his disciples like Antonio Nigro, colleagues like Ernesto Vila, and his one-time neighbours in Barrio Sur. She gathers information from different sources including an account by the artist Jorge Damiani. She travelled to the Ramot Menashé kibbutz, where Gurvich lived and where his mother and father are laid to rest, and she met his erstwhile companions who remember him tending the sheep with a rifle over his shoulder to scare off wolves or enemies, and who remember him painting.

She uses her own life experiences to achieve empathy with her character since Haber is herself a Uruguayan Jew, the daughter of immigrants, and she too lived in Israel and worked on a kibbutz. She interprets things the artist wrote; some of these are notes about his state of mind that he just jotted down, but others are in a more reflective spirit and convey his ideas about how he saw his art, his life and his trade. She submerges herself in writers he liked, such as Antonio Machado and Shalom Aleichem. She uses many books on Jewish culture in order to

Sketch for Jewish man in Lithuania
c. 1973
felt-tip pen on paper
20 x 12,5 cm

[1] This reference of the three Jewish figures is taken from a lecture by the Spanish writer and scholar of Jewish culture, Leopoldo Azancot: Marc Chagall: a Jewish life, 1999, Juan March Foundation, Madrid. Gurvich never actually changed his name in Israel as other Jews did. Yuski is a Yiddish diminutive, not Hebrew, and Gurvich was also called this by his Zionist Marxist friends in Uruguay.

go deeper into the interpretation of ethnic and religious symbols. She brings in the writings of other notable Jews like the philosophers Raymond Aaron and Isaiah Berlin, the sociologist Samuel Eisenstadt, and the father of psychoanalysis, Sigmund Freud, for their experiences and comments on the subject of Jewish identity. And lastly she is an art historian armed with new codes to understand Gurvich's work, which is a vital part of her whole effort, and she processes all that information. Her main thesis is quite clear: to understand the artist's change of direction towards his Jewish roots we must immerse ourselves in Jewish culture in general, in the experiences of Jewish immigrants in Uruguay, and in the experience of being involved in kibbutz life and in the construction of the State of Israel.

It is no coincidence that this book should have appeared now, at the start of the 21st century. For the past two decades we have seen ethno-cultural minorities striving to gain recognition for their own cultures and seeking to avoid assimilation into the dominant culture of the land they live in. Today, groups of immigrants and their descendents, sub-national minorities and native peoples, are working to re-create their cultural identities. They are asserting their political right to not disappear and to make visible their contributions to the national states they are part of. This has been called the politics of recognition or the politics of identity, and it is the backbone of the theory of multiculturalism. This book is a great example of that trend, as I will now explain.

Soon after the end of World War II, in a 1946 text entitled *Reflections on the Jewish Question*, Sartre criticized the French policy of assimilation because in attempting to salvage the Jews as human beings it destroyed them as Jews, "This means that it is an effort to separate the Jew from his religion, his family, his ethnic community, and to place him in the melting pot of democracy, from which he shall emerge alone and naked because each product is solitary and similar to all the others. In the United States this is called a policy of assimilation."

This was the dominant policy in the West toward the Jews and towards ethnic minorities in general. It was geared to emphasising their identity as citizens of the nation, and confining their cultural identity to the domestic and private sphere. Some Jews fell into line with this and adopted a strategy of assimilation as a way to protect themselves, even at the risk of allowing their culture to be eradicated. But today there is a shift towards multiculturalism, and many countries have modified their assimilation policies and reacted positively to pressure from numerous cultural communities that live in the same land and want their cultural identity rights be supported and their contributions to the country to be recognized.

Uruguay is a relative latecomer on the international scene but this movement is evident, as can be seen from four laws enacted in the last six years. There is Law 17.817 (2004) to "Fight against Racism, Discrimination and Xenophobia", which in article 2 explicitly condemns discrimination based on "...race, skin colour, religion, national or ethnic origin". Also Law 18.059 (2006), the "National Day of Candombe,[3] Afro-Uruguayan Culture and Racial Equality", where it is laid down in article 2 that the State recognizes and values "...the contribution made by the Afro-descendent population to the building of the nation and to the composition of Uruguay's cultural identity". The third is Immigration Law 18.250 (2008), which states in article 14 that "The State shall respect the cultural identity of immigrants and their families and shall promote their maintenance of links with their country of origin." And lastly the 2009 "Charrúa[4] Nation and Indigenous Identity Resistance Day" bill, which promotes "The recognition of the indigenous contribution and presence in the national composition process".

Sketch for Jewish festival (Pesach)
c. 1973
Watercolour on paper
9 x 14.5 cm

This book is in harmony with this broad multicultural context. It is like a new effort to retrieve and recognise the diverse cultural forces that were involved in building Uruguay, and it does so by focusing on the Jewish dimension of one of the country's outstanding artists of the last century.

Specifically Jewish elements and themes did not emerge in Gurvich's work until his first trip to Israel, but from then on they featured more and more. Among the many Jewish motifs he employs there are some that pertain to festivals and holidays, as in *Bocetos para Festividad judía (Sketches for Jewish Festival)*, a watercolour from 1973. The scene is dominated by a bearded patriarch dressed in his blue robe, and there are rustic peasants sharing the bread and wine at a rectangular table alongside a seven-branch candelabra. There are also numerous versions of *Composiciones del Kibutz (Compositions of the Kibbutz)* from the 1956 to 1970 period; they have ladders going up to the heavens, sheep, carts and the Bible. And in the more specific 1969 ink drawing *Qué pesado es ser judío (It is hard to be a Jew)* we see a patriarch in his enormous overcoat carrying the weight of a tree of life on his back, and again there is the ladder, the scrolls of the *Torah*, the Bible and the candelabra.

A whole range of themes from Jewish religion appeared in Gurvich's work including Genesis, the Sabbath, Sarah the matriarch, many events from the Bible, Cain and Abel, Isaac, Jacob, Jesus as a great Jewish martyr, the feast of *Hanukkah* that celebrates the liberation of Israel from Seleucid domination, the Passover that commemorates the end of Jewish slavery in Egypt and the start of the Exodus, and the *Sukkot* festival, which recalls the Hebrews' struggle to survive during the Exodus. This book offers an in-depth analysis of how all these Jewish motifs appear in Gurvich's work, and of what they mean.

One cannot emphasise enough that there is not just *one* monolithic and homogenous Jewish culture. As happens with all cultures, Jewish culture is being constantly reinterpreted in each context —historical, geographical and personal. For this reason, we cannot talk of its essence —a term so favoured by orthodox believers and fundamentalists in any belief system. Nevertheless, we *can* talk about Jewish culture because it embodies a specific ethnic history and it has its own symbols, its land, its religion, its common language and its catalogue of rituals. All of these serve to distinguish it from other ways of understanding the world and give rise to a feeling of belonging. And this is what many of its adherents, some in very unfavourable conditions, wanted to transmit to the new generations so that Jewish culture could carry on through time.

Gurvich was a person with many identities but two stand out, the Uruguayan-Jew and the Jewish-Uruguayan, which is sometimes called a "scripted identity" and is based on an experience shared by other descendants of immigrants in Uruguay such as Armenians, Lebanese or other Jews. Here, and also in other respects, there is a strong parallel between Gurvich's life and work and that of Marc Chagall, for whom he had the greatest admiration. Chagall was a Russian Jew, born in Vitebsk, and like Gurvich he lived in a ghetto (at the end of the 19th century). He fled from anti Semitism and migrated to France, where he declared he had been born again. When he travelled to the land of Israel for the first time —before the State was founded— he discovered his Jewish roots. He was a Jewish Russian who bore witness to his Judaism and was conscious he had to transmit that cultural and military experience if Judaism was to endure. His personal endurance and survival, and Gurvich's, becomes that of all Jews. Like with Gurvich, a large part of his work was based on and inspired by Jewish culture, but each of them interpreted this in his own particular way and merged it with many other influences including surrealism, constructivism, Paris, Russia, Jewish immigration, Montevideo, Cerro, to name just the most obvious.

It was in this way, through their art, that they made a contribution to keeping their culture alive, but they also made a contribution through how they lived and the things they did. In 1999 there was an exhibition in Spain called *Marc Chagall: Jewish Traditions* which aimed at "Showing how Chagall's art was based on Jewish culture and traditions." Gurvich, with his Uruguayan and Jewish cultures, deserves the same, and that is precisely what Alicia Haber achieves in this book.

FELIPE AROCENA is Doctor of Social Sciences and essayist. His specialization areas: multiculturalism, history and society in Latin America, globalization and identity, sociology of culture and public opinion. Author of several books, among which are: *William Henry Hudson Life, Literature and Science*; *Cuban interviews: stories of a divided nation*. He is a lecturer in the Faculty of Social Sciences of the Universidad de la República, Uruguay. In 2001, he won the Annual Award of Literature of Uruguay (Literary Essay category).

End notes

1   1933-1938. Gabriel Terra (1873-1942) was elected to power in 1931, led a coup d'etat against his government in 1933, enacted a new Constitution in 1934, and ruled by dictatorial decree until 1938.

2   A neighbourhood in western Montevideo where immigrants from East Europe settled, and where Gurvich lived part of his adult life.

3   Afro-Uruguayan music genre.

4   Native indigenous people of the land today known as Uruguay. Many of them were killed in the infamous Salsipuedes (literally Get-out-if-you-can) massacre in 1931.

Fantasy world
1967
oil on plaster
38 x 29 cm

Game of mirrors

Gerardo Caetano

The life of José Gurvich (1927-1974) had as many different colours as his marvellous palette, and one of Alicia Haber's great virtues in this book is that she guides us wisely on the voyage to discover them and thus we acquire a deeper insight into the painter's vision and his work. It is an opportunity to delve into an identity that houses a cluster of identities, a complex and fascinating collection that can revive roots and dialogues we thought were irretrievably lost. Gurvich himself gives us a key indication when after his parents died he feared he might be left without roots, but then he found the right way to rediscover them, "You should seek for the other in the mirror, the other that walks with you."

In this book Alicia Haber invites us into a sort of game of mirrors. Her main aim is to focus on the components of Gurvich's identity that are to be found in Jewish subject matter. He always had these elements inside him, but it was only after a quite radical search that he managed to integrate them intensely into his compositions. And at the same time he was able to discover himself in a holistic way, affirm as never before his creative freedom and attain the peak of his art. Haber explains that her main objective is to identify and clarify "Gurvich's Judaism and his creative work with Jewish content." And throughout her very rigorous research, she always worked with the basic hypothesis that there is a crucial link between the time that Gurvich, with his solid Torres García training, "...began to explore other paths of expression and define his own language, iconography and subjects," and a profound re-awakening of his Jewish identity, with all the many components that go right down to his roots.

It is no coincidence that the author had to travel and move around to track down the clues in this search. She had to go to many places, partly because Gurvich liked travelling and the puzzle of his life involved living very intensely in different locations. And the author herself had to tackle this more radical dimension and research the inner impact these journeys had on the painter. As Cirlot says, a journey "...is never merely moving, but involves the tension of the search and of the change that underlies that movement".

Alicia Haber speaks about this in her introduction, "...I visited the Ramot Mensahe kibbutz and acquired a feel for this place where the artist lived, worked and painted. In addition I interviewed many of his Uruguayan, Argentine, Chilean and European friends and companions, I travelled to Tel Aviv, Ramat Aviv and Jerusalem to talk to people who knew him and to see pieces of his work that they have... I saw many of his compositions that were new to me, on the kibbutz and in private collections in Israel and other places, and I studied them with a particular eye on their Jewish iconography. This enriched my knowledge enormously, it was a new source of nourishment, and it led me to new ways to understand Gurvich's work, this time with a more precise approach as regards time, space and subject matter... During this process I became involved with, and renewed my enthusiasm for, the whole area of symbology. I read very widely about festivals, the Bible, new studies on identity and multiculturalism, and new perspectives on Masada, the kibbutz movement and Zionism. And as I followed this learning path I also triggered one of the most significant aspects of being Jewish..."

The author's approach is a combination of rigorous research and genuine evaluation of subjective and emotional content, which is inevitably risky but makes this book extraordinarily persuasive. This persuasiveness comes from talking about concrete things, which is the route to understanding Gurvich. How else could we really enter into an artist who invited us, who invites us, "Not to see what the eyes see, but to use them for what our spirit wants to see"? There is no doubt that this was the correct choice (besides being perhaps inevitable) and the beneficiary is undoubtedly the reader.

With this approach, Haber undertakes an exhaustive examination of the main components of Jewish identity that came to the fore and marked the great positive change in the life and work of José Gurvich. She explains how the world of the kibbutz influenced the artist and provided a source of great cultural wealth and meaning, and she does this by taking us to the place itself, to the microcosm of Ramot Menashé and the utopian ideals of the socialist Zionist pioneers in Israel. She brings out the ideology and the day-to-day social solidarity of that life, how public art was highly valued, and how the artist became immersed in that society, which emerged so much in his compositions. And it is this same cult of work and the desire to build a society based on ideals that links the worker-artist in Cerro in Montevideo with the shepherd in Ramot Menashé. And it is this crossroads of identities that triggered the changes in Gurvich's art. As Haber points out, in no way was it accidental that *Carta al hombre (Letter to man)* from 1967, this "...pictorial declaration of his vision of life", should be firmly set in the context of the kibbutz.

It was also the authentic umbilical link with his mother that led him to a more affectionate attitude to Jewish tradition and an openness to the very particular world of Israel in the 1960s. The book relates how Totó (the painter's wife) and his friends at that time saw how when Gurvich found out about his mother's illness he brought more "...explicitly Jewish subjects and religious scenes" into his work. And it was this transmission of Judaic elements from his mother, this tradition that was so special to him and such a source of pride, that enabled him for example to bring more religious themes into his art including specific references to traditional Jewish festivals. For Gurvich this profusion of religious motifs was also a way to permanently evoke his mother, an instrument of emotion and love to confirm his full adhesion to a humanist message that was completely in harmony with the utopian values of the kibbutz that he so loved and wanted to share. Traditional and patriotic Jewish festivals appear in many of his better-known compositions, which shows how he established a synthesis with his roots in the primordial world of Jewish traditions, but gave them a new, secular interpretation.

Another tremendously important Jewish component in his work was the whole question of anti-Semitism, and in particular the terrible scars left by the Shoá (the Holocaust). Although Gurvich and his family were direct victims of anti-Semitism, he did not bring this or the Shoá into his work in any systematic way. But these terrible tragedies had a very deep effect on him, they were contemporary situations and events, and he involuntarily inherited such an emotional burden that, as Haber says, "He wasn't the same after Nazism", and there are many images of pogroms and repression in his work. He admired Mordechai Anielewicz and the other heroes of the Warsaw Rising, but he could not paint or show resistance to the Nazis in his art, perhaps because he was simply overwhelmed by the sheer enormity of the genocide. In any case, faced with the Shoá and its far-reaching repercussions and implications for Jewish identity (and for all humanity) in the post-war era, the artist opted to reaffirm his links to Jewish traditions and values as the best way to expresses resistance and a response to the Nazi project to annihilate all the Jews, and to all anti-Semitism. His series of compositions on the theme of "It is hard to be a Jew" express this commitment most profoundly.

Another image that recurs frequently in Gurvich's work is Jesus, and this also has to do with the artist's increasing immersion in Jewish traditions and identity. He shows he values this legacy by the way he includes it in his most common representations like in *Javer kibutz (Chaver Kibbutz)*, *Martir en un pogrom (Martyr in a pogrom)* or *Anciano rabino judío (Old Jewish rabbi)*. The figure of Jesus becomes "An emblem of suffering, torment and flagellation", which has a direct connection to anti-Semitism and specifically to the Shoá. In fact there was a long tradition of this motif in Jewish painting because showing Jesus as the victim of suffering was a valuable weapon in the struggle against anti-Semitism in Western Europe, a tool in resistance against persecution, which was usually perpetrated by people who called themselves Christians. As Haber notes, Gurvich took this image from a painter he greatly admired, Marc Chagall.

It was after he re-discovered his Jewish roots that José Gurvich was finally able to realise his vision and "...open a window into nothing, in infinite space..." as he put it. He was able to take the rich inheritance he received from Torres García and project it towards hitherto unexplored horizons, which was perhaps the best way he could possibly have paid tribute to his teacher and at the same time pass on his legacy with full creative freedom. In a metaphor comparing the relation between a child and his parents with that between a disciple and his teacher, Gurvich said, "Every birth has a father and mother... it is a case of having parents .... and of freeing yourself from them."

In this task, which was in no way easy, Gurvich with his newly re-discovered Jewish roots was finally able to display the full range of his artistic freedom, and he constantly insisted how important imagination is in creative work. He wrote for the catalogue for an exhibition at the National Fine Arts Committee in 1967, "My greatest pleasure is the creative game from which freedom of image and freedom of space emerge ... Art does not reveal the truth, it is not committed to reality, art is an invention of man and man expresses himself through it. Expression is giving form to feeling and intuition, it is the path where reason does not go ... To find life I had to leap into free space with just one hope, that in the dark depths of space I would find my own voice. It was then that my imagination ran wild through endless galleries, laying bare an unsuspected world, a world of adventure that I wandered through full of anguish and joy, full of voices that sing the song "Yet always" with echoes, forms, colours and feelings..."

As Haber so consistently demonstrates, it was when Gurvich came into direct contact with Jewish subjects like the kibbutz, the context of Israel in the 1960s, the world of his parents' primordial traditions and the troubled re-creation of Jewish identity after the Shoá, that his "creation of new languages" was triggered. And it was also this liberating force that enabled him to fully assimilate and be comfortable with the two complementary and converging sides of his identity, the Uruguayan and the Jewish. That is why this book, which goes so deeply into the whole question of Jewish identity and its decisive influence on the work of a major artist like José Gurvich, also deals with Uruguay. As the author puts it so well, "To live as equals in democratic societies in the Diaspora it is not necessary to pay the price of eroding all differences or renouncing identity. On the contrary, differences can be emphasised, which is what Gurvich did, and integrated into multi-faceted identities, which in his case meant being intensely Jewish and intensely Uruguayan."

GERARDO CAETANO is a Historian and Politologist, Ph.D in History. Academic Coordinator of the Observatorio Político del Instituto de Ciencia Política, Universidad de la República (Uruguay). Researcher and Professor (Grade 5) at the Universidad de la República. Teaches postgraduate courses (Master and Doctorate) in national and international universities. Consultant of several international institutions (UNESCO, PNUD, FLACSO, OEA, Unión Europea, UIP, IIDH, OEI) He is the author of more than 200 books and has received several Uruguayan and international awards. He is a member of the Real Academia Española, the Consejo Superior de la Facultad Latinoamericana de Ciencias Sociales (FLACSO), the Consejo Latinoamericano de Ciencias Sociales (CLACSO). He is President of the Centro Unesco of Montevideo and Academic Secretary of the Consejo Uruguayo para las Relaciones Internacionales.

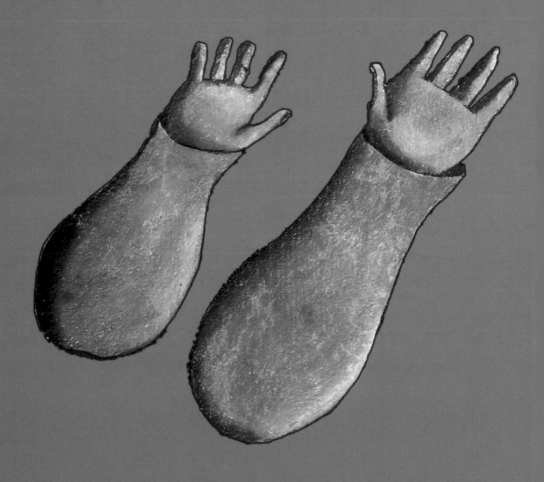

JOSÉ GURVICH
AND THE JEWISH IDENTITY

Alicia Haber

Introduction

In his early years, José Gurvich (Lithuania, 1927 - New York, 1974) came to prominence in the Torres García Workshop and developed his own style in Constructive Universalism, but starting in 1954 he gradually incorporated more and more Jewish subject matter into his work. He was a Uruguayan-Jewish artist of Lithuanian origin, he was fully integrated into Uruguay and he loved the country and made cultural contributions to it is several fields – most of all in visual arts – and then he took this new path and changed his iconography and his artistic expression.

When I speak of Jewish subject matter, I mean everything involving the symbology that Gurvich absorbed from tradition and his experiences of kibbutz life, such as the candelabra (menorah, hanukkiya), the Star of David, the scrolls of the Law, people on the kibbutz (chaverim) flying, kibbutz hats, awassi sheep (which Gurvich tended when he was a shepherd at Ramot Menashé) and many other elements. He used these symbols in murals, in ceramics, in paintings of imaginary scenes and in pictures that are almost abstract, and not just in his work in Israel but also in what he did in Cerro (Uruguay) and in New York. However, it was his first stay in Israel (1955) that triggered this process and propelled the artist deep into his Jewish heritage. His subject matter includes symbols and motifs clearly derived from his life on the kibbutz, but he also tackled a wide range of subjects that have to do with the ongoing, dynamic construction of his Jewish identity like biblical themes, festivals, scenes of sabbatical celebrations, pogroms and expressions of the idea that "It is hard to be a Jew". I stress this point because, since Gurvich's death, people who know little about the question of Jewish identity have misinterpreted his work and spread misunderstanding about it. The Jewish subject matter in his work can be found in images of Jewish festivals, of pogroms, of Lithuanian villages, of rabbis or biblical scenes; it is far more than just six paintings he did on commission in New York.

This book is about Jewish subject matter in the widest sense of the term, and my approach is to start from the moment in 1955 when Gurvich began to bring this aspect of his identity very intensely into his compositions.[1]

To this end, I analyse the experiences that stimulated him to develop, and describe the contexts in which these forces within him found expression in his work. From studying his art I uncover his growing interest in Jewish themes and I work back in time and research the basic origins of his identity. I examine the aspects of Gurvich's life that left lasting impressions, his inherited knowledge and his primary learning,[2] which started in Yezne (Jieznas), the Jewish-Lithuanian village where he was born and spent the first five years of his life.[3]

Menorah couple and flowers on the kibbutz, detail

One crucial element in his make-up was the Yiddish language, his mother tongue, and he spoke it to the end of his days. And as the sociologist Alain Medam[4] explains, Yiddish[5] is more than just a language, people live in it, it is inhabited, and it has baroque, archaic, poetic, prophetic, intimate and conspiratorial dimensions. The Jews in the ghettos of Eastern Europe had a long history of being marginalised; they did not have the right to their own place, they were expelled, isolated, confined, stigmatized, trapped, limited and segregated against their will, and (according to Medam) Yiddish, this semantic no-place, was a place. This sociologist maintains that the language itself is integrated into these people's lives in a unique way because it is their home, with the warmth of its sayings and the cunning of its humour, and it is a reserve, a treasure, a mother, a matrix and a memory. And because it is written with Hebrew letters,[6] Yiddish is laden with memories and emotions, with minority pathos, and it lives on in those who speak it and those who no longer do so. This is also the reason why it has been examined and analysed so much by sociologists, historians, psychoanalysts, fiction writers, the Jews themselves and also gentiles.[7]

For Gurvich, the traditional culture (Yiddishkeit) passed on by his parents, mainly by his mother, was very important, as were his childhood and adolescent experiences in the Jewish environment of the Barrio Sur neighbourhood in Montevideo where he grew up. He was very attached to his sister Miriam, who influenced him with her Marxist Zionist Judaism, and he also had links with the Zionist Socialist youth movement Hashomer Hatzair. In this study I pay particular attention to the next phase of his life, his three trips to Israel when he stayed on the Ramot Menashé kibbutz.

My research shows that Israel played a key role in how José Gurvich constructed his identity. It was there that his feeling of belongingness, of fraternity and continuity with the Jewish people, developed and intensified, and this included the historical dimension, the recognition that he shared in a common past and had ethnic ties. He underwent a process of having his memory mobilised.[8] I came to see how he remembered the events of that context with fondness and affection. He was in communication with the long-remembered traditions of the land and of ancient and mythical times, and it was an essential place for ethnicity, a semantic ground,[9] a richly-laden territory,[10] where he had roots pervaded with history, stories, testimonies, epics, folklore, beliefs, heritage, myths, ceremonies, commemorations, celebrations and costumes.

I was also aware of how the kibbutz moved him, how it was that this rural commune became another important reason for identifying with his Jewishness. The characteristic dynamism of the Zionist movement was channelled through the kibbutz and it flowed with full force. The philosopher Martin Buber stresses that the capacity of inventiveness, the construction of a new world, the productive autonomy, the social equality and the very fact of working the land, were unleashed. And at the same time the kibbutz was a metaphor for the new kind of Jew. Medam presents the image, which I share,[11] of a ship travelling from the ghetto to utopia, a ship that is in anamorphosis.

In Ramot Menashé, Gurvich experienced Jewish traditions in what was for him a new context, they had a different nature, and he went through the process of anamnesis and rediscovered treasures from the past like the Shabbat (Sabbath). As Medam said,[12] "Nothing is more musical than the simple silence of a Shabbat." Abraham Heschel[13] commented, "The Shabbats are our great cathedrals … The meaning of the Shabbat is to celebrate time more than space. Six days a week we live under the tyranny of things in space, on the Shabbat we try to become attuned to holiness in time."

Another aspect that I deal with in this book is the influence on Gurvich of anti-Semitism, which he experienced as a boy in Jieznas and which found its most terrible expression in the Shoah, the holocaust of World War II and the extermination of six million Jews. Gurvich, like all of us post-war Jews, was a victim of the Shoah. For him and for all of us this is a key element in the construction of our identity. And this touched him very closely indeed because a large part of his extended family perished in the massacres in Lithuania. When he was in Israel he met many survivors of the Shoah on the Ramot Menashé kibbutz, and this intensified the impact of that event in his life. As numerous people I talked to in my research testified, Gurvich was marked with that burning brand.

There are other significant aspects to the painter's Jewishness, like his famous sense of humour and his feelings about Shalom Aleichem. And there are facets of his personality that show he belonged to this ethno-cultural group; some are indescribable and cannot be exactly defined but are recognizably Jewish such as his liking for adventure, his urge to go beyond the limits, his freedom of imagination and his dreams of other realities. Much of this is the heritage from centuries in the ghettos of the Diaspora, and it came out in his art, which broke boundaries and went beyond the limits. He had a trait that the Jews of the Diaspora developed over centuries, the ancient need to look for other horizons that nothing could imprison, not persecution nor humiliating oppression nor forced confinement in the ghettos. These were free regions of the mind that no one could take away such as study, spiritual speculation, the ability to go further and generate new points of view, the instinct to challenge received wisdom. Gurvich had all this, and while still keeping his feet on the ground he was able to hurl himself into the air like the figures in his paintings, and he could investigate and sublimate and exalt these other regions of experience. He lived in Uruguay, which is a land of freedom, but he inherited a sense of limitation from his ghetto beginnings and

Shabbat
1966
ink, pencil on paper
20 x 13 cm

Jánuca, sketch
1968
ink on paper
12.5 x 20 cm

he also inherited the means to transcend all restrictions just as Jews all down the centuries have transcended their situation. And this was an indelible characteristic, a way of being that makes the Jews of the Diaspora different.

I conducted numerous interviews and I gathered information about how Gurvich was with his Jewish friends, about their experiences with him in Montevideo and in Israel, and this has enabled me to get to know him, to follow his tracks, and to uncover just how much he was a Jew in the full sense of the word. Like all the people I talked to, like all the sources I checked, I believe that his whole identity was deeply anchored in his being Jewish.

My main aim is to enhance people's understanding of Gurvich's work, to make his art more accessible, but I also want to foster knowledge about Jewish culture, about the traditional festivals and myths and legends in the Bible. Therefore I elucidate aspects of the painter's iconography, I try to explain the symbols and thus make it easier for people to understand and enjoy his art.

Gurvich's creative work is steeped in Judaism. As I document his career as a painter it will emerge that the greater part of his life's work is evidence not only of his creative imagination but also that he was most profoundly influenced by his cultural heritage. This can be seen from the photographic reproductions of his art that are available in Uruguay, Israel, the United States and Argentina.

In tackling this whole subject there is no way to avoid the multiple facets of the artist's identity and the many different ways there are to understand the condition of being Jewish. I take the reader into a world of heterogeneous Jewish identities that are mobile and changeable. I start from the basic premise that identity is always under construction, always in a state of being modified and redefined, and that a fundamental component is the person's relationship with the other, with what lies beyond. Therefore it is essential to see Gurvich in the context of his place and time, and this includes an appreciation that Uruguay is a multicultural[14] society in which diversity is accepted and valued as a resource that can stimulate the imagination, and as a rich storehouse of treasures from many communities and their traditions. It is important not just to focus on Gurvich's Jewishness, which is so evident in his art and so obvious in his personality, but also to stress the value of diversity, pluralism and differences in his influences.

In addition, I realised it was important to bring in other voices, other points of view, other ways of reading the artist's work, and I invited various people to contribute to this book. These are Joséphine Balken, a connoisseur of Gurvich's work; Nisso Acher, Director of the Permanent Chair of Judaism at the Catholic University of Uruguay; Isaac Margulies, an expert on the Talmud; and Manuel Tenenbaum, an outstanding Uruguayan intellectual and specialist in Jewish history.

In my research I had many interviews with the artist's wife, Julia Añorga de Gurvich (Totó), and with his students and friends in Uruguay. I also visited private collections and I discovered a wealth of drawings and sketches I had never seen before: pictures of kibbutz life, Jewish festivals, the "It is hard to be a Jew" theme, Moses, and many more recurrent motifs.

Thanks to the Gurvich Foundation, I was able to go to Israel and Switzerland and I visited the Ramot Mensahe kibbutz and acquired a feel for this place where the artist lived, worked and painted. In addition I interviewed many of his Uruguayan, Argentine, Chilean and European friends and companions, I travelled to Tel Aviv, Ramat Aviv and Jerusalem to talk to people who knew him and to see pieces of his work that they have. I went to Switzerland to talk to the Israeli artist Naftali Bezem, who was very close to Gurvich.

Jánuca, sketch
1968
ink on paper
12.5 x 20 cm

On these travels I saw many of the painter's works that were new to me, on the kibbutz and in private collections in Israel and other places, and I studied them with a particular eye on their Jewish iconography. This enriched my knowledge enormously, it was a new source of nourishment, and it led me to new ways to understand Gurvich's work, this time with a more precise approach as regards time, space and subject matter.

It is important to review an artist's work at different times, to take a Heraclitean approach, to accept that art is open to many interpretations and we are never the same when we confront it again. And when we come to a work, we circumscribe our interest to certain aspects of it, we are at a new point in time in our own lives and we have a different perspective. And this is what I did when I saw works that I knew and also ones I was hitherto unfamiliar with, and it enabled me to bring other views and opinions into my reactions.

Gurvich was very open to change. Starting on his first trip to Israel he showed just what a permeable and flexible being he was, able to expand his horizons and break free into new variations. And this is what emerged from my research, and what can be seen in this book, the tremendous range of metamorphoses he underwent. Gurvich knew how to go deep into changing worlds, and to do so in an original way, and to let life stimulate his imagination, emotions and sensitivity.

An analysis of his work shows a certain fidelity to his teacher, Joaquín Torres García, who did not try to set limits on him. And perhaps this is why he was always able to listen to other voices and see the value in other approaches. He was very open to ideas including those he found in the work of Paul Klee, Pieter Brueghel, El Bosco, Marc Chagall and Joan Miró.

Gurvich was inspired by the poetry of Antonio Machado and from reading Shalom Aleichem. His work is full of Jewish iconography but he also tackled Christian subjects like the seven deadly sins and the parable of the

Sketch
1966
ink on paper
12.5 x 20 cm

Figures in space
n.d.
ink on paper
15 x 11 cm

blind (Luke 6:39), although in this case his inspiration was more Brueghel's oil painting (1568) than reading the New Testament. As an artist, he did not exclude, he included, he added, he incorporated and he embraced life with all its local as well as its universal spirit. He blended different elements together, he linked them and put them in new settings, he connected and fused them, he united very different worlds and realities, he painted his kibbutz with different atmospheres and in the most varied times and spaces.

In my research I came upon a wealth of evidence of his versatility, expressive energy, variety of resources, originality of outlines, fantasy, formal richness, constant searching, deepening reality, transfiguring reality, and many other dimensions of his work. He was intelligent enough to know how to go beyond the obvious, beyond narrative and folklore, and move into metaphorical expression that gives rise to a variety of possible reactions and can be interpreted in many different ways. This shift into a more imaginative approach is evident in his work starting when he was on his second trip to Israel, and we can see how the absurd, the weird, the illusory and the irrational came into his creative vision. He embodies dreams, fantasy, lyricism, spontaneity and surprise, but he anchors this in day-to-day reality as the most prominent feature.

I researched Gurvich's life, and there are some features that parallel my own experiences, quite apart from the fact of being Jewish. I had two stays in Israel in the 1960s, and on one of those trips I lived and worked on a Socialist secular kibbutz for six months. In this book I have inevitably evoked the Israel of the 1960s that he and I knew, which until the changes that started in 1967 was so idealistic, so utopian and so socialist. Before the 1980s, the kibbutzim were still much as they had been in the beginning. When I tackled the subject of Gurvich I inevitably relived my experiences in Israel and on the kibbutz and recalled what we were like in those years, how we were in the years of my adolescence. However, while I have not lost those feelings and I have given them their due weight in this book, I also updated my knowledge from the social sciences and from research by experts in various fields and from various points of view. So this book is also based on a new bibliography by French, Israeli, United States, Uruguayan and Latin American writers. In short, I have tried to be as objective as possible.

During this process I became involved with, and renewed my enthusiasm for, the whole area of symbology. I read very widely about festivals, the Bible, new studies on identity and multiculturalism, and new perspectives on Masada, the kibbutz movement and Zionism. And as I followed this learning path I also triggered one of the most significant aspects of being Jewish, the desire to learn, which from time immemorial has always been valued and treated with the greatest respect. "If a man does not increase (his knowledge), he will decrease (it)." (1:13) "Let your house be a meeting place for scholars, and sit in the dust at their feet, and drink up their words with thirst." (1:4) This is what our sages teach in the Pirkei Avot.[15] As the famous essayist Ahad Ha'am wrote, "Learning, learning, learning, that is the key to Jewish survival." And besides learning about Gurvich I have learned from him, from his art, from our common roots, from our feeling of belonging, from the past, from our shared historical fate, and from the Jewish and Uruguayan identities that unite us. And there are many more aspects that the reader himself will add to the multi-faceted work of this Uruguayan-Jewish artist.

This process is still going on, Gurvich leaves enough doors open for us to delight in his work and interpret it. And my job is unfinished, it will go out of my hands and there will be others who do further research and find new interpretations

End notes

1   There are many publications about Gurvich's rich Torres García style production, his portraits, his still life paintings and other work. I have dealt with these periods of his life in other books, as have other authors, and these are noted in the bibliography. There are also interviews with friends and colleagues from the Torres García Workshop and artists and friends outside Jewish circles, which again are noted in the bibliography. In this book I have concentrated on Gurvich's Judaism and on Jewish subject matter in his work.

2   Candau, Joël, Memoria e Identidad, Serie Antropológica, Buenos Aires, Ediciones del Sol, 2008.

3   There are several studies on life in those villages, which were called shtetls, including Rachel Ertel, Le shtetl, la bourgade juive de Pologne: de la tradition à la modernité, Le Régard de l'histoire, París, Payot 1982.

4   Alain Medam, Mondes Juifs. L'envers et L'endroit, Paris, Presses universitaires de France, 1991.

5   Which combines elements of German, Hebrew and Slav languages.

6   Medam, op. cit.

7   Régine Robin, L'amour du yiddish: écriture juive et sentiment de la langue, 1830-1930, Paris, Le Sorbier, 1982. Sherry Simon, "Mémoires en partage", Voix et Images, vol. 34, No. 1, (100) 2008, pp. 33-41. http://id.erudit.org/iderudit/019402ar

8   Candau, op. cit.

9   Medam, op. cit.

10 Ibidem.

11 Medam, op. cit. p. 84.

12 Ibidem.

13 Abraham Heschel, Les bâtisseurs du temps, Paris, Éditions de Minuit, 1957. Abraham Heschel, The Sabbath: Its Meaning For Modern Man, New York, Farrar, Straus and Giroux, 1975.

14 Multiculturalism in Uruguay is a research programme in the Sociology Department of the Faculty of Social Sciences of the Universidad de la República, Uruguay. http://www.multiculturalismoenuruguay.com. Responsible for the project: Dr. Felipe Arocena. Research: Mg. Sebastián Aguiar, Dr. (candidate) Rafael Porzecanski, Mg. Mónica Olaza, graduates Victoria Cestau, Juan Cristiano, Mariana Zina, Adriana Topalián, Anna González Schmit, Leticia Carro and Pablo Silva.
    Publications: Felipe Arocena, "Elogio de la diversidad", ed. Enrique Mazzei, El Uruguay desde la sociología V, Montevideo, Universidad de la República, 2006; Felipe Arocena and Sebastián Aguiar (editors), Multiculturalismo en Uruguay. Ensayo y entrevistas a once comunidades culturales, Montevideo, Trilce, 2007; Felipe Arocena, "La contribución de los inmigrantes en Uruguay", Papeles de CEIC, 2009/2, Spain, Universidad del País Vasco, 2009; Felipe Arocena, "Dilemas para construir democracias multiculturales", in Relaciones No. 301, Montevideo, June 2009; Felipe Arocena, "How Immigrants Have Shaped Uruguay", in Culturales, No. 9, Universidad Autónoma de Baja California, Centro de Investigaciones Culturales-Museo, Mexico, January-June; Felipe Arocena and Sebastián Aguiar (editores), Multiculturalismo en Uruguay. Ensayo y entrevistas a once comunidades culturales, Montevideo, Trilce, 2007; "Elogio de la diversidad", El Uruguay desde la sociología V, ed. Enrique Mazzei, Montevideo, Universidad de la República, 2006.

15 Pirkei Avot (Ethics of the Fathers) is one of the most important books of Judaism, with thoughts about morality and ethics by the greatest thinkers in history.

1. Jewishness

1

Jewishness

The feeling of being Jewish pervaded his being. José Gurvich had a multiple, heterogeneous, Jewish identity that was built in stages, enriched in various scenarios and through different experiences in his native Lithuania, then Montevideo, Israel and finally New York. It came out in his art, from his three stays on a kibbutz, an Israeli collective farm[1] called Ramot Menashé[2] (Menashé[3] heights). It came to the fore on his first trip to Israel in 1954 and it flowered with particular intensity after 1964.

José Gurvich was born in 1927 in Yezne,[4] a Lithuanian *shtetl*[5] (a small, predominantly Jewish village),[6] in the bosom of a traditional Ashkenazi family (Jews from Central and Eastern Europe). His closest kin were his parents Jaie Galperaitas and Jacobo Gurvicius, and his older sister Miriam.

His mother tongue was Yiddish, the Ashkenazi vernacular language, which is a combination of Hebrew and High German with some Russian and Polish expressions. He never forgot this language, he used and enjoyed it with his family and friends in Montevideo, and he later spoke it with many people, in particular European immigrants and refugees, when he lived in Israel and New York. With Yiddish he received and passed on elements of a centuries-old culture, a very special spirit ranging from high culture to everyday usage including humour – which he treasured greatly as he loved the typical jokes and the popular sayings that had been passed down for centuries from generation to generation. Yiddish was a very important factor when it came to feeling and expressing his Jewish identity.

The family – Gurvich, his parents and his sister - emigrated to Montevideo in 1932, and in the first two decades of his life he lived in a Jewish environment both at home and in the neighbourhood. His mother, Jaie Galperaitas, was crucial to the development of his identity. She kept *Shabbat*, the Sabbath, the holy day of rest, and celebrated every festival; she prepared the traditional Ashkenazi meals and observed the religious rules, the *kashrut*,[7] about diet and cooking. These are laid down in the *Torah* (the Pentateuch, the first five books of the Bible), and like every practising Jew, Jaie followed them as they established a closer relationship with God, with holiness, with the definition of what is sacred and profane, and with the division of the pure from the impure. By respecting them Jaie, like every religious Jew, raised the simple act of eating to a more transcendent plane. She added spirituality to life in how she considered what she was going to buy, how she was going to cook it and how the meals tasted. Every time she fed her

Sketch of rabbi
c. 1973
felt-tip pen on paper
10 x 15 cm

family –including her beloved son[8]- Jaie remembered and made them remember their identity and the ancient legacy they had inherited. And she linked these things with history and other Jews around the world. By keeping to these diet laws Jaie showed how strongly, consciously or unconsciously, she insisted on believing that you are born with a history, with belongingness, and that you should not break with the past or with your identity. And she transmitted this spirit to her children, even though they later opted for secular ways of being Jewish.

In the Gurvich home the essence of the *shtetl* was preserved, especially thanks to his mother. They kept what is known as *Yiddishkeit*, which consists of a number of identifying elements associated with the use of Yiddish including religion, traditions, ways of being, feelings, moods, emotions, behavioural traits, the practice of *mitzvot*[9] (sacred prescriptions), the conception of family, and valuing generosity, humility and empathy. And it was also in their way of talking and everything that could be called the Jewish way of living of the traditional Ashkenazi communities in Eastern Europe, communities that were tragically wiped of the map in the Nazi genocide in World War II.

Gurvich left home at the age of seventeen but he only moved a short distance and he used to see his mother every day. He was living in the *ken*[10] of the *Hashomer Hatzair*,[11] and his mother missed him so much she would go by there and shout, "Yoshale, Yoshale,[12] don't you think you'd be better off at home?" and he would answer, "Don't bother me, Mom." His wife, Julia Añorga de Gurvich (Totó),[13] says that in fact he was living just round the corner from his parents' house.

His wife and all his friends and colleagues say that Jaie Galperaitas always loomed large in her son's life and was of crucial importance in his education. The intimate bond between the two of them continued when he moved away, when he married, started his own family, went to live in his own house in Cerro, had students, and later lived on the Ramot Menashé[14] kibbutz.

According to the Uruguayan painter Yuyo Goitiño, "...The cultural element was present because his mother was a very religious woman, she was a Lithuanian peasant with exceptional human qualities. And at Jewish festivals she prepared all the Jewish meals and invited her son's friends."[15] Many people remember him from that time, like the artist Ernesto Vila, and Isaac Gliksberg,[16] a renowned expert on the life of immigrants in Barrio Sur who himself lived there with his parents and siblings for many years, and who studied the subject. Vila, who was one of the artist's disciples, says, "Gurvich was Jewish in his very essence; and family life and Jewish meals were very significant. He took many of his pupils to his parents' house, which surprised us, his young followers. They spoke Spanish badly. Normally at home they spoke Yiddish."

In his childhood and youth, Gurvich lived in Isla de Flores, Durazno and Rio Branco streets in Barrio Sur, a neighbourhood of Montevideo where Jews still practiced their traditional customs. It was one of the areas where Jewish immigrants in the early post-war period settled. He was in constant contact with other Jews, and many of the friendships forged in those years lasted his whole life. He was very connected with other Jewish people in the area, he used to visit their homes, and many were religious families that invited him to participate in traditional festivals such as the *Shabbat*.

Gliksberg tells us that this neighbourhood where Gurvich lived was dynamic and self-sufficient, and the Jews supplied themselves with everything they needed in all aspects of life. Everything was there, first and foremost housing, very humble houses like tenements with several families sharing the bathroom and kitchen, and at the start this was the situation of the Gurvich family. They were in a one-storey house from the early 20th century, a small tenement with a hallway and a central courtyard that the rooms looked onto. Seven or eight families lived there. They went there straight from the ship with their few belongings. On the voyage they made friends, their *schifbrider* (ship brother) or *schifshwester* (ship sister), and these people went on to become like real brothers and sisters and fill the painful void of those other family members they missed so much, left behind in Eastern Europe. They remained close to these friends, this new family, throughout their lives.

In the neighbourhood there were institutions, synagogues, the immigrants' club, the houses where they prayed with *minyan* (a *Yiddish*

Evocations of the shtetl, detail
1970
pencil on paper
30 x 22 cm

word indicating the presence of ten men, which was the minimum needed to conduct a ceremony or pray) and the Sholem Aleichem library. They could go there to read, to have tea with other Jews, to catch up on the news, to find out what was going on in the world and in Montevideo, to share information about jobs or housing, and all this naturally forged bonds of friendship and solidarity among them.

In Barrio Sur and Centro there were institutions not only for religious people but also for the secular leftist unionists who leaned towards communist thinking. The ideological spectrum of those impoverished Jews in the neighbourhood was very diverse, but all the while Yiddish and Jewish culture was intensely maintained. The people in general wanted to preserve their cultural identity, they wanted to fit in but not be assimilated. In fact non-religious Jews with left-wing views sent their children to Yiddish schools after the normal Uruguayan school day because they wanted to preserve their culture and identity. There were also humble shops to buy the ingredients for the traditional kosher meals. The Jews took over many shops in the area, grocery stores and small businesses, and also there were bookshops to buy religious products and books in Yiddish. In those days and for a long time after, the Mercado Central (Central Market) was the place to go to find everything for traditional dishes. The butchers there slaughtered the poultry in accordance with religious rules so it would be kosher, and the products the Ashkenazi needed were all on sale including herring, rye bread, sour cream, poppy and cumin. There was a weekly street market in Barrio Sur and the main languages were Yiddish and poor Spanish. Some bars were only for Jewish men, and Yiddish was the norm. The life in the *shtetl* of the 1930s and 1940s was imported with many of its singularities, and Yiddish was so predominant in people's homes and around the neighbourhood that some immigrants never learned Spanish properly.

In the "Chile" state school where Gurvich went, Jewish children made up a sizeable group. At Rosh Hashanah (New Year) and Yom Kippur (Day of Atonement), the classrooms were half-empty and teachers did not mark the Jewish pupils absent. Some football teams in the neighbourhood and at school were made up of mostly Jewish children. Judaism, both religious and secular, was a source of pride and joy inside and outside the home. It naturally spread all over the neighbourhood and was evident on the streets where adults and children, children first, began to mix with gentiles and even played Jewish festival games with them with their symbolic toys such as the *sevivon or dreidel* (spinning top). Jewish Mothers welcomed their children's gentile friends into their homes —Gurvich's mother did this— and invited them to share tea with *latkes* (a kind of potato fritter, also made of cottage cheese) and to have them to dinner, and in this way lifelong friendships were born.

At home, after a hard day, the parents sat and chatted nostalgically about the *shtetl* or the Jewish quarter of the European city they had left behind, or their family back there, or of the dangers of Nazism. Later on the conversations were about the vicissitudes of the persecution, and then, when they learned about the concentration camps, anxious speculation about what might have happened to their relatives.

When they finally found out about the genocide, they experienced it in their own names, they wept for their own names, for their parents, uncles, brothers and nephews. It was part of their everyday life. They experienced the Second World War very intensely, it was always on the front page in the Yiddish newspapers published in Montevideo, and they talked about it with their neighbours and in their clubs and synagogues. There were committees supporting the allies, there were anti-Nazi meetings, and many people used to gather in front of the La Mañana-El Diario[1] building to read the updated news and listen to a Yiddish radio programme. Many of them, like Gliksberg, say they always mourned for the family they never saw again, the family that was murdered by the Nazis. And this applied to almost every Jewish home. Gurvich grew from boyhood through his teenage years and became a young man while this was going on, the experience was unrelenting and all the Jewish families suffered. And certainly he too was immersed in these feelings because his family was so profoundly affected.

Gurvich was permeated with Jewishness, it came in though his pores, from morning till night, in the family home and in the extended home that was the neighbourhood. These influences were already there after his five years in the Lithuanian *shtetl*, and in Montevideo the assimilation process went on. Those years are the most formative part of our lives, the times we always remember, and Gurvich never forgot them.

Through his sister Miriam and her friends, who later became his own friends, he had a lot of contact with a Marxist-Zionist Scouts youth movement called Hashomer Hatzair. Totó says, "He lived in the *ken*, in the attic at the Hashomer Hatzair, a sleeping loft where there was hardly room for a bed. He went there because he did not have a place to paint at home as his mother was always complaining that he made everything dirty." He got to know the *Hajshara*[17] of the Hashomer Hatzair in Florida very well. When he was living in the *ken* he made many friends and he widened his circle and deepened his sense of Jewishness.

He was also in contact with Jewish culture in many community activities like drama, conversations in Yiddish, and initiatives to raise funds. Israel Gantz remembers that "On another occasion a very im-

---

[1]   Morning and evening newspapers, respectively. El Diario was one of the top-selling newspapers in the 1950s.

Lithuanian village
1969
oil on canvas
37.5 x 45 cm

Shtetl. Scene in Lithuania
1969
oil on canvas
40 x 50 cm

Kibbutz scene with moon

c. 1964

ink on paper

13 x 19 cm

portant Jewish theatre company came, and Mauritius Muller, who was already a critic in Marcha,[II] went to see them. The company was in need of extras so he recruited his brothers Leopoldo and Martin, Gurvich and myself, and we took part in it. Gurvich and I spoke Yiddish."[18] Ganz recalls that in the 1940s, Gurvich joined a theatre group which performed Jewish plays in Yiddish, "... he made the sets for us, very original ones, incredible, and his sister was also in the group, and Leon Biriotti, who composed the music."[19] Ganz says that in 1946 he went to a fund-raising event that the young Jews of the Hashomer Hatzair organization were taking all over the country, to buy a farm in San Luis.[20] In his teens Gurvich started to work but he remained close to the community; his first job was in a Jewish-owned factory.[21]

A friend from his kibbutz days, Vera Jordan, who had already met him in Montevideo,[22] said "He felt very Jewish, he spoke Yiddish with his mother and father, he drew inspiration from reading Shalom Aleichem, and everybody thought he had a very Jewish sense of humour.[23]

Another very strong element in Jewish identity was the birth of the State of Israel in 1948. This was discussed everywhere including in the Hashomer Hatzair, and it became a powerful force in Gurvich's bond with his sister and friends and neighbours in the community. Israel became a mythical place that would finally lay to rest the image of the Wandering Jew. This was the end of the Exodus, the ultimate response to the insecurity caused by anti-Semitism, and there would be no more pogroms,[24] persecution or discrimination. This was the Promised Land, and it is known by many names: *Moledet* (native land), *Ha'Aretz* (land), *Eretz Israel* (land of Israel) and *Medinat Israel* (State of Israel). That spirit was vitally important in the first decades of the State of Israel, and it sent emotional reverberations throughout the Diaspora.

Finally the cherished dream of the Zionist movement[25] had come true. This was a nation-oriented movement whose aim was bring into being an autonomous, sovereign Jewish State, a nation with its own territory in the ancient lands of the Bible, and this finally came to pass. The Jewish community in Uruguay, including the Hashomer Hatzair and Gurvich and his friends in the neighbourhood, celebrated the event. There were a few dissenting voices, but the Jews in Uruguay have always had close links with Israel, and the creation of the State was a ray of hope in those years. The horrors of the Nazi genocide showed how important it was for the Jews to have their own State. They had hoped for and needed a homeland more than ever, and now it actually existed.

When Israel came into being there was an explosion of enthusiasm among Jews all over the world, and the community in Uruguay reacted

II   Uruguayan leftist cultural and political weekly magazine, founded in 1939.

in a very sensitive way with feelings of loyalty, identification, and reverence at the appearance of this peculiar country.

In the circles where Gurvich moved there was excited talk about the chance of *aliyah* (moving to Israel), the validity of the Diaspora, the future of anti-Semitism in the world, the ideas of Theodor Herzl (the main theorist of Zionism[26]), Jewish identity, the kibbutz experiment, and Socialism and Marxism in a Zionist form.

Another fundamental subject in the family and in those circles was the Holocaust, in which six million Jews were exterminated by the Germans in World War II. A better term for this is *Shoah* (disaster, calamity) as it was not really a sacrifice but a crime carried out by the Germans and their collaborators from many European countries. This horror was an almost tangible presence in the homes of Jewish immigrants, above all those that had left their families behind and now knew that most of them had been annihilated.

Gurvich carried his Jewish essence in his soul and in his being. He had always been Jewish, although like most Uruguayan Jews he was not particularly inclined to religion. However, at that time his Jewishness was not reflected in his art. Before he travelled to Israel Gurvich did not show any particular interest in putting this culture into his work. Ganz says,[27] "At the time I knew him, when he was in the country and at the Torres García art school, he would never have thought of a picture with a Jewish subject. But in fact he ended up producing paintings with Jewish religious themes." Judaism did not appear in Gurvich's art until he finally set foot in Israel.

Construction hoy-es (with menorah)
c. 1960
ink on paper
13 x 19.5 cm

Israel

The experience of going to live in Israel at the Ramot Menashé kibbutz and getting to know the country brought on a big change in Gurvich. He was deeply moved and his art was transformed, and this is evident from the work he did there. These painting show the enormous impact that the country and the kibbutz had on him. The Argentine painter and one-time Gurvich pupil, Adolfo Nigro[28] said, "His experience as a shepherd on the kibbutz was decisively important in the development of his work." In Goitiño's opinion, "...the trips to Israel were the trigger for Gurvich to find his Jewish roots."[29]

It is very difficult for a Jew to visit Israel and not be changed by the experience. The feelings of exaltation, enthusiasm and happiness that the country aroused in people at that time was very special indeed. Those were the first decades of the State, in many ways they were the pioneering years, a time of hard work and amazing growth, and the atmosphere was the very epitome of idealistic purpose. Nobody who went to Israel like Gurvich in the 1950s and 1960s could have remained immune.

Mural project

c. 1955

watercolour and ink on paper

10.5 x 20 cm

Kibbutz drawing

c. 1955

ink on paper

12.5 x 21 cm

When he went, the country was imbued with tremendous idealism, which was at its height in the 1950s and 1960s and went on. The Mapam,[30] the ruling Zionist Socialist Party at that time, consolidated the natural feelings that accompanied the impressive birth of the new State. Prime Minister David Ben-Gurion,[31] a dominant figure in the early years, was a secular Socialist Zionist and the key architect of a civil State religion, and he broadcast idealistic messages of social justice and equality that acquired messianic connotations. The predominant concept was that the new State should have moral and ethical purposes that were useful to Jews and to humanity as a whole. Israel ought to be an example, a light for the human race, and it was right that it should be constituted in a new place where a new Judaism could be constructed. From a modern perspective it is obvious that these utopian ideas were a burden, but in those days they were received with intense enthusiasm.

Gurvich saw how socialist Zionism was a revolution because it not only founded the State but also embodied ideals related to aspects of public, community and social life. Like all Jews who went to Israel in those years, he was impressed by this booming country and these new generations making sacrifices and dedicated to the task of building a nation, dedicated to developing a new society and imbued with the destiny of a national mission.

In Israel and on the kibbutz he found he was in harmony with the way society was being built because he had great sympathy for socialism. According to Totó,[32] the only time he voted in Uruguay he voted for the Partido Socialista (Socialist Party), and this political stance was something he shared with Antonio Machado, his favourite poet, the writer who influenced him most. Machado was an important figure for Gurvich, "... my friend, Machado my friend, I feel you and love you as you have revealed the deep feelings of the soul and the murmur of spring to me, and the cycle of human love, my friend, my brother, of the immense sea, of the journey with no return.[33]" Machado was Spanish, he was a socialist, and he supported the Spanish Republic and the political left in their struggle for social equality.

Israel had a series of socialist governments from when it was founded until 1977, and it embarked on a programme of far-reaching changes in the area of social equality. There were tangible concrete achievements, such as strong trade unions. The State owned the means of production, 90 percent of the land, the big companies were state-owned and there were socialist organizations such as the kibbutz, the *moshav* and *Nahal*.[34] Rural socialism was not only viable but triumphant, and there were profound changes in the people's way of life.

Solidarity and the asceticism of the pioneering spirit were much admired and appreciated. Voluntary organizations developed and spread widely, there was intense mutual support, the spirit of self-sacrifice was an important factor and the common good was the highest goal of all. The civic virtues of the redeeming pioneer, manual labour and collective agriculture, were extolled. Israel endured decades of self-sac-rificing work and the people suffered hardships and scarcity. There were restrictions on consumption and the people lived in simple, humble, modest, frugal conditions. It was only in 1968 that hardship and short-ages were finally left behind. Amos Oz, the celebrated Israeli writer, recalls that when he first went to Paris in 1969, his French friends were surprised that in Israel there were only two kinds of cheese, "white" and "yellow."[35] And this frugality and simplicity continued for years.

Gurvich had always been an austere man and he was attracted to this kind of context, he was very happy with the simple life in Israel. All these dreams and these realities moved him deeply, as he said many times and as he expressed in his art. He admired the country's achieve-ments and left testimony to them.

The years of consolidation (1958-1968) were particularly success-ful, and non-Jews as well as Jews were very impressed with the coun-try's growth rate. The State expanded enormously, there was mas-sive immigration, and Israel became the protecting home for Jews who survived the Holocaust and others fleeing from persecution in Arab countries. Israel's population grew from 800,000 in 1948 to more than two million in the 1960s and three million in the 1970s, and this unleashed a great creative effort. Continuous change was essential to be able to tackle the thousands of problems of refugees and immigrants; these were permanent challenges which called for constant construction.

New schemes were needed, the people had to plan, invent, impro-vise and modify as they went along. This was a birth, the birth of some-thing new, something that had never been tried before, and the people had to be energised and have their inventiveness given free rein.

The land was revolutionized. Fuelled by the rural mystique of Zion-ism there was progress in agriculture, and irrigation systems were built on an extraordinary scale. The agricultural sector managed to meet the population's needs and the surplus was sold abroad, by the mid-1960s Israel was an exporting country and in two decades exports doubled. The country's Gross Domestic Product (GDP) rose spectacularly. Indus-trial development began and metallurgical, electronic, chemical and machinery industries were founded. A second port was built, at Ash-dod, and this made trade even more dynamic.

Universities, hospitals, and primary and secondary schools were built, and the fantastic *Israel Museon*, dedicated to Jewish art, was in-augurated, which was a real milestone. The Weiszman Institute was already earning a reputation for research, science, and technology, and

Free composition at Ramot Menashé (unfinished), detail
c. 1969
watercolour, ink on paper
43 x 35 cm

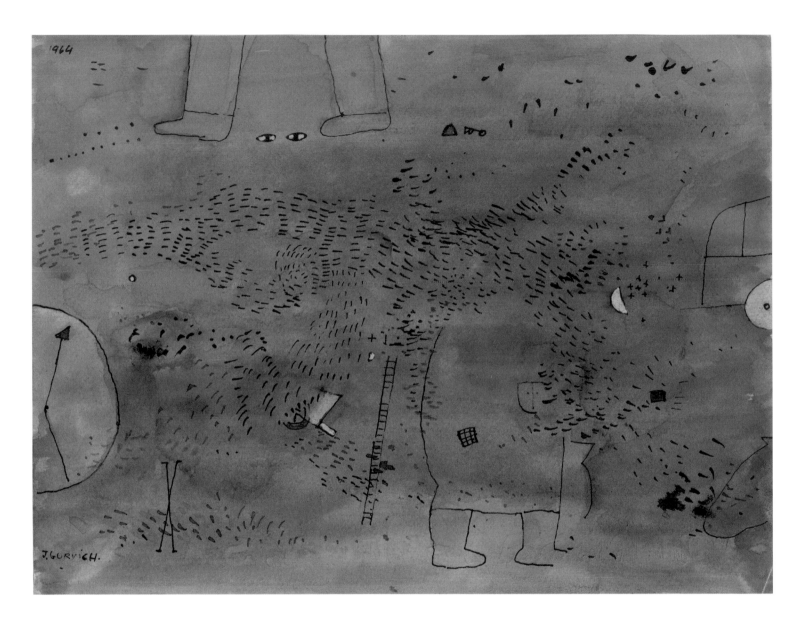

Nocturne
1964
watercolour, ink on paper
16.5 x 21.5 cm

when it started producing its first inventions it was launched on a distinguished career and gained world-wide recognition. In the 1960s the Hadassah University Hospital in Jerusalem started to excel in the field of medicine,[36] and it went on to shine even brighter. Israel is a small country with few natural resources, but by backing scientific research and education it soon won international recognition for its scientific and technological achievements.

Since 1958, Israel has been sharing its technological discoveries with many countries and taking part in international cooperation programmes. The Centre for International Cooperation (MASHAV) of the Foreign Relations Ministry has been active in Asia, Africa, and Latin America. Thousands of agriculture experts have been sent abroad on long- and short-term missions. Irrigation experts are sharing their know-how with students in a number of countries, grant programmes have been implemented to study in Israel, and cooperation has been extended in many fields.

Those decades were relatively peaceful, although Israel did fight the Sinai campaign of 1956 and there was Fedayeen terrorism, which consisted of Arab armed militias that infiltrated into Israel, especially from 1948 to 1965, and carried out sabotage and assassinations. In addition, there was always a latent threat from the Arab countries, which did not recognize the State of Israel. At every opportunity, dignitaries in Arab countries made speeches and incited the crowds with exhortations to eradicate Israel, to wipe it off the face of the earth.

According to Abba Eban,[37] the most fruitful period of modern Jewish history[38] was from 1957 to 1968. There was a lot of dreaming and utopian thinking but there were many concrete achievements too, even though these were not perfect and modern historians, with hindsight, have criticised many of the things that were done.[39]

Gurvich was aware of what was going on in Israel not only on the kibbutz but in other places, as he had many friends in other cities. He worked in Tel Aviv at various times and on each trip he saw how the country was growing and developing, and he was filled with genuine admiration for it.

All nations have their founding myths, the original principles and traditions that become part of the people's collective memory, and Israel was no exception. Gurvich found himself immersed in that new culture, in those new myths, he absorbed them during his three long stays in the country, and they are echoed in his art.

This was a period of strong cultural and social construction,[40] it was an effort of almost mythical dimensions and it had happened before, during the time of the *Yishuv* (the settlement of Zionist pioneers under Ottoman and British rule in the first *Aliyot*[41]) when the first immigration began before the State of Israel was born. After 1948, there was a State civil religion that coordinated a common vision and drew together people who were born in Israel, people who undertook *Aliyah* (immigrated) and people like Gurvich who came to spend some time in the country.

One strong element in the process of constructing Israel was the teleological direction of Zionism and the idea of continuity from antiquity right up to the present day, and this meant a total change from the Diaspora of the past. Israel was infused with a sacred spirit that was not religious. The name Jerusalem is connected with Zion, Mount Zion, and even in Biblical times this symbolised the homeland. Zion as a place was linked to that ancient era, to Israel's age of glory, as well as to the history of the people who founded the modern State without divine intervention.

Sketch for painting of Cain and Abel

c. 1973

felt-tip pen on paper

15 x 10.5 cm

Abstract man

1954

oil on cardboard

32.5 x 31 cm

Socialist Zionists considered that they represented historical continuity. They talked about rehabilitating the land of the *Tanakh* (Bible) because it was a return to Zion. A new society made up of immigrants was building a national identity and culture, and they sought their roots in the past. As Yael Zerubavel says,[42] the nation based itself on collective memories of recovered roots. Modern Hebrew society had to establish a different identity from that of the Diaspora so it made an explicit connection with the ancient land of Israel, which it glorified with a positive, romantic, and idealized vision.

A key element was the language. *Eretz-Israel*, the land of Israel, constructed its own language which was not the Yiddish of the Diaspora but modern Hebrew.[43] The man who transformed Hebrew into a living language was Eliezer Ben-Yehuda.[44] For seventeen centuries Hebrew had mainly been confined to religious or literary contexts, but he reinvented it and created a thousand new words, and this generated a unifying factor of great significance because this invention or re-creation became the everyday language, and it has continued to grow in an ongoing process.[45] The Hebrew language[46] is a recipient of traditions and sensitivities, a powerful spreader of heritage, and while the people who learn it and use it today may have a more secular perspective, they have a direct link to biblical texts and to things that were written thousands of years ago.

The use of revived Hebrew was amazing for anyone from the Diaspora who came to Israel in the 1950s and 1960s. Like all of us, Gurvich was astonished, and the Hebrew letters and phrases that appear in his early work are evidence of this. First, there was surprise at something novel and unusual; an entire country in which every written and spoken thing was in Hebrew. And then there was the emotion, it was enthralling to see for the very first time streets with Hebrew signs, Hebrew newspapers, stamps in Hebrew with biblical symbols, bookstores packed with books in Hebrew, and Hebrew typewriters. In addition, there was the very special symbolic act of adopting new names. This is what the *olim chadashim* (new immigrant) did (and still do) when they arrive in Israel, they baptize themselves in pure Hebrew and thus get rid of the derogatory connotations of surnames they have been forced to use for centuries.

Some of Gurvich's Uruguayan peers Hebraized their names. That language, which had been virtually extinct in daily life and was only used in religion or in literature, was alive again and blossoming, growing more every day. In 1966, a writer who wrote in Hebrew, S. Y. Agnon, received a Nobel Prize and went on to achieve great literary stature. It was most moving to see, and as Zerubavel[47] says, everything changed, there was Hebrew literature, Hebrew youth, Hebrew work and Hebrew schools.

Another aspect was that everything that made up Jewish culture in the Diaspora was only used at home or within the community, but now it was on every corner, on every street and on every building. Suddenly, wherever you went there were murals with subjects such as the twelve tribes,[48] and the Star of David was on the flag, on ambulances and hospitals, as decoration on gates and railings, or as the insignia on ships and aircraft. And all that iconography begins to appear in Gurvich's work.

As Shlomo Avneri[49] explains, Gurvich witnessed the creation of new rules and a public focus on mythologisation and fascination with the land,[50] which was a very strong feature of the new country.[51] At that time, knowing about the geography and making trips to different parts of Israel became a passion, a hobby for everyone, and this is still the case. Religion permeates everything, it is an unavoidable force, and although the country is secular its traditions are of religious origin. Even though orthodox religious Israelis were and are a minority in percentage terms, the weight of religious tradition was and is very powerful. There are examples of religious practices everywhere; the *Shabbat* has been kept as the national day of rest, Jewish wedding rites have been retained, the main religious festivals are public holidays, funeral traditions are respected, male circumcision is practiced, and *kashrut* (the religious rite at meals) is compulsory in public places.

For Gurvich, to be in Israel meant to ingest, from morning to night, words, names, facts, stories, and places that have biblical connections. They were part of everyday life, in the most natural way. The Bible, the *Tanakh*,[52] resounded in the daily lives of non-believers as well as believers, institutions are named in honour of biblical figures, and for many the use of biblical names was and is like being born again.

This whole mythologisation was promoted in a great effort by the State, and Ben-Gurion was a key figure in this process. He encouraged the members of the government and the army to Hebraize their names based on names in the Bible,[53] he campaigned for the streets around government offices have biblical names, the medals given to soldiers had the names of heroes from the Bible, and he encouraged painters, sculptors, musicians, writers and teachers to study and draw inspiration from the Bible. But the people did not resent this or feel it was something imposed, they accepted it with pride. Secular Jews were (and still are) encouraged to know about the *Tanakh* because of its great literary value, its ethical lessons, the teachings of the prophets and the deeds of its heroic figures.

The sacred books constitute the central document of Judaism. The Bible contains the symbols and the key developments, it is a source of discussion about a whole range of subjects, it is in effect a spiritual home, and all Jews have known the Bible stories since childhood be-

Kibbutz
1967
pastel on paper
21 x 27 cm

Composition with religious symbols at Ramot Menashé, detail

cause it was read not only by religious Jews but by secular Jews as well. It has been used to develop study methods for children so that it would become an integral part of their lives. The sacred books are a historical, legal, ethical, literary, linguistic, geographical and artistic framework, and they are the inspiration for literature, songs, music and the visual arts.

The State fostered the setting up of secular Bible study groups, and among the *kibbutzim*, and even among anti-religious Marxists, it had (and still has) great cultural significance.[54] And because the *Tanakh* was read, used and interpreted in the Hebrew land while a new Jewish State was being created, it acquired other connotations, other reverberations, and it was transformed into a powerful factor in unity and self-identification. It has been consecrated as the paramount cultural source for Israel. Gurvich did not have to go very far for the *Tanakh*, the Bible, to come into his life. The kibbutz he lived on was called Menashé, which was one of the legendary twelve tribes, one of the sons

Several plans, detail of Moses receiving the Torah

of Joseph. Almost every place he visited was named in the Bible. The children he lived with and many of the *chaverim* had names taken from biblical texts, and the new Hebrew words had their roots (*shoresh*) in those texts. If he listened to songs, many were inspired by the Bible, for example, by *Shir-ha Shirim* (the Song of Songs). Every festival was named in the *Tanakh*.

When Gurvich sent a letter he might find a great king or biblical hero on the stamp, like David, Judas Maccabeus, Samson, Saul, Simon Bar Kochba or Solomon. Proof about passages in the Bible was uncovered whenever there was an archaeological dig. Biblical heroes such as Samson, Gideon, Saul, David, and Solomon were spotlighted and exalted, as were the uprisings of the Maccabees against the Seleucids, the wars in Judea against the Romans, and all the liberation movements. In this State effort, national and political aspects were stressed and the religious aspects of the stories and legends were minimised or eliminated. There was a selective reconstruction of the past and the new Hebrews were seen as the descendants of those ancient heroes. They too were *ivrim* (Hebrews), and the word *yehudi* (Jew) became secondary. With this emphasis on historical and mythical rather than religious roots, it was easier for a lay Jew like Gurvich to feel he was part of that identity.

Gurvich wrote in a letter, "Strong, simple men, with such a love for their land, this new kind of Jew who was born here is completely different from us. He has no religion, he is not interested in metaphysics, he is sometimes slow thinking but he is positive and practical. They are called *sabras*, which is a fruit from the pine tree with thorns on the outside but very sweet and soft on the inside."[55] This was how he res-

cuadrado, estoy leyendo un autor italiano, Ignacio Silone, te recomiendo el libro (Fontamara) y Pan y Vino), a mi me dijo mucho, mucho.....

Aquí, los días son pesados, con un Sol!! que te quita la energía, ahora ¿crees eso de que el sol se alimenta de nosotros; pero, no te imaginas, lo agradable que resulta al atardecer, una brisa! una serenidad de las las onduladas, suaves y pedregosa colinas que nos rodean, te invade una serenidad y querer a las plantas, y bichos, flores.....y niños, cuántos niños a esa hora, es cuando se reúnen con sus padres, la alegría! que libertad reciben, son completamente I independientes, por ejemplo tu ves un niño de 3 años salió de su dormitorio, lavarse, peinarse, comió solo, y recorrer el Kibutz, y cuando se le antoja ver a ir a sus padres, los niños de 7 años, los ves manejar caballos, burritos etc. y a los 12 o 13, años los ves arriba de un tractor o camiones admirable!; hombres, fuertes, simples, con un amor a su tierra, este nuevo personaje de Judío nacido, aquí se diferencia totalmente de nosotros, no tien religión y no le interesa la metafísica, es a veces lento en el pensar, es positivo, práctico, y se los llaman Sabres, que es una fruta de los pinos, con espinas por afuera, pero muy dulce y blando por dentro, voy a comer y vuelvo a continuar la carta. espero algún día terminarla y mandártela, ~~trato de ir pensando al tierra~~ a algunas

ponded to a new discovery he made, the *sabra*. According to Amos Oz, "This fruit has stamped its mark on the landscape and on history," and it had a special value in the new Israel and in the kibbutz society.

A new generation of Jews was emerging, heroic, courageous and daring, transcending all boundaries, making marshes and deserts fertile. The Zionist ethos was in the process of projecting this key notion of the healthy young person, strong, robust, daring, honest, direct, ideologically committed, pragmatic, and willing to defend the State to the very end. In fact this concept grew to mythological levels and set up the *sabra* as an ideal. It was a hegemonic construction from those years that also revealed the aspirations of the Zionists in Europe. It was a social construct, a powerful myth to underpin self-image, education and socialisation.

In those years there were many archaeological discoveries and they inevitably had an enormous impact and repercussions because of their implications for national unity and the sense of belonging. They were deeply moving because they bore witness to thousands of years of history in this land, they yielded traces of the past with ancient symbols, and they confirmed some biblical texts. The remains of cities, synagogues, fortresses, cemeteries and *mikvot* (the plural of *Mikvah*, the ritual bath to attain purity[56]) were unearthed. In the excavations, a whole array of artefacts were found including coins, vases, mosaics, ceramic lamps, Jewish folk art and inscriptions. There were also examples of decoration with traditional symbols venerated for many generations like the pomegranate, the palm, the *menorah*, the Holy Ark, the seven fruits named in the Bible that symbolise the fertility of Israel (grape, date, pomegranate, barley, wheat, fig and olive), and the *shofar* (a horn played at New Year and on the Day of Atonement). These finds were inspiring and they were a valuable source of iconography for the new art, such as Gurvich's painting.

The depths of the earth yielded up cultural treasures that were thousands of years old, the legacy of centuries of architecture, art and crafts, and also fortresses and citadels built at the time of the kingdoms of Israel and Judah. There were synagogues and their ornaments with different images, mosaics with geometric patterns, fruit, animals, birds, the zodiac in Hebrew and the scene of the so-called sacrifice of Isaac, the *Akedah* (Genesis 22: 1-19), among a myriad of other treasures.

Masada was a landmark in archaeological excavation. Between 1963 and 1965, evidence was found there about the Jewish uprising against the Roman forces occupying Israel, and this confirmed what the Romanised Jewish historian Flavius Josephus had written.[57] Masada[58] was a milestone because of its impressiveness, its historic richness, the symbolic value it acquired and the findings that were unearthed. This revolt is famous: the rebels entrenched themselves at Masada in an at-

Project for a painting of the kibbutz, detail
c. 1973
watercolour, ink on paper
35 x 43 cm

Shabbat (with scene from Jacob's dream)
1973
tempera on paper
25 x 30 cm

tempt to regain their freedom and sovereignty, to resist Romanisation and to put a stop to attacks on Jewish religion. The war lasted from 66 to 70 A.D., but resistance dragged on until 73 A.D. when the Romans defeated the last rebels.[59] The end was very tragic. According to Flavius Josephus, the rebel leader Eleazar ben Yair ordered the fortress to be set on fire and everyone inside it to be killed. The story (and the myth) is that ten men were chosen to kill all the others because suicide is forbidden in Judaism. The last man had to break this commandment. The archaeological expedition led by Yigael Yadin found evidence of the rebels' Jewish life, how they practised their religion, that they read the Bible[60] during the fighting, that they founded a synagogue, that they used the two ritual baths, and how they showed their spirit of independence by minting coins[61] with inscriptions such as "Shekel of Israel" and "Jerusalem the Saint".[62]

When Gurvich was in Israel, Masada made a great impression on him. It became a symbol of the Jewish people's yearning for freedom and self-determination. It represents the will to remain Jewish and to die for that identity, and thus to save the land. One of the great unifying slogans in Israel was "Masada shall never fall again", and it has tremendous meaning for the Jewish people not only in Israel but throughout the Diaspora. And this significance becomes even more intense when we see it in the dreadful light of the Holocaust.

The story of Masada was essential in forming the identity of the Zionist Jew, in his pride, his bond with the land, his roots, his will to struggle for that land until the end if necessary, even though recent historians have raised doubts about what really took place.

There were other excavations that were essential for national feeling like those that yielded evidence of the rebellion of Shimon Bar Kochba against the Roman Empire (132-135) in the second Jewish-Roman war. Bar Kochba founded a Jewish sovereign State which lasted three years. The uprising was put down with terrible cruelty by the Romans in 135 A.D., and that was the start of the Jewish Diaspora. Archaeological expeditions found traces of these heroic events,[63] and they were very significant because the rebels' fight to the death became a symbol of brave national resistance. There are findings that prove several aspects of Bar Kochba's rule, including his famous coins. Because he longed for independence, Bar Kochba minted his own coins with Jewish motifs and inspiring inscriptions such as "Year one of the Redemption of Israel" and "For the liberation of Jerusalem". These coins soon became popular images in Israel and part of the country's national imagery.

Another milestone was the discovery of the Dead Sea Scrolls.[64] These originally belonged to a Jewish sect, probably the Essenes, and they contain the oldest Hebrew texts of the *Tanakh* and a total of nine hundred documents, including evidence of the second temple in Jerusalem.[65]

Archaeology became an Israeli passion and made a massive contribution to the so-called civil religion,[66] which was an ideological tool that met the mythic-poetic needs of a nation and revolutionized the country's consciousness. Old images became part of modern life. Archaeology became a central pillar of secular identity, one more way to embrace the land, to take part in the digs, to learn the geography, to establish contact with our ancestors, and to fortify the connection between the present with the past. That is still the situation today, and there was even more emphasis on it during Israel's early years, the time when Gurvich was there. He saw how the past floods the land of Israeli and there is no way to avoid it. It starts with an excavation or a chance discovery, then one find after the other comes to light, and each is one more reason to love the country. Archaeology united the Jews and still unites them with thousands of years of their history and with passages from the Bible.

In Israel the past is always present and each trace nourishes a sense of continuity. For secular people it was important to verify that the Tanakh can in fact be a source of history, even if only occasionally. The poet Avraham Shlonsky,[67] in an apparent paradox, wrote, "We came here to start from the beginning because we came here to continue the way."

It is not difficult to imagine the atmosphere of fervour, emotion, unity and love for their roots that these events awakened in the new State. The effect of the discoveries was amazing because the news spread quickly in the most varied ways, and all you had to do was take a few coins out your pocket to find the replica of the grape clusters or the four-string lyre from the Bar Kochba period, or a replica of the *menorah* from the Arch of Titus in Rome. This was one of the ways the State of Israel forged links with and celebrated its past in Zion, which was its land. It used images from archaeological findings in many everyday contexts like posters, illustrations in school books and *Haggadot* (plural of *Haggadah*, a book recounting the exodus from Egypt), and right from the beginning of the 1950s many motifs from the distant past were to be found on coins and stamps.[68]

From very early on there were postage stamps with scenes of Jewish festivals, images of geographical locations such as the Negev desert, cities like Jerusalem or Petah Tikva, *Rosh Hashana* (New Year), portraits of heroes like Theodor Herzl, the founder of Zionism, or Max Nordau, another crucial figure in Zionist history, portraits of writers such as Sholem Aleichem, Jaim Najman Bialik and Eliezer Ben-Yehuda, the philosopher Maimonides, and pictures of the land of Israel, its scenery, its native birds, its flora and fauna. In those early years there were not many tributes to religious figures; one of the few was Baal Shem Tov, the founder of Hasidism.[69] The country's modern attainments were also

Explosion
1965
tempera
33 X 46.5 cm

publicised on postage stamps, as happened with the outstanding scientific achievements of the Weiszman Institute, for example. So the postage stamp became yet another key factor in the development of the nation's identity.[70]

Like every new state, Israel had to create its emblems, but it was a special case because it took them from an enormous long-standing storehouse of culture. It surrounded itself with collective representations that could be recognized and take root, and these were based on a rich heritage of tremendous symbolic importance[71] that was right there, under their feet, in the land of their ancestors. These symbols of identity were provided by history, archaeology, folklore and religion, and they were projected in the modern State. And Gurvich was immersed in that process.

Judaism in the Promised Land

Judaism pervaded all aspects of life in Israel, and the State promoted and developed it as a civil religion. Gurvich consciously or unconsciously, deliberately or otherwise, absorbed knowledge from these sources, and this experience stimulated and revitalized his identity. He expressed this developing consciousness in his artistic work at the Ramot Menashé kibbutz.

His first stay there (1955-1956) was very intense and exciting because it was just a few years after the country was founded and it left an indelible mark on him. Afterwards, during his other two stays, in 1964-1965 and in 1969-1970, he saw the country and the kibbutz growing rapidly. He was able to actually experience how a nation with a defined identity was created and grew. He was hugely impressed by the Israel of the two most exciting decades, the 1950s and 1960s, and he kept receiving fresh doses like new layers on top of his Lithuanian experiences, his mother's religiousness and his Uruguayan Jewishness.

Those experiences set him off on a progressive conscious or unconscious search for the heritage of Judaism and for new elements, the revived symbolic load generated in the new State. This wide range of symbols and images was implanted in Jewish migrants who came to live in the country, that is to say people who undertook the *aliyah* (to ascend), and also in people who just came to visit. The experience was very moving for Gurvich because he lived in Israel for a long period and took part in a special Israeli invention which was the collective farm or kibbutz.

This meant working and living with *chaverim* (comrades) in the idealistic framework of a Marxist Zionist Hashomer Hatzair community, which is what Ramot Menashé was at that time. The people there were still dedicated to the emergence of a new kind of man, to social

Kibbutz I
c. 1956
watercolour, ink on paper
13 x 21 cm

equality and to changing society, and these were burning questions that were debated were discussed. He shared this experience with members of his family, and because he was always very attached to them the impact of that way of life was deeper and more intense. On his first trip he was with his sister Miriam and her family, and on the other two, besides them, there were also his wife Totó, his son Martín, his mother Jaie and his father Jacob.

These visits affected him profoundly, as they did all who had similar experiences, because those were dreamy, romantic, altruistic times full of lofty ideals. However, this idealism started to progressively disappear in the kibbutz movement after the 1980s,[72] as it did in all of Israel after 1967, gradually at first and more markedly in recent years.[73] But Gurvich was there in the glorious years, that unparalleled time when there was genesis, movement and dynamic building, and the atmosphere of constant invention and vitality favoured and promoted the part of his character that was geared to change, innovation, creation and metamorphosis.

From those experiences he imbibed challenging new stimuli for this identity, fresh elements that were unknown in the Diaspora. He was nourished spiritually by the new symbolic repertoire based on tradition, on the founding representations that strengthened the people's will, aspirations, interests, expectations, memories and hopes for social change. Gurvich felt and experienced this exposure to the agglutinating power of the symbols of Jewish tradition. And this power was very pervasive, it was a national effort to mould the people's attitudes and guide them, and in this process many characteristics of Judaism were emphasised and raised to transcendent levels to foster a sense of belonging to the new State. This generated genuine respect among the population, it fostered integration, it stimulated union, it legitimised the social order, it galvanised people to make a combined social effort, and the core values and the world vision of that Jewish country were passed on to the next generation and to new arrivals.

The birth of Israel wrought far-reaching changes in all the Jews of the Diaspora, and Gurvich was no exception. Israel is crucially important in the definition of Jewish identity, and this is expressed as support, solidarity, and defending its existence and its fight for freedom and survival. Since the State came into being, to be Jewish has meant having ties in one way or another with Israel, different bonds depending on each individual and each Diaspora community. Israel unifies Jews all over the world, whether or not they agree with its domestic or foreign policy, with its political parties, the conflictive status of Israeli Arabs, the Palestine question, social problems, or the successive governments and their decisions. And this applies to Jews even if they have not undertaken *aliyah* (moved to Israel), even if they love and identify with the countries where they were born and live. Gurvich did not undertake *aliyah*, he identified with Uruguay and loved it, he was as Uruguayan as they come, but at the same time he established a great bond with Israel.

In a way Israel has taken over the role that religion played in the old Jewish communities of the Diaspora. In our modern, secular world it is a secular point of reference, it defines what is called *Klal Israel* (all Israel), an expression that indicates a sense of fraternity, of common destiny. Jews use it to denote the fact that they are a people, a united group, regardless of their different attitudes to religion, of the countries they live in, of their heterogeneity, of their different ways of ex-

Ramot Menashé
1970
watercolour, indian ink on paper
45 x 57.5 cm

Chaver and chavera
1973
tempera, indian ink on paper
21 x 29 cm

Kibbutz composition
1964
watercolour on paper
16.5 x 21.5 cm

pressing themselves, of their varied ideologies or opposing opinions. They are a human mosaic, and all together they make up the Diaspora and Israel.

For Gurvich, Israel was an extremely encouraging and stimulating context. He was in harmony with the prevailing spirit and those experiences had a big impact and repercussions and ramifications in his artistic languages. He developed very intense, fervently artistic expressions of Judaic content, above all during his second and third stays in the country, and this content became a main subject in his art and gave him an iconography he used for the rest of his life.

He worked very intensely with Judaic symbols and themes in numerous compositions depicting kibbutz life, man and woman, the cosmic man, the creation, the traditional festivals and so on. His creative world was filled with *Menorot* (seven branch candelabra), the Star of

Kibbutz
1967
pastel on paper
21 x 27 cm

David (*Magen David*, the hexagram which represents King David's coat of arms or one of his emblems), the Ten Commandments, Hebrew letters, trees of life, and also *chalutzim* (pioneers) working under the burning Israeli sun and the hills of Menashé, where the Ramot Menashé kibbutz is located.

He progressively built up a symbolic repertoire with strong Jewish overtones from the kibbutz. The kibbutz was the place from which he looked at the world, from which he expressed his thoughts about life and the cosmos. He embedded his universal messages in this real setting so it is the environment from which connotations and subtexts emerge, and he went on doing this even when he was living in Cerro or in New York, or working on other things. Jewish and kibbutz symbols can even be found in a very imaginative work like *Pareja* (Couple, 1967) which is an urban context painted in an oneiric-surrealistic style. There are symbols such as the *menorah*, the seven branch candelabra that has a raised central arm to dignify the *Shabbat*, ladders ascending to the celestial sphere, *chaverim* (comrades) on the kibbutz, Israeli sheep, and the hand of the Creator touching that of the first man (citing Michelangelo in the Sistine Chapel), and these images also appear in other paintings that have nothing to do with the kibbutz or Jewish subject matter.

In the kibbutz setting he conveys his world view, so the sins of human beings and their vices and virtues, for example, are worked into his art. There is an eye at the top, or many eyes, which are references to spirituality, to ethical values that are above us and see us and judge us

Couple, detail

like God or a supreme being, there is the original universal couple like Adam and Eve, an allusion to love, and there is suffering represented by the crucifixion of Jesus or his stigmata.

But the world Gurvich projects also includes a whole range of other subject matter like trees of life, love for work, the capacity to create, the faculty of dreaming, time indicated on a clock, the need to ascend using ladders, the terrestrial and the celestial, the immanent and the transcendent. There is the theme of constant birth and transformation, and biblical quotations, Torres García-like symbols, memories of Lithuania and scenes of festivals.

He put in some verses by his beloved Antonio Machado, the Spanish poet, references such as "*SSSS oíd al viento…*" accompanied by the image of a woman calling for silence, a figure that subsequently appears in many works, but without the poem.

After 1969 he included more and more religious connotations as a tribute to his mother, who had an incurable illness. We find the *Erev Shabbat* (the eve of Saturday) ceremony, and biblical scenes from Genesis such as *Akedah* (the binding of Isaac, wrongly named the sacrifice of Isaac), Sarah's pregnancy, Sarah's death, Cain and Abel and Jacob's dream. He did a series of the most important celebrations in Judaism, events that are crucial in kibbutz life and in Israel, sacred days that his mother always observed when he was a child.

Another subject that attracted him was "It is hard to be a Jew". This is based on a saying by Shalom Aleichem[74] (Shalom Rabinowitz), the most beloved of classic Yiddish writers and one of Gurvich's favourite authors, whose pen name means "Peace be upon you", the traditional Hebrew greeting.

The painter tackled all these subjects in his own, highly idiosyncratic way. He generated a metamorphosed reality and a fluctuating world, he dealt with subjective content and he presented fantasy images loaded with emotion. He invented multiple figures that proliferate and quiver in his compositions, which have incredible energy, vitality, joy and dynamism. Life itself throbs in all his work.

The major change that Israel inspired in his art involved new formal schemes, diverse approaches to composition, and ways of using colour that were different to what he did before. His colours were vehement, animated, communicative, luminous and effusive, and he created compositions of various types, undulating, dotted, with spheres, with small lines. He used dynamic graphics, ovoid shapes and curved rhythms. He explored many forms and modes of composition, he successfully tried new routes to expression. He expanded his idiosyncratic pictorial and drawing resources and added an original way of handling ceramics, collage and objects. He was nothing if not versatile and changeable.

Kibbutz composition with couple, detail

The physical location that triggered this sea-change in his art was the Israel he came to know at that special time. There was a quasi-religious fervour in the air and he immersed himself in the exalted emotions of joy and enthusiasm that held sway during the first decades of the life of the new State. At that time there was a special mystique that bound the people firmly together, and this is what Gurvich fed on.

Kibbutz daydream
1966
oil on canvas
30 x 40 cm

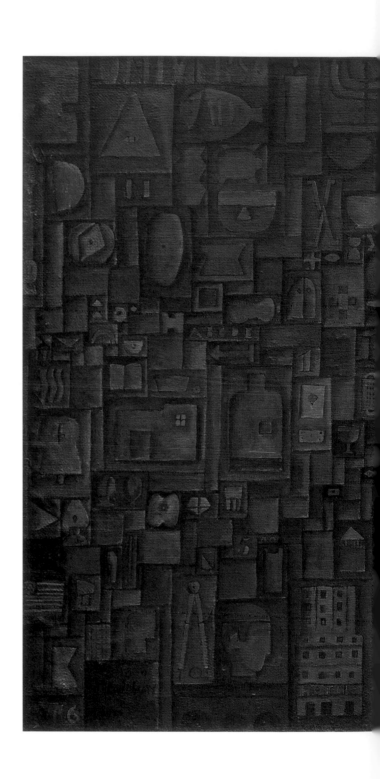

Construction with sun
1962
oil on hessian
98 x 180 cm

Universal couple at Ramot Menashé
c. 1965
oil on wood
130.5 x 41 cm

Construction with Star of David
1957
painted and incised wood
30.5 x 16 cm

Fantasy world on white background
1966
oil on canvas
60 x 80 cm

Creation in collage
1967
oil, fabrics on canvas
55 x 75 cm

Couple
1967
oil on plaster
39.5 x 30.5 cm

Kibbutz composition
1967
mixed technique on paper
21 x 29 cm

The creation
1970
oil on canvas
45 x 53 cm

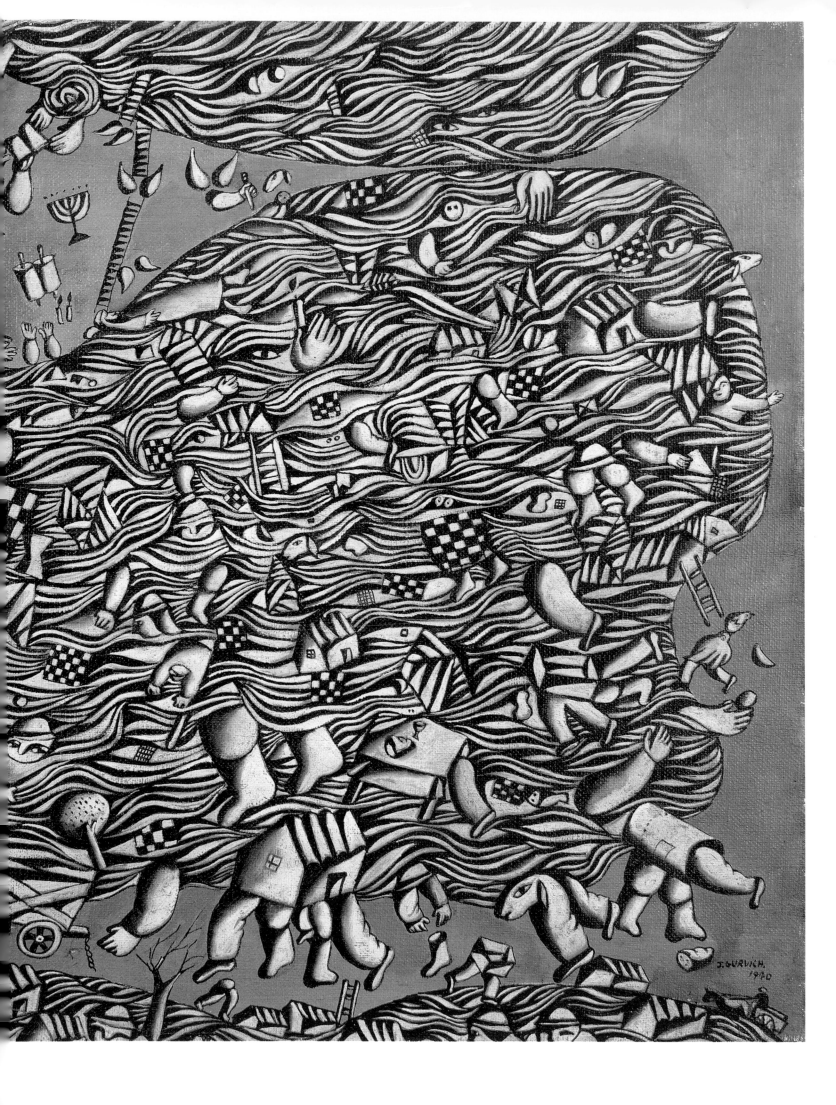

World of images
1972
oil on wood
60 x 92 cm

End notes

1 Kibbutz (plural: kibbutzim): Israeli rural commune founded by young Socialist Zionist Jews from Eastern Europe. The first one was Degania, which was set up on the shores of the Sea of Galilee in 1909. There were many more, and the original kibbutz model continued until the 1985 crisis, after which it underwent progressive modifications. It is a voluntary collective community and in the early days it was agricultural, private property did not exist and the community was responsible for all the needs of its members and their families. It is based on democracy, humanism and equality of opportunity. It is a unique social system and one of the greatest achievements of Zionism. Socialist or Marxist ideology (depending on the kibbutz) played an important part, especially before 1985. There are also religious kibbutzim. The members of a kibbutz had a missionary and pioneering spirit. A kibbutz can have from 30 to 1,500 members. See Ernest Krausz (editor), Sociology of the Kibbutz - Studies of Israeli Society, vol. II, New Brunswick , Transaction Books,1983.

2 Ramot Menashé, the heights of Menashé, kibbutz located in Northern Israel. 'Ramot' means 'height' in Hebrew and 'Menashé' is the name of one of the twelve Jewish tribes in ancient Israel. This kibbutz is between Mount Carmel and the Valley of Jezreel, it was founded in 1948 by Polish pioneers and survivors of the Holocaust and it also received Austrians, Romanians and a large contingent of Argentines, Uruguayans and Chileans.

3 According to the Bible, one of the sons of Joseph. Menashé was one of the tribes that received lands in Israel.

4 Since the villages in Eastern Europe were often invaded their names vary according to the different invading countries. It is Jieznas in Lithuanian, Yezne in Yiddish, Ezno in Russian, Jezno in Polish, and it is also known as Jezna, Yezna, Yeznas, Eznas, Iyeznas and Jeznas.

5 Shtetl in Yiddish refers to Jewish villages very typical of Eastern Europe. The shtetls territory, the cherta osedlosti, was marked off in accordance with a Russian Imperial decree. It included what are now parts of Poland, Lithuania, Belorussia, Bessarabia, Ukraine and Western Russia. Jews were forbidden to live outside that territory, and there – in that segregated, apartheid environment – a very peculiar Ashkenazi culture developed.

6 The shtetls were wiped off the map during the Nazi genocide of World War II when 6 million Jews were killed and with them whole cultures, a way of life, and the predominance of Yiddish, a language that united the Jews.

7 Kosher means "ritually correct" and the word kashrut is derived from it.

8 This emerges from everyone I interviewed for this book: his wife Julia Añorga de Gurvich, his friends and colleagues at the Ramot Menashé kibbutz, and the Uruguayan painters that were welcomed into his home in his Montevideo years.

9 Mitzvah (plural: mitzvot): a number of religious precepts that a Jew must carry out in daily life. There are 613 commandments.

10 Youth Zionist Movement members' meeting centre.

11 Hashomer Hatzair, a Youth Zionist Marxist Movement, was founded in Eastern Europe in the Polish province of Galicia in 1913. Its ultimate goal was to move to Palestine, settle there and work as pioneers to create a socialist nation based on social justice and equality. During the war they were partisans, resisting in the ghettos. Mordechai Anielewicz was the heroic leader of the Warsaw ghetto uprising. The members of Hashomer Hatzair distinguished themselves during the resistance in Hungary, Lithuania, Slovakia and other areas. In Palestine they formed part of the Haganah, the liberation army, and the Palmach, shock troops in the War of Independence.

12 Diminutive de Yosef - José, in Yiddish.

13 Author's interview with Julia Añorga (Totó) for this book. The author has interviewed Totó many times since the 1990s.

14 His mother emigrated to the Ramot Menashé kibbutz in 1962 to live with her daughter Miriam and her family, and later on José Gurvich's father followed.

15 "Héctor Yuyo Goitiño, La alegría de pintar", in Daniel Rovira Alhers, Proximidades: testimonios sobre el pintor José Gurvich, Montevideo, José Gurvich Foundation, 2003, p. 159.

16 Author's interview with Ernesto Vila, July 1999. Author's interview with Isaac Glicksberg in 2010. I am very grateful to him for all the knowledge he so generously shared about Jewish life in Barrio Sur and downtown Montevideo during the 1930s and 1940s.

17 Rural collective farm with agriculture teaching.

18 "Israel Ganz: Adolescencia y amistad", in Daniel Rovira Alhers, op. cit., p. 23.

19 Ibidem. p. 25.

20 bidem .

21 Author's interview with Julia Añorga, February 1999.

22 Ibidem.

23 Interview with Vera Jordan in Montevideo.
24 Pogrom: a word of Russian origin. It means to destroy or demolish, and is used in reference to the attacks on Jewish populations in Russia, especially towards the end of the 19th century in Kiev and Odessa, and in the 20th century (1903-1906). There were many pogroms in other areas, some were famous, like Kishinev in 1903, and later there were more during the Russian revolution in 1917.
25 The term Zionism was invented by Nathan Birnbaum in 1890. It derived from the name of the mountain near Jerusalem (Zion) and it has since become synonymous with Israel. According to Zionism, the Jews are a nation; they are defined as sharing a culture, a common past and a history, and they aspire to populate the land from which they were expelled. Zionism has variations; it may be practical, synthetic, socialist, revisionist or religious. The main Zionist theorist was Theodore Herzl, although the idea began to take shape before him, and it has a history and a basis. However, it was halted by the enormous wave of anti-Semitism, the terrible pogroms in Russia at the end of the 19th century and by the shock caused by French anti-Semitism in the Dreyfus case, which split France between 1890 and 1900. This was all the more disturbing because France was a democracy, a republic, an educated and modern country, based on human rights, not at all like the authoritarian and backward Russia of the Tsars. The movement's founding Zionists felt that life in the Diaspora was very bad as the Jews were limited by anti-Semitism, not integrated, restricted by exclusion in a distorted socio-economic structure, and in addition they were a long way from Israel, which reduced the feeling of belonging. The solution to the Jewish problem was to create a national sovereign State where the life of the people would be reborn in all its dimensions. Exile – from a secular point of view – had to end without waiting for the Messiah, it had to depend on human effort. This Zionist programme eventually led to the creation of the State of Israel.
26 Theodore Herzl was the founder of the Zionist Organization, set up during the First Zionist Congress in Basle, Switzerland, in 1897. He wrote The Jewish State (1896). Theodore Herzl, El Estado Judío, Buenos Aires, Prometeo, 2005.
27 Ganz, op. cit., p. 21.
28 Interview with Adolfo Nigro in Buenos Aires, September 1999.
29 Goitiño, op. cit., p. 159.
30 Socialist Zionism had many variations, some Marxist, like the Mapam, which is associated with the Hashomer Hatzair, and others of more labour leanings like the Mapai. The Mapai Mifleget Poalei Eretz Yisrael (The Worker's Party of Eretz Israel) came into being in 1930. The leader was David Ben-Gurion and the spiritual leader was Berl Katznelson. They created constructive Socialism based on pioneering ideals and political pragmatism. They were the dominant force in the country until 1968. They later merged with two other left-wing parties, Ahdut HaAvoda and Rafi, and formed the Labour Party.
31 David Ben-Gurion (1886-1973) was Prime Minister and Minister of Defence (1948-1953 and 1955-1963). He proclaimed the independent State of Israel in Tel-Aviv on May 14, 1948. In 1920, he founded the Histadrut – the central workers union - and he also founded the Mapai Party, which won the elections many times and governed Israel between 1948 and 1977.
32 Author's interview with Totó, 2009.
33 Alicia Haber, José Gurvich: El mundo íntimo del artista: dibujos, bocetos, escritos y acuarelas, Buenos Aires, Homage exhibition at the Borges Cultural Centre, December 1999, p. 83.
34 Nahal, a special unit in the Israeli Armed Forces. Their task is to care for and defend the agricultural areas.
35 Amoz Oz was born Amos Klausner in 1939, and like many Israelis he changed his name to Hebrew. He is a renowned writer, novelist and journalist, and he is important for his pacifist stance. He was one of the founders of the Israeli pacifist movement Shalom Ajshav. He is a literature professor at the Ben-Gurion University in Beer Sheba, in Neguey, and a member of the European Academy of Science and Arts. In 2007 he received the Prince of Asturias Prize for Literature.
36 Israeli medical research is among the most advanced in the world. Apart from Hadassa, medical research institutes were founded at the Ben-Gurion University, the Bar-Ilan University, the Technion, the Israeli Institute of Technology, the University of Tel-Aviv, the Weizmann Institute of Science and the Hebrew University. This research stands out for its development of sophisticated technology for diagnostic and treatment procedures based on microcomputers, laser surgery instruments, electronic medical equipment and computerised monitors. It has also made numerous contributions to domestic and international medicine in cardiology, genetics, neurology, ophthalmology, neonatology, gerontology, and telemedicine, to name but a few notable examples.

37 Abba Eban was a renowned figure in Israel. He was a member of the Mapai Labour party. Eban graduated from Cambridge University in England and he was a politician, statesman, diplomat, academic, writer and speaker, Israeli Ambassador to the United Nations and the United States, Minister of Education and Culture, Minister of Foreign Affairs and a Member of Parliament.

38 Abba Eban, Heritage: Civilization and the Jews, New York, Summit Books, 1984.

39 Laurence Silberstein, New Perspectives on Israeli History: The Early Years of the State,New Perspectives on Jewish Studies, New York, NYU Press, Judith Gertz, Myths in Israeli Culture: Captives of a Dream, Parkes-Wiener Series on Jewish Studies, Mitchell Valentine & Company, 2000.

40 Charles S. Liebman, "Secular Judaism and its prospects", Israel Affairs, London, Routledge, vol. 4, Nos. 3 and 4, spring 1998, pp. 29-48.

41 Plural of aliyah, meaning to ascend, to immigrate into Israel. The first aliyah was in 1882 and was organized by the Zionist Movement.

42 Yael Zerubavel, Recovered Roots: Collective Memory and the Making of Israeli, National Tradition, Chicago, University of Chicago Press, 1995.

43 A language linked to the synagogue and religion, although there were Hebrew writers.

44 The foundations of current Hebrew were laid between 1881 and 1921. In November 1922, the British authorities in Palestine recognized Hebrew as the official language of the Jews.

45 All immigrants from all over the world soon learned the language in ulpan (an institution set up in 1949 for intensive teaching, and it is still a pillar of the aliyah) and they quickly integrated into society.

46 The Hebrew renaissance is one of the most notable successes: three thousand people spoke the language in 1940 and today 8 million speak it.

47 Zerubavel, op. cit.

48 The twelve legendary tribes in the Bible. According to Genesis, Abraham fathered Isaac, he begat Jacob or Israel, he in turn had twelve sons: Ruben, Simon, Levi, Juda, Isacar, Zabulon, Joseph, Benjamin, Dan, Neftali, Gad and Aser, and these fathered the twelve tribes of Israel. After the Exodus and return from Egypt, Joshua divided the Promised Land (the land of Canaan, Judea and today's Israel) among the twelve. After the captivity of Babylon, ten of the tribes disappeared.

49 Shlomo Avineri, "Assessing Zionism: Zionism as a Permanent Revolution", Union of Jewish Students, 8 April, 2003. http://www.doingzionism.org/resources/view.asp?id=1355

50 Charles Liebman and Eliezer Don-Yehiya, Civil Religion in Israel: Traditional Judaism and Political Culture in the Jewish State, Berkeley, University of California Press, 1983, p. 74.

51 Shlomo Avineri, op. cit.

52 Tanakh: acronym for the books that make up the Bible. In Hebrew, the Torah consists of the five books of Moses.

53 Liebman and Don-Yehiya, op. cit., p. 94.

54 Yuval Dror, "Teaching the Bible in the schools of the Labour and the Kibbutz Movements, 1921-1953", Journal of Jewish History, School of Education, Tel Aviv, TeTel Aviv University, vol. 21, No. 2, June 2007, pp. 179-197.

55 A letter written by Gurvich.

56 Carried out by women before marriage, after menstruation and giving birth. To this day, the mikvot are built in all orthodox communities.

57 A Jewish historian named Joseph ben Matityahu (Jerusalem circa 37 A.D. – Rome circa 100), who Romanized himself in order to survive. He told the story in his book, The Jewish War, in which he focuses on the rebellion that took place between 66 and 70-73. The book was written between 75 and 79 A.D.

58 The spot was identified in 1842. The main discoveries were between 1963 and 1965 in an expedition led by Yigael Yadin. This project was organised by the Hebrew University, the Israel Exploration Society and the Department of Antiques and Museums of Israel.

59 Today the story of what happened at Masada is quite controversial. One academic who sought to expose the myth was the sociologist Nachman Ben-Yehuda, Dean of Social Sciences of the Hebrew University. See: Sacrificing Truth: Archaeology and the Myth of Masada, Amherst, NY, Humanity Books, 2002, The Masada Myth: Collective Memory and Mythmaking in Israel, Madison, University of Wisconsin Press, 1995.

60 Papyrus with Biblical texts.

61 The rebels minted five thousand coins in their effort to achieve autonomy and freedom.

62 Seven hundred ostracon, pieces of ceramics or stone, with Hebrew inscriptions, plus ceramics, stone pots, arms, textiles and skeletons.

63 They were found in particular in the Judea desert between 1952 and 1961.

64 The Dead Sea or Qumran scrolls. They were found in a cave of the same name near the Dead Sea in 1947 by Bedouin shepherds. Later on more were found and Israel was eventually able to acquire them.

65 From 200 B.C. to 65 A.D. Found in caves, they are new theological sources and provide knowledge of various elements of Judaism. They were written by scribes from a dissident sect, and they contain hymns, prayers, writings, and rituals for an ascetic, strict, devout life. They are testimony to a communal, isolated and self-sufficient existence.

66 Civil religion. See Charles Liebman and Eliezer Don-Yehiya, Civil Religion in Israel, op. cit.

67 1900-1973.

68 From 1950. There are books with the findings for academics and for the general reader.

69 In that period, it is noticeable that there is an overall absence of religious figures.

70 Designs from those decades are cited. The process continued, but the iconography of the postal stamps reveals a variety of cultural emphasis.

71 Bronislaw, Baczko, Los imaginarios sociales. Memorias y esperanzas colectivas, Buenos Aires, Nueva Visión, 1991.

72 The kibbutz was subject to progressive changes and the crisis came in 1985. They still exist but they no longer have the structure that Gurvich knew.

73 Israel went through various periods of change. After the Six Day War there were problems with the settlements on the West Bank, and since 1977, when the Labour Party lost the elections and the right-wing led by Menachem Begin came to power, the changes were accentuated.

74 Shalom Aleichem (Pereyaslav, Ukraine, 1859 - New York, USA, 1916).

2. Ramot Menashé

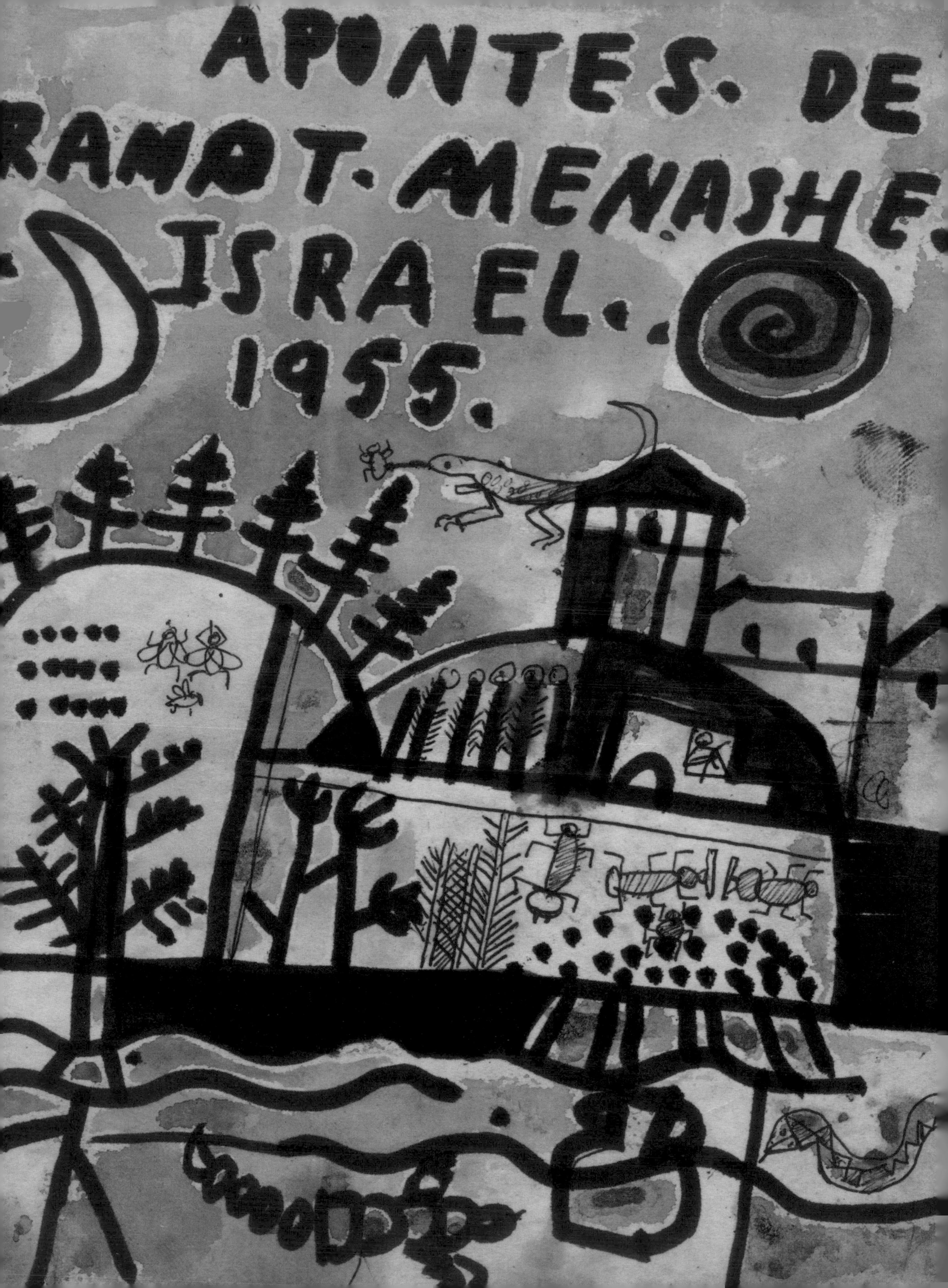
APONTES. DE
RAMOT. MENASHE.
ISRAEL.
1955.

Sketches of Ramot Menashé, Israel
1955
watercolour, ink, pen on paper
20 x 16.5 cm

2

Ramot Menashé

When Gurvich went to the Ramot Menashé kibbutz he experienced at first hand just what the kibbutz movement meant at that time. This was a new kibbutz, it was set up after the State came into being, so it had the pioneering characteristics of something being born and growing, and it was infused with the peculiar devotion of the Marxist ideology of the youthful members of the Hashomer Hatzair, who were from the same generation as the founders.

At that time the kibbutz movement was a vitally important element in the new country. It was successful as a collective undertaking, it was still at its height, and for a long time the kibbutz lifestyle was admired throughout Israel. It was considered an example to be emulated and a microcosm of Israeli society when socialist Zionism was supreme. It represented an icon and a reason to be proud, a model community that put universal values into practice. Members of the kibbutz acquired the aura of a symbolic elite and they felt they were in the vanguard. As an institution, the kibbutz movement was one of the most prosperous sectors of the Israeli economy, and that model prevailed for decades.[1]

Gurvich was part of the most important community experience in the world, one of the most innovative social experiments of all time. It had enormous moral, social and political prestige, and it was geared to consolidating a State that in those years was dedicated forging an egalitarian society. He was immersed in the construction of the new Jewish identity in the framework of a rural commune.

As Melford E. Spiro, Joseph Ben David, Daniel Katz and Naftali Golomb have said,[2] the kibbutz movement aimed at nothing less than the creation of a new man. They believed that human nature was essentially good but had been corrupted by bourgeois values and urban civilization, and once the excrescence of capitalism and urbanism was removed society would change into a community based on love, kindness, comradeship, altruism and the good of the group over the good of the individual. The kibbutz was an instrument in the Zionist revolution, not an end in itself, and its purpose was to move all of Israel in an egalitarian direction. In that sense it was utopian, it had the greatness of dreams, it was how the State of Israel put its ideals into practice. It was an attempt, and to a great extent it succeeded, in creating a socio-cultural system in which cooperation, fraternity, equality and the abolition of social classes prevailed. Until the changes that took place in 1985, the kibbutz was a great extended family, an organization based on the voluntary work and commitment of its members, with no system of formal sanctions and with great motivational dynamics. Ideology played a key role and the movement acquired an almost sacred aura, a symbolic meaning.[3] It was a non-dogmatic organization and it was always very flexible, very creative, with the ability to adapt itself to new situations.

Gurvich was interested in the aims of the kibbutz; he identified with the idea of a commune focused on people being equal, based on common property, collective control of the means of production, self-management, and the system of deciding all questions at general assembly meetings.[4] Ramot Menashé simply breathed equality; in sociological terms what had been established was qualitative socio-economic parity.

Ramot Menashé looked after its members and took care of all their personal needs in the framework of the commune's economic capabilities. And all the members of the kibbutz contributed their own personal resources and work. An individual's success was not judged in comparison with other people but in terms of their own needs and expectations. The kibbutz took care of educating the children and adults, of leisure, health, the disabled, people of the so-called third age, and of housing, transport, diet, culture, sports and clothing. There was total solidarity. People were given tasks depending on their age and their inclinations, so long as these were in line with the community's needs, and the limitations of peoples' health situation and age were respected in the communal project. The kibbutz looked after people who did not have families, widows and widowers and the unmarried, and it integrated them all into community life. The kibbutz had an excellent education system, but besides that informal education was always regarded as very important.

Gurvich participated in the community with great enthusiasm during his first stay when he went alone and afterwards on his second and third stays when he went with his family. He took part in the group cultural excursions to concerts, music shows, theatre and all kinds of top-level events. Most of what was put on in Tel Aviv or Jerusalem was shown to the kibbutz *chaverim* as a group, in a kibbutz theatre or some other selected place. They went by truck. Totó[5] remembers as if was yesterday the emotion they felt when they went with the *chaverim* to hear Beethoven's Ninth Symphony performed by a great European orchestra in the Caesarea Roman amphitheatre right on the Mediterranean, under the stars and in moonlight, and with the scene lit up from many boats on the sea. They travelled quite often to see different shows at the Ein Hashofet kibbutz theatre, concerts, chamber music, dancing and ballet. There were also cultural events at the kibbutz library, especially exhibitions. These activities were important artistically because there was a concerted effort to generate a local identity and a cultural ethos. The whole kibbutz movement put great emphasis on the value of art in society.

Another important element was the artistic decoration of the dining halls, which were a key space for socialising and communal life, and of the public places where festivals were held. Gurvich did two murals at Ramot Menashé, one on a wall and the other a great painting on a board, and both were in the communal dining hall. He also painted the concrete outer floors of the children's house, the Beit Ieladim, which was a kind of constructivist structure. On these occasions, like at other times when he did work for public spaces, he followed the guidelines of his teacher Joaquín Torres García[6] and his own ideas about public art.

It was inevitable that Gurvich would admire the kibbutz movement given his personality and principles and the fact that it was so successful. He worked as a shepherd and he took part enthusiastically in every activity. As the Argentine artist Adolfo Nigro[7] explains, "He never disowned his working-class origins, and this life experience identified him with the people. His sensitivity was rooted in the people's culture. His close friend and neighbour, Nativo, was just a common worker. In addition, when he shared the experience of the kibbutz in Israel he did so at the Ramot Menashé, which had a community and socialist philosophy. And it was this, his world, the world of the common people, that he expressed in his art."

And the kibbutz was a complete solution for him because he did not have to worry about making money or supporting his family or the other concerns of daily life; all this was taken care of by the community. After his daily work as a shepherd he could dedicate himself without restrictions to his art.

A very important subject that interested him greatly was the role of work, not just in everyday life but also in the educational system of the kibbutz and all the kibbutz mythology. The cult of work[8] and the slogan "Do it for yourself" came to be of prime importance. This is the notion that physical work is valuable as something that redeems the individual, it is almost regarded as sacred, especially work on the land, which is considered the most productive kind. All these beliefs were inspired by the spiritual leader of the Israeli labour movement Aaron David Gordon (1856-1922), who created the "work religion",[9] and by Dov Borochov (1881-1917)[10] and Meir Yaari (1897-1987), whose motto was "Hands first of all".[11] The central focus here is to appreciate the non-instrumental value of work, the idea that work is prized for itself, as a personal achievement. This amounts to an occupational system with ideological roots. The Jewish tradition and Bible reading, which are very important in Israel even among the non-religious, underpin this view. In the *Torah* and in religious thought there is a belief that work generates the world for the kingdom of God, and this work ethic is emphasised in the writings of many Jewish thinkers.[12]

Gurvich must also have found encouragement in Machado's poetry because the writer too admired work for its own sake. Both believed

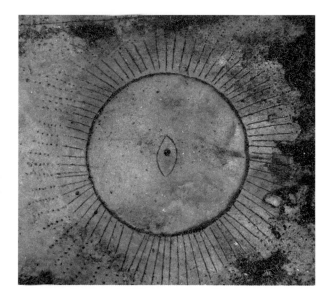

Beit Ieladim Ramot Menashé, detail

Homage to the kibbutz, detail

Mural project
for the Ramot Menashé kibbutz
1955
watercolour on paper
20 x 16 cm

Kibbutz in ochres and whites
1965
oil on wood
10 x 18 cm

Kibbutz
c. 1955
oil on wood
9 x 19 cm

Mural project
c. 1955
oil on wood
62 x 130 cm

Ramot Menashé, the water tower and the menorah
1970
watercolour, ink on paper
18 x 24 cm

that it dignified life, that there had to be a moral attitude towards work. Other principles that Gurvich shared with Machado were equality and people's commitment to solidarity, and these were the very principles had were put into practice on the kibbutz.

You say nothing is created?
You should not care, with clay
from the ground, make a goblet
for your brother to drink[13]

Gurvich could see the tangible results of these idealistic efforts. He saw the Ramot Menashé kibbutz, newly born, poor, the earth still full of stones, with everything still to be done, and he saw it changing and progressing. He collaborated very intensely and he was amazed and dazzled at the efforts his sister, his brother-in-law, his close friends and the other *chaverim* were making. The verve, the enthusiasm, the spirit of optimism in those years of his kibbutz experience at Ramot Menashé, is reflected in his writing, paintings, drawings and ceramics. He could see how the kibbutz was growing economically as the years went by. One of the key elements in this prosperity was the fact that the *chaverim* were devoted to work, even if it was demanding and meant self-sacrifice, even if it was carried out in the most unrewarding conditions.

Totó says, "He really liked the kibbutz. With a dose of idealism he called it the most perfect system of human cohabitation. He was of socialist fibre and Israel motivated him and moved him. He felt at home there."[14]

Vera Jordan says,[15] "Those were hard times on the kibbutz, mainly on his first trip, there was still *tzena*[16] (scarcity)... But he was delighted to see how the kibbutz was developing, a barren place with no trees was turning into a forest. This was dazzling for him, and it was all done by just six women, including myself... Many people found it difficult to bear the hardships of that life but Gurvich did not mind, and when somebody criticized or complained (as I did), he cheered us up. He was deeply involved, he admired the effort, he pointed out the positive side, the good things. He admired the achievement, he felt part of it and he enjoyed his work. And he cared about equality, which is what we were building; people living from their work trying to achieve a society without hierarchies. He adapted very well to the tough life of the kibbutz, without comforts and where hard work was a must. He was a great worker and he was liked for that; he lived with that spirit of great work."[17] Vera explains that *Yuski*, "...lived very modestly in one of the most undesirable places on the kibbutz, a small electricity transformer room, and that was where he painted. Those adverse conditions did not bother him and he never complained, he always exuded great happiness on all his stays at the kibbutz and in Israel. He felt completely fulfilled, in his work as a shepherd, on the kibbutz itself, with his the friends and with his painting. He very much liked to walk in the hills of Ramot Menashé with the sheep, with his friend Nehemias and with Rudi Heyman, who was a very cultured character, a real ideologist, a Jew of German origin, a musician who played the *chalil* and who was the founder of the Hashomer Haitzar in Montevideo."

The Israeli artist Naftali Bezem recalls, "He loved his work, he always had a smile on his face, he talked about his friends, about God, about nature; he had a smiling soul. I remember Gurvich being very happy in Israel and on the kibbutz. He radiated joy, happiness and spiritual peace. All matters of money and economic problems to

On the Ramot Menashé kibbutz
1964
pencil on paper
20.5 x 15.5 cm

Ramot Menashé with clock and couple flying, detail
c. 1972
ink on paper
49.5 x 29.7 cm

Kibbutz life
c. 1956
watercolour on paper
20.5 x 16 cm

do with maintaining his family disappeared. It was peaceful living in the community. There might be quarrels about everyday matters or over a football match, he had that Latin American energy and passion for the game, but he found a world in which he could paint and create. The kibbutz offered solutions, and many aspects of family life were taken care of like clothes, food, the daily budget and housing. The children were cared for like treasures, they were the darlings of the kibbutz and their parents could rest. Gurvich felt he was much loved in the kibbutz, like at home, and he was in contact with the land and the sky. Nobody bothered him, there was nobody on his back."[18]

Composition
1966
oil on canvas
58 x 73.5 cm

His colleague Eva Kaufman explains, "In Israel he was always very happy with his sister and her family, their parents and his great friends. He liked kibbutz life very much. He felt at home in Israel. He always told me how good he felt at the kibbutz, he worked with the sheep there, which didn't bother him, he obeyed orders, and in the long hours of solitude he painted and then stayed on in his rough shed, completely happy. He told me that no one else wanted to work taking care of the sheep, but he really liked it and he gladly accepted the job."[19]

Two *chaverim* on the kibbutz, Boris and Maia Blinde,[20] who met Gurvich when he was a child, have this to say, "He never pretended to be a *chaver* on the kibbutz and nobody tried to make him one. He had close friends and everybody loved his family. He was an institution on the kibbutz. A lot of his family were also there, first his sister, his brother-in-law and his nephews, and then his parents and his great friends. He felt happy among those *chaverim*, five hundred souls, parents and children, Chileans, Uruguayans and Poles. He liked simplicity, community life, meals all together, taking tea with everybody."[21]

Totó remembers, "His friends were on the kibbutz, those of the *ken* period in Montevideo, and the Uruguayan members of the kibbutz knew him quite well from Montevideo, and there they forged friendships and were very kind to him."[22] Gurvich's life there was full of surprises, just like childhood. He wrote, "... And the children, so many children at that time, and what joy they show when they run to meet their parents! They are so free, they are completely independent. So, for example, you see a three-year old boy leaving his room alone, having a wash, combing his hair, eating alone and wandering around the kibbutz, and when he feels like it he goes to see his parents. The seven-year-olds ride horses and donkeys, and when they are twelve or thirteen you can see them up on a tractor or a truck. That is impressive!"[23]

The mystique of nature was part of the kibbutz *Weltanschauung*, and the fact that it was a rural setting was always important for Gurvich. He was born and grew up in a small peasant village, and as an adult in Montevideo he chose to live in Cerro,[1] a rugged part of town away from the built up area. He was always attracted to nature, his childhood memories were associated with rural life, "I remember, on the long road back into my childhood, hides that smelled like horses, a pungent smell."[24] Bucolic feelings were very important for him and he was free to develop them there. He wrote, "...you cannot imagine how pleasant a breeze and the undulating, gentle, stony hills around us are at dusk. Serenity pours into you and you want to love the plants, the creatures and the flowers."[25]

Gurvich forged new connections with Jewish tradition, which was deeply-rooted in him because of his childhood experiences, and he asserted that identity in a context that suited him because he was secular, rural and socialist. Of course, like all of us who experienced the kibbutz at that time, he idealised it. Today, with hindsight, people can see the achievements and failures of the kibbutz system with a more critical eye, but it should be said that although it was not a perfect system, it aspired to be one. Muki Tsur[26], a writer, thinker, teacher and *kibbutznik* (member of the *kibbutz*), expressed it in this way, "The kibbutz is not an ideal society, but it is built on ideals."

---

1   A neighbourhood in western Montevideo, home to Eastern European immigrants. Gurvich lived part of his adult life there.

Chaverim working
c. 1956
oil on wood
34 x 47 cm

Con mi trabajo de pastor, tuve oportunidad de sentir el campo, y el sol!! de Israel, aunque esta ocupación, parece tan apacible, poética, y tranquila, nada de esto; primero, tienes que ir armado, y con mucho cuidado, pues te tienes que alejar del Kibutz, y esto trae peligros, los lobos que aquí abundan tanto, chacales, pues cuando te toca salir a las 4 de la madrugada en que la luna esta colgada todavía, y los posibles árabes fronterizos, que a veces vienen a robar o causar disturbios, todo esto, y la sensación de constante peligro del las víboras, con esto se requiere especial cuidado, pues si te pican, no cuentas el cuento. Pero a pesar de todo, te acostumbras y vas con cierta tranquilidad. Por hoy basta tengo mucho sueño, y mañana hay que trabajar. ¡ha me olvidaba se me rompió el mate! cuanto lo sentí!!

Hoy he cambiado de cuarto, es pequeño, con una ventana ~~hacia~~ hacia el occidente, sol en la tarde, tengo una radio que tocará tenerla 2 meses, (como no hay todavía suficientes radios como para todos, se turnan). con algunas cerámicas que me hice, una mesa, cama y silla completan mi

Domestic scene with primus stove at Ramot Menashé

c. 1956

oil on wood

41 x 31 cm

The Kibbutz in his Art

On his first visit to Ramot Menashé, Gurvich captured life on the kibbutz and Jewish symbols in many ways. He quite naturally made notes and kept a record of what daily life was like, and he did constructivist paintings with kibbutz subjects and Jewish symbols in them. He integrated the world of the kibbutz into his constructive compositions, his artistic legacy from the Torres García Workshop, and thus created a vision with symbols. He did a series of naturalistic drawings that are like Torres García's but have been released from the rectangular format and have Jewish symbols, and he also did freer compositions too. He painted portraits, one of the most outstanding of which is *Dama que piensa* (Lady who thinks).

Some of his works that show what kibbutz life was like are *Atardecer en el kibutz* (Dusk on the kibbutz, 1955), *Proyecto para mural en el kibutz Ramot Menashé* (Mural project for the Ramot Menashé kibbutz, 1955), *Composición del kibutz* (Kibbutz composition, c. 1955), *Homenaje a Brueghel* (Homage to Brueghel, 1956), *Composición del kibutz* (Composition of the kibbutz, 1956), *Paisaje del kibutz* (Kibbutz landscape, 1956), *Trabajando en el kibutz* (Working on the kibbutz, 1956) and *Kibutz Ramot Menashé* (1956).

In addition to his best-known paintings he left a series of sketches and numerous drawings. There are folders containing naturalistic and geometric landscapes, notes about housing on the kibbutz, and sketches for compositions with colour details. One example is a drawing of a huge human figure, a man sowing under a burning sun with rays of light, which seems to echo elements from Van Gogh.

There are many drawings and compositions with images of sheep, some with elaborate details of rams, studies of their heads, horns and shapes. Gurvich captured the great spiral horns, typical of males and of some females, the rusticity and robustness of the animals with their characteristic tails, their great, fat, greasy bodies adapted to survive in the heat of Israel, and the long, wide ears that are so heavy they cover part of the face. He drew awassi dairy ewes, high-yield milk producers that are mentioned in the Bible and are among the oldest sheep in the world. He spent hours watching them grazing and he developed a bond with the animals that was to show up in many of his subsequent compositions.

He did other naturalistic sketches of hens, goats, horses, cats, dogs, singing birds, owls, trees, fruit, wells, carts, the water tower, the stables, men peacefully returning from work, chaverim at their daily tasks, gathering the seed. He sometimes included some writing: The little donkey did not want to go to...

The blazing Israeli sun is a major force in this rural environment. That persistent sun, which for eight months of the year shines, warms, im-

Lady who thinks (Aída Melman)
1955
oil on canvas
85 x 55 cm

Rest at Ramot Menashé
c. 1956
oil on wood
34 x 48 cm

Miriam
c. 1956
oil on wood
67 x 97 cm

(at left)
The sower
C. 1955
watercolour, pencil on paper
20 x 15.5 cm

Rams
C. 1955
watercolour, ink on paper
20.5 x 16 cm

(at left)
Sheep grazing
C. 1955
watercolour, pencil on paper
20 x 16 cm

Chicken coop
C. 1955
watercolour, ink, pencil on paper
16 x 20 cm

poses itself and tires people out, and the high summer temperatures, made a big impact on Gurvich, "We have heavy days here, and the sun! It takes away your energy. I now believe that the sun lives off us."[27] This can be seen in his art; he turned up the heat, his range of colours began to change and his paintings became warmer and more intense. This is typical of almost all painters who come to Israel and remain for some time or settle in the country. And in Gurvich's colourful scenes of the kibbutz we can see this process of chromatic transformation; he did bright compositions with strong yellows, intense reds, burning suns spinning like spirals, and the land quivering with vivid hues.

These pictures show the plain, basic truth of what life was like in those days, rigorous asceticism in the middle of the countryside and in the collective farm experiment. And in the rural life of these urban Jewish immigrants we can feel their energy as they struggle in pursuit of an ideal of a new kind of man, not Diaspora man, but Jews making a great effort to build a new world in an adverse environment in those pioneering years, battling with the land, bereft of bourgeois comforts, dedicating themselves to a mission. What emerges from Gurvich's work is his

Resting
C. 1955
watercolour, ink, pencil on paper
17 x 22 cm

Kibbutz landscape
c. 1956
watercolour, pencil on paper
20.5 x 16 cm

Kibbutz scene
1956
watercolour, ink on paper
22 x 17 cm

Kibbutz
1956
watercolour on paper
15 x 21 cm

Kibbutz scene
n.d.
watercolour, pencil on paper
25 x 35 cm

Kibbutz scene
1956
watercolour, pencil on paper
25 x 35 cm

Sunset on the kibbutz
c. 1955
oil on cardboard
26 x 36 cm

Kibbutz
c. 1956
watercolour on paper
15 x 21 cm

Kibhutz II
1956
watercolour, ink on paper
15 x 22 cm

Children and Chaverim at Ramot Menashé
1956
watercolour, graphite, ink on paper
23.5 x 33 cm

Shepherd on the kibbutz
1955
oil on cardboard
24 x 34 cm

Kibbutz
1957
oil on canvas
40 x 52.5 cm

Kibbutz landscape
1956
watercolour, ink on paper
16 x 20.5 cm

Still life with landscape
c. 1956
oil on cardboard
50 x 67.5 cm

Ramot Menashé
1955
oil on cardboard
40.5 x 52.5 cm

Ramot Menashé with moon
oil on cardboard
1956
33 x 47 cm
(Double-sided painting)

Chaverim at Ramot Menashé
c. 1956
oil on wood
33 x 47 cm

Ramot Menashé and its chaverim
c. 1956
oil on cardboard
24.5 x 33 cm

Scene at Ramot Menashé
1957
oil on canvas
41.5 x 50 cm

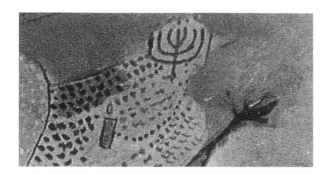

Kibbutz rhytms, detail

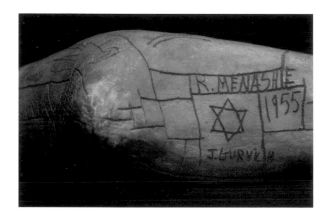

Ceramic
1964
pottery
23 x 13.5 x 6 cm

Dancing (Rikudim)
n.d.
pencil on paper
15 x 20.5 cm

love of the land, his friendship with the *chaverim*, praise for farm work, a reverence for physical labour, a fondness for nature, the tenderness that the animals aroused on him, the bucolic feelings the kibbutz and its environment awoke in him, and the beautiful hills of Ramot Menashé in the background. Many of these oil paintings, drawings and watercolours are testimony in the sense that they are evidence of life in those years and how rudimentary it still was.

Gurvich employed a whole range of symbols. One was the *menorah*, the seven branch candelabra with one arm raised to represent the *Shabbat*. He painted it and drew it in compositions in a Torres García style and he accompanied it with Hebrew letters and used different layouts. The image would never leave him, and this was no coincidence because it is an image that acquired special significance when the State of Israel was set up, and it became an essential symbol in the new country. It evokes restored Jewish sovereignty. Metaphorically, it is "rescued" from the Arch of Titus in Rome where it features as a sign of Roman rule over Israel. So Gurvich chose a fundamental element that Israel cherishes, a most significant object that throughout history has been a most important and venerated symbol, it is mentioned in the *Talmud*,[28] it is rich in connotations and is linked to the original tree of life, the seven branches of the Tabernacle and the seven days of the creation.

Another symbol in the artist's work is the Star of David, which was already widespread in the land. It alludes to the Shield of David, it came to prominence in the 19th century but it had a previous history and was already in use in Prague in 1354, when the Emperor Charles IV granted the Jews the privilege of having their own flag. From that time on, Jewish communities used this star in cemeteries and in house decoration. The flag with the Star of David was designed at the first Zionist congress in Basel in 1897, and a new history for the star began. Secular Zionism accepted it because it is not associated with religion and was a relatively new symbol. In the opinion of Gershom Sholem,[29] when secular Zionists chose the Star of David they did so because it was already widely diffused in the communities, it had no religious associations, it did not carry memories from the past, and as a symbol it could represent hope for the future and something new. On the other hand, after World War II it acquired other connotations because it was used by the Nazis to label and humiliate the Jews during the *Shoah*, it served to identify them in the campaign to persecute and annihilate them. But in the end it became a symbol of honour because life and identity persisted and went on in spite of Hitler, Germany, Nazism and anti-Semitism. According to Scholem.[30] "From suffering and torture it illuminates the path to construction and to life, the way that leads from humiliation to exaltation." It became an emblem of identity and unity, of honour, of dignity and of pride. It was chosen for the flag of the new State and of the *Magen David Adom* (the Is-

Ramot Menashé and burning sun
1956
oil on cardboard
45 x 34 cm

Kibbutz composition (1966), detail
(Gurvich playing the chalil)

Shepherds (playing *jalil*)
n.d.
pencil on paper
14.5 x 10 cm

raeli Red Cross). The socialist Zionism that ruled in those years promoted it, and since then it has always been an important emblem of Israel. It appears frequently on craft work, jewellery and ornaments. And it is significant that Gurvich used it, since it shows how visible and relevant it was and is as a symbol in Israel.

Another subject in his drawing and painting is the *Chaverim*. He shows them in scenes with Israeli dances and in traditional costumes in folk dances (*rikudim*[31]). And yet another identifying element that attracted him was the *chalil*, the wooden flute so typical of local folklore. He painted himself playing this instrument, as in *Composicion del kibbutz* (Kibbutz Composition, 1966) and in that same work we can see the *hora* (an Israeli dance). Gurvich was experimenting with the flute; he learned to play it and took it with him when he went to tend the sheep. This shows yet again how much he loved music; in his youth he played the violin, and in Israel he played the *chalil* out on the pasture. He wrote on one composition, "My friend, look, play and listen to this song. I have just found its melody, a song that I have always carried in my soul, listen, watch, play it ...I'm staying here ...and I am going to look for another tune..."

The presence of these images in his work indicates the period and the context. Gurvich lived at that special time when there was an emphasis on the value of new instruments, new music, new dances and the creation of an Israeli folklore, and he brought this into his art. Music and dance played an important role in the construction of national identity. There had been Jewish folklore, known as *Yishuv*, in the land since the time of the first pioneers, the arrival of the Zionists in Israel, and more so since the 1930s when the British were in control. There was a repertoire, music, lyrics and choreographies that were basic elements in the Israelis' lives and very important on the kibbutz. This was a conscious Zionist effort to create a new folklore for the new mother country, another symbol of unity to help underpin national identity.[32]

Poetry was important too, and biblical texts were a valuable source in this field. Hebrew composers were encouraged to create new works and there were incentives for this like constant folklore programmes on the radio and songbooks. *Shirei Eretz Yisrael* (the songs of the Land of Israel), with songs written between 1920 and mid-1970s, was distributed. The lyrics and poetry had to do with daily life, love for Israel, the traditional festivals, love, comradeship, and praise for the land and the pioneers. For decades, and precisely in the years that Gurvich was in Israel and on the kibbutz, the people sang those songs and danced the new dances (the *hora*, the *debka*) everywhere and in a very natural way. These songs and dances were useful for social integration, they brought people together, and the choreography and costumes served to reaffirm values like equality and simplicity. The new dances had a great impact not only in Israel but in the Diaspora, they were taught in the youth movements, and since then and for decades they have been part of the bond that binds the Jews together. Gurvich already knew them from his days at the Hashomer Hatzair *ken*.

Gurvich did not speak Hebrew, but from the start of his Israel experiences he used the language as a reference framework and he wrote the name of the kibbutz in it, for example. And he used it in his art as well; in a painting on card we find "Ramot Menashé". This must have been a trial for him for many reasons; he had never learned the language, he did not know the alphabet, the writing or the sounds, and Hebrew must have brought back memories of his native Lithuania since Yiddish has the same writing, and many Yiddish words are of Hebrew origin. In the *shtetl* where he lived as a child there were religious books with Hebrew writing at his grandparents' house, there was his mother's prayer book, and later at his home in Montevideo there were books in Hebrew. In Israel he was reunited with Hebrew, in another context and with a different usage, and the symbolic strength the language gave to the new State had a powerful impact on him.

When Gurvich turned his hand to pottery he first made the typical objects, abstract shapes that suggest animals or fish, and shapes of women that seem to be Neolithic figures and are linked together with cords in cavities, and they enter each other with curvilinear hollows, some merely touching, others fitting in. He created dense figures, organic and sensual shapes, and he made some pottery in a Torres García style. He left many sketches, composition studies for those pieces with indications of the colours he would use.

In his sketches he drew couples and the shapes of birds, sheep and oxen. At first this was in a naturalistic style but we can see how the creative process developed, he became more abstract and we find reversed circular shapes, others that are tubular and interwoven, sketches of couples, allusions to love and sex, stylized female shapes, hips, breasts, eyes, Torres García style figures, and squares for vases and jars. In his folders of drawings with ideas for ceramic work there are also kibbutz scenes. And besides all that, he made basic, utilitarian pieces like a cruet stand with a salt cellar and pepper pot.

The Conquest of Freedom

In 1964, on his second trip to Israel, Gurvich went with his wife Totó and his son Martín. For part of that year he worked on the kibbutz as a shepherd, and he also lived in Tel Aviv for a while, preparing an exhibition in the Katz Gallery. Totó recalls, "One of the missions of the trip was to introduce Martín to Gurvich's mother Jaie and his sister Miriam, who the child had never met. It was also very important for his grandmother because Irit, the other granddaughter, Miriam's daughter, did not speak

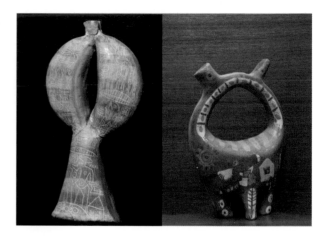

Ceramic
1964
engraved pottery
23 x 13.5 x 6 cm

Kibbutz ceramic
c. 1955
pottery
25 x 16.5 x 8 cm

Construction in red and black
c. 1955
tempera, pencil on paper
25 x 18 cm

*Universal being
at Ramot Menashé
1964
oil on wood
77 x 50 x 2 cm*

*Universal beings
at Ramot Menashé*
c. 1964
oil on wood
64 x 48 x 4 cm

World of images and figures
c. 1966
oil on wood
40 x 30 cm

Spanish, she spoke Hebrew. Gurvich was delighted to be on the kibbutz with his father Jacobo, his mother and his family. He made an agreement with the kibbutz community; it was impossible for him to stop painting, it was his life, so he worked half the day for the kibbutz and then painted. He set up a workshop in the *jazeira*[33]. He bought reams of fabric in Haifa and closed up the place to make it darker because there was too much light. For many months it is not cold and it does not rain so there was no problem. In the winter he painted in the family room[34] and in summer in his workshop. He painted in the morning and went to the fields in the afternoon."

In the beginning his compositions were influenced by the Torres García style and he used the grid in very dynamic and complex ways. Sometimes his work was abstract, sometimes figurative, and more and more he brought in kibbutz motifs and Jewish symbolism. Then he started to move away from this Torres Garcia influence and towards fantasy, and this is when his most original stage began. This can be seen in numerous oil paintings, tempera pictures and collages from his kibbutz days and from when he was in Cerro. His outstanding work from this period includes *Pareja construida en* B/N (Couple built in black and white, 1964), *Pareja besándose* (Couple kissing, 1965), *Mundo fantástico con fondo negro* (Fantasy world with black background, 1966), *Formas geométricas en colores puros* (Geometric shapes in pure colours, 1966), *Pareja* (Couple, 1966), *Pareja cósmica* (Cosmic couple, 1966), *Mundo de imágenes* (World of images, 1966), *Mundo de formas y ritmos* (World of shapes and rhythm,1966), *Universo de imágenes en collage* (Universe of images in collage, c. 1966), *Mundo fantástico con fondo blanco* (Fantasy world with white background, 1966), *El muno de las bolitas en* B/N (The world of marbles in black and white, 1966), *Pareja con rayitas en* B/N (Couple with stripes in black and white, 1966), *Pareja casi besándose* (Couple almost kissing, c. 1966), *Composición con reloj* (Composition with clock, 1966), *El robot* (The robot, 1966), *Hombre astral concéntrico* (Concentric astral man, 1967), *Formas, símbolos e imágenes* (Shapes, symbols and images, 1967), *Pareja y universo* (Couple and universe, 1967), *Hombre cósmico en colores puros* (Cosmic man in pure colours, 1967), *La Creación en collage* (The Creation in collage, 1967), *Mundo fantástico en colores puros* (Fantasy world in pure colours, 1967), *La Creación en colores puros* (The Creation in pure colours, 1968), *Formas geométricas en colores puros* (Geometric shapes in pure colours, 1968), *La Creación* (The Creation, 1969) and *La corriente de la vida* (The flow of life, 1969).

He worked tirelessly, and Totó witnessed the process, "He had a method: he bought several notebooks of various sizes in Haifa, in the Arab neighbourhood, and he carried the small ones all the time, he took notes of everything and systematized his work. He observed every detail, he tried to capture them in drawings and afterwards did tempera paintings. He was interested in the whole, every element of the kibbutz, all

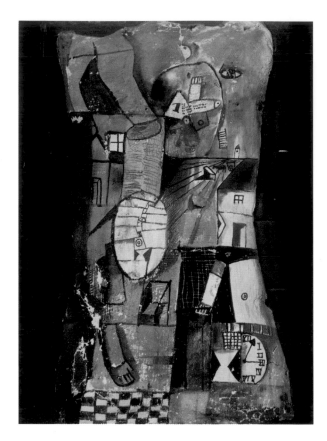

Symbolic construction

c. 1964

mixed technique, wood, hessian and plaster

56 x 47 x 6 cm

Kibbutz scene

1970

watercolour on cardboard

34 x 25 cm

of reality. He took notes and then did drawings, which at the beginning of that second trip were still composed in a constructivist style but were already moving away from traditional constructivism. He kept to the golden section (sectio aurea), but the grid sometimes opened up and varied and this was the start of what was later the cosmic dawn. He told me, "I feel that I am making a path but I do not want to take steps into the void, I want to be sure, to free myself." The drawings were growing, they were moving towards watercolours and tempera compositions, and this was happening very fast. He worked with great intensity, he created a platform for the comprehension of what he saw, and then for the transmission of this with the elements already absorbed by his eyes, his mind, and his brush. His training in those years was extremely intense. Then he moved into tempera work and Jewish iconography began to emerge, symbols, the wonderful light of the kibbutz, the hills of Menashé, nature, workers, and the fields. He was putting everything in his compositions. Things began to levitate and he no longer feared that they might get out of hand because he had the composition rule and the golden rule implanted in his eye. What levitates does not lose contact with reality, it is rooted, it has roots, it is terrestrial, and everything he did is anchored in reality. His flying figures are from the kibbutz, they reflect reality and do not come from another dimension, and Celia the *metapelet* (caregiver) is there with her huge *tojes*.[35] What he painted does not belong to a weird, ethereal world or the hereafter, which is why his peasants are bulky, and in this he reveals his admiration for and kinship with Brueghel and has the essence of a sculptor. Yepes discovered this characteristic in Gurvich as far back as the 1960s and he insisted that the artist had a sense of volume, shape and space that was worthy of a sculptor."[36]

Totó recalls that "...after his trip to Europe he started to do things as if they were floating, appearing, and he gradually began to separate the figures and make them more free flowing, more floating. When we went to Europe and to the State of Israel in 1964 and 65, in what people usually like to call the "Gurvich takeoff" period, he started doing landscapes of the kibbutz but in a constructivist style, but I would say this construction was cut or clipped, not orthodox; it was loosened. With his paintings of the kibbutz and of the land he started the transformation into something more fluid and the figures began to fly. And it happened because he did not use the orthogonal line, he left it behind, it was hidden. He did this in his workshop, and he mostly used temperas. He did a very interesting collection of tempera work. And afterwards in Montevideo, when he went back in 1965-66, he started to work on everything in tempera. Then he began to use oils and did the figures from what everyone calls "the time of the kibbutz", with flying and floating things. It was a whole process that gradually took him there. When he was on the kibbutz he continued with his constructivism but he did it in a more open way; he always did something related to the constructivist style."[37]

According to Jorge Damiani, "His trips to Israel allowed him to "be more free". And it is in the middle of that new geographical location that new elements emerge in the painter's work."[38]

What makes these new compositions special is their simultaneity of times in space, assorted images, abundance, a profusion of uneven figures, the incorporation of the fantastic and the absurd, and evidence of oneiric tendencies. Fragments of reality are transfigured, and things and beings are caught in imaginary dialogues. Gurvich interrelated body segments and objects, animals and things, to make up a whole, and he created composite figures like the "house-leg", the "house-female body", the "window-arm" and the "sheep-shepherd". His world is filled with overlapping shapes, like hands that give fruit and people walking with other figures inside. Arms come out from the windows of kibbutz houses, and young *chaverim* are just tiny figures in the background with no thickness that contrast with hypertrophied figures or big faces in the foreground. There are intricate shapes such as occupied-faces and settlements, a sun with a hand, an arm with a key, a cosmic couple inhabited by symbols, limbs falling apart here and there with their own life, mobile legs, dynamic fragments of bodies, *chaverim* heads with the characteristic *kova tembel* (hat), and inverted figures. The wind embodied in a face, sheep, burning suns, moons, day and night, clocks, ladders, carts, tables, *chalilim* (wooden flutes), towers, musical notes, wheels, trees, all these among so many other images make up his iconography on board, on fabric, in drawings, in watercolours, tempera compositions and in plaster.

A very common subject in Gurvich's art was the world of rural work and its tools. These compositions are full of images that proliferate and spread, there are bodies that seem to escape from the picture, others that seem attracted to a magnetic centre, and all these fantasy characters and things are features of his everyday world. There are substantial, overlapping, weightless figures together in a variegated space, with totalities and fragments. It is an imaginative world, but daily reality is an essential, prominent feature. Gurvich never left it aside. He loved to transcend everyday life but he constantly harks back to his love of the land and of farm work. Reality and fantasy come together in different time frames. The animate world is mixed with the inanimate, everything is on the same level, the parts and the whole. In some works the tiniest things are expressed, and Gurvich does what Italo Calvino calls "crushing reality." The dread of emptiness, the *horror vacui*, is paramount.

In Gurvich's art there is an interplay or dialogue between different spheres –the sphere of work and that of love in the couple, between terrestrial and eternal time, between everyday life and the transcendent, between the earth and the cosmic plane, between present and past, order

Two men
1966
gouache on cardboard
33 x 47 cm

Working on the kibbutz

c. 1964

watercolour on paper

10 x 16 cm

Work, couple and sheep

1964

watercolour on paper

12.5 x 9.5 cm

and chaos, Israeli folk dances and Torres García-like symbols. Gurvich fused a variety of subjects and in some compositions he cited venerated works of art such as Brueghel's "The Blind leading the Blind", which alludes to the incompetence and ignorance of people who follow useless leaders, who let themselves be led and go far along a path into darkness, fumbling, with a poorly-equipped guide: an idea that derives from a New Testament parable. Gurvich criticizes irrationality, the lack of common sense, senselessness, the foolishness of following a leader unquestioningly, the stubborn over-confidence that leads to the wrong place, to an abyss, and this is still a topical subject. He also shows us the myth of Adam and Eve, and the trees of Paradise laden with fruit.

Some human figures fly and others walk, and they are shifting, located in changing landscapes, never just in one place, and this in a way echoes the Diaspora and the history of the Jews. Very often there are figures filled with fragmented images that inhabit them, they are bulky and transparent and they carry supplementary elements, scattered realities. Their skins tell a story, they have superimposed images, sometimes in the form of a palimpsest.

There are particles, molecules, fragments form and weave themselves into the ground or go up to dizzying heights, they join together and disperse, matter is converted into energy, everything germinates. Each element is a shape being born which metamorphoses, there is a feeling of infinity and ongoing creation that transcends the limited reality of the physical world, of the fact that things must end. There is continuity, there is the spiral –one of his favourite symbols– which he was already using back in his Torres García period.

In several compositions he has ovoid shapes from life, and these intertwine or contain symbols, faces or figures. There are trees pregnant with fruit, the green and blue faces of loving couples who have other realities, bubbles containing houses and figures, brewing micro-shapes, fertile spheres. He forged an exuberant reality, filled with multifarious elements, an exultant world throbs inside each balloon, as if the whole of reality was about to conceive. Gurvich set up a fantastic world in the shape of tiny balls in which energy flows, like in *Hombre astral* (Astral Man), and there are echoes of everything that originates, that is brewing, that is in the process of beginning.

There are paintings made up of points and undulating planes in which primary colours dominate, and the dazzling Israeli summer sun imposes itself. These elements express the vibrancy of life of the kibbutz, and this is emphasised by the movement of images and accentuated by the changeable waves Gurvich uses in the composition. That enterprising, tireless, shifting, busy, vivacious kibbutz world is stirred up under the omnipresent sun, which dominates the space.

When Gurvich transformed space with structures defined by irregular curves he generated a kind of discontinuous and intermittent sinuosity and twisting, and this lent great mobility to the composition, as can be seen in *Homenaje al kibutz* (Homage to the kibbutz). We discover a populated world within each undulating sub-space, and increasingly there is a feeling of changeable waves that quiver. The lines and sub-spaces inter-penetrate, they interweave, they do not follow a uniform line, and this increases the feeling of pulsing. In this way there are echoes of the land that is worked and is peopled with images. This features in many pictures of couples and in *El sueño de Jacob* (Jacob's dream).

Kibbutz composition with eggs, detail

He was very versatile in his range of expression; some works are almost abstract compositions with tiny lines, very dynamic and synthesized, with small, loose symbols. Or small lines with a certain geometric order predominate, graphics encapsulated in rectangles, and a subtle presence of figures and symbols. Gurvich employed a subjective spatial dimension, he developed fluid spaces and broke with temporal and spatial coordinates. His inner freedom allowed him to create blue sheep, red or green faces, alterations of scale, hypertrophy in some figures and hypotrophy in others, and to generate ascending bodies that defy the laws of gravity.

He attempted to feel space as if it moved, to capture it from many points of view with an eye that was mobile, that shifted and looked through space. He speaks in waves, folds and furrows. And in his writing he describes this, "The painter, the active protagonist of space, is moving and not fixed. He captures reality from many points of view and then pieces it together in an ideal of art with an eye that moves or looks through it. He extracts voices that are still unheard... My shapes appear told and sung like in tales ... My shapes adjust to the folds and furrows left by the everlasting waves of a breeze that appears and disappears like wind in the leaves."[39]

He generated a heterogeneous and intricate world, in full motion. His is a hectic reality. His vertiginous world vibrates and throbs. There are scenes of developing hurly-burly; we feel the strength of the whirl and the swirling impetus. The images exude continuity and messages of cyclical return.

His work is full of life and he shows us a universe of work, it is busy, lively and enterprising, as was Israel, as was the kibbutz. It is a vision of humanity and the cosmos that is swift and vivacious, that lives in a whirl of shapes, in an atmosphere of vibration and bustle, there is change, liveliness, activity and action. He expresses universal energy and focuses on every living thing, on terrestrial and cosmic energy. He transmits messages of encouragement, he values drive, dynamism and strength. He communicates freshness, vigour, joy and happiness. He exalts vitality, he demonstrates spirit and he expresses joy for everything that consolidates existence.

Triptych.
Painting lesson,
detail

Jacob's dream,
detail

Kibbutz II
1956
watercolour, ink on paper
15 x 22 cm
detail

Cosmic couple in black and white,
detail

Cosmic couple,
detail

Kibbutz composition
c. 1966
watercolour, ink on paper
24 x 32.5
detail

Hanukkah, detail

In all his compositions Gurvich always deals with life. Sometimes he does this with a symbol like the egg, which is a true exaltation of the organic, of nature and of birth. The egg is a way of paying homage to Bosch and Brueghel, but it is a long-standing, universal emblem of immortality and the origin of life. Gurvich wrote, "Everything has the right to life."[40]

At other times he transmits the message in other ways. He came upon a dead tree trunk out in the country and this prompted him to construct an image to use it, to revive it in art. In the many versions of *Jánuca* (Hanukkah) there are numerous characters that sprout and give new life to this image, that grant it existence.

In his work he expressed his vigorous vision of the world, his enthusiasm for change and his feeling for what is dynamic, and this was fostered by the great volatility and growth that was all around him in Israel and in the rural, productive development of the kibbutz, where dreams came true thanks to the dedicated work of the *chaverim*. These subjects moved him, just as they affected Antonio Machado, and Gurvich was greatly inspired by hope for the renovation of the land, he was enthusiastic about the re-establishment of life cycles, he was concerned with the rebirth of fertility in the fields, he was always yearning for change and in love with revitalised nature.

In his figures and images Gurvich might have expressed, consciously or unconsciously, the fragmented identities of the modern Jew. There are the tensions, ambiguities, nuances, heterogeneities and changes in modern Jewish identities; they figure in metamorphic, unstable, numerous, interrelated and miscellaneous elements in his work. The Jews of the Diaspora live in many spaces and many times, and this may be why he expresses a total present in his paintings, he includes yesterday and today, and yesterday blends into today, which creates an association of separate times and places. His compositions can be read as a testimony to the paradoxes that enrich those identities and make them difficult to delimit within clearly defined borders.

His flying figures may in some way be echoes of the Diaspora experience, of relocation, of the artist being uprooted and travelling. Flight suggests the nomadic aspect of the Jews in history; it often figures with this meaning in the work of Marc Chagall, whom Gurvich admired. To fly is to forget, to escape from being marginalised, from insecurity, anxiety and anguish, and thus flying could be a metaphor for fleeing. Flying could also have positive connotations like being above the real world that traps people, the world of contingency and routine, and being able to reach for possibilities that invite us to create, to imagine, to dream and to shape something new, which is what Gurvich did. Flying is also associated with the poetry of Machado, who imagined that in heaven the soul is transfigured, and who dreamed about going beyond the world."[41]

Chaver and chavera
c. 1966
tempera on paper
34.5 x 48 cm

I love subtle worlds,
weightless and gentle
like soap bubbles.
I like to see them painted
with sun and deep-red, and fly
under the blue sky, and shiver
suddenly and crack.

VII
It is so easy to fly, so easy!
It is all about not letting the ground
get close to our feet.
Valiant feat; flight! Flight! Flight!

VIII
To fly without wings where there is all sky!
Write this joyful
thought: To stop, to stop the world
in between the toes,
and then wind it up anticlockwise
to see it spin in the void,
reddish and cold,
and silent – there is no music without wind.
Sure, sure! Poet and bugle
are that short-winded!...
Only silence and God sing endlessly.

Kibbutz
1973
watercolour, ink on paper
21 x 27 cm

Kibbutz scene
1973
watercolour on paper
21 x 27 cm

Kibbutz composition
1970
ink on paper
17 x 23.5 cm

Letter to man
1967
ink on paper
39.5 x 29.5 cm

Letter to man, detail

Carta al hombre (Letter to Man, 1967) is a kind of pictorial explanation of Gurvich's vision of life. He locates the whole composition on the kibbutz, and it is quite revealing that he should choose that context as he valued it so much. He brings a number of subjects together in this intricate work. On the one hand there is the cosmic, the universal, the oneiric and the imaginary, suffering, the primordial couple, love, family life, work, country humility, music, identity (which is present in the ancestral symbols), the clock and time. On the other hand there is the mobility of pulsing life, of nature, of the capacity to build, deadly sins, Machado's plea for silence, the egg announcing birth and renovation, the terrestrial and the ascendant on the same level, so the daily reality of human beings is interrelated with the fantastic. The painter himself is also there, he becomes a walking palette with two legs and a great body represented by the palette, as if his calling had invaded his being and taken him to the most diverse destinations. Gurvich painted images of ladders, which allude to the possibility that human beings may ascend. There is also a microcosm of miniscule organisms, and references to ineptness, crassness, backwardness and incompetence that echo the idea of the blind leading the blind (an image based on Brueghel).

In this work the characteristic elements of his vision of the world are quite clear: his belief in the possibility of metamorphosis, his commitment to the energy of life, the feeling of vertigo in existence, his praise of permanent and constant activity and his admiration for the impetus that human beings have. Moreover, he is fascinated by the vivacity and mobility of reality, he enthuses about the capacity people, objects, nature and animals have to combine harmoniously, and we feel how he has faith in building fantasy worlds created by the imagination. The words of Italo Calvino in *Six Memos for the Next Millennium* seem to have been written to describe what Gurvich transmits, "An essential parity between everything that exists … the celebration of the unity of all things, inanimate as well as animate, the combination of elementary figures, the variety of living forms …the frantic spectacle of the world … the dissolution of the compactness of the world."

In the context of another, somewhat different and smaller version of this painting, also entitled *Carta al hombre* (Letter to Man), Joséphine Balken, a friend of Gurvich and a connoisseur of his work (who has also contributed an essay to this book) has this to say, "This painting is one of the clearest examples of G's conception of his own creative process in that it transmits the way the artist's world vision in relation to his existential surroundings is passed on, since G searched fervently for the most direct communication possible with other people. I believe that G was always very concerned about that relationship; it was a very strong inner need, to use his artistic work as a means of communication to establish bonds of common humanity with people.

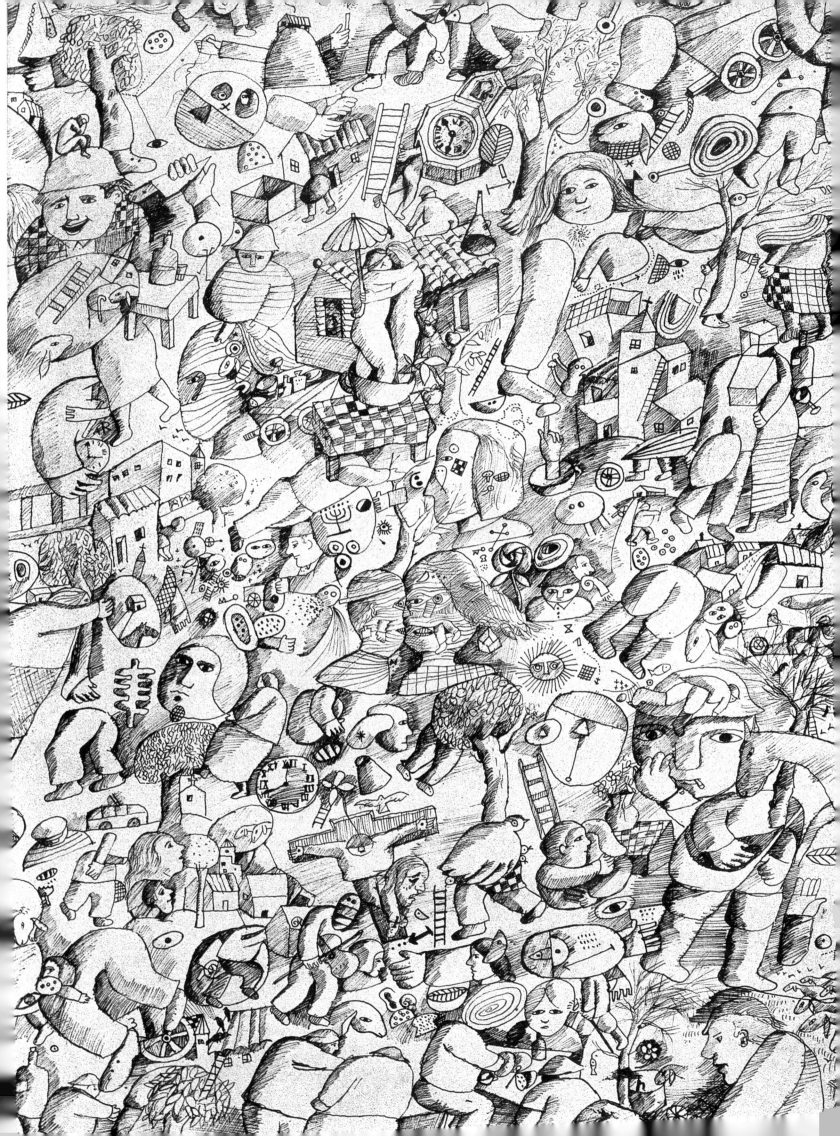

Couple
1966
mixed technique
30 x 38 cm

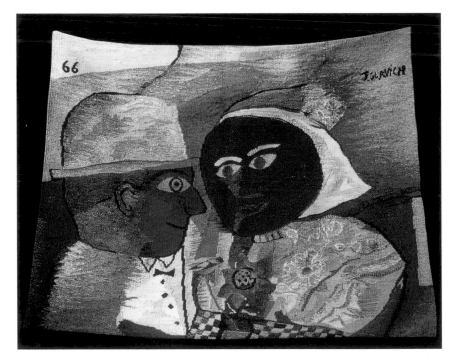

Tapestry couple
c. 1966
wool tapestry
made by Ernesto Arozteguy
90.5 x 115 cm

Kibbutz scene
1970
watercolour on cardboard
25 x 34 cm

The eye of God
1965
gouache on cardboard
33 x 47 cm

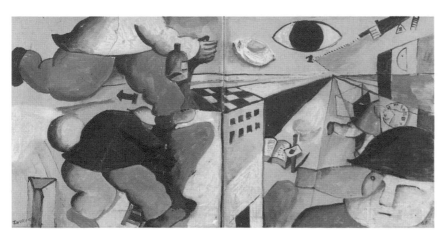

Two painted tiles
1965
oil, tempera on tiles
16 x 31 cm

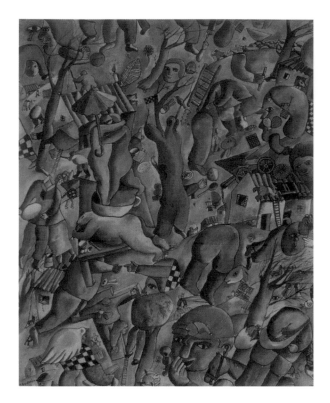

Letter to man
1967
oil on canvas
61 x 51 cm

"One of the principles underlying G's work in all its aspects is simultaneity of perception as a result of a random process of sensations (especially visual ones) that are combined with each other, and this enables the artist to create a personal, individualized organization of the world around us.

"I believe that he was first trying to establish contact and then to find the way to transmit the first stages of a kind perception that was more spontaneous and direct, more original, with less subsequent intervention of the intellect. In this way we have the pleasure to participate in a perceptive dynamic, to be in movement, like a source of elements that assemble in a harmonious way and thus pass on the incredible richness of the primary act of perceiving. Sensations of the present and the past are mixed without much rational organization, which is exactly what G tried to avoid so that he might reach the most genuine nature of human beings and try to apprehend it in its totality.

"Thus the great perceptive wealth and the dynamism of the different details in the painting, which are expressed in space by the dynamism of the rhythm, are like the sounds of an orchestra, in a somehow melodic harmonization of shapes, colours, meanings and symbols.

"I remember him pointing out, with his usual good humour and a cheeky twinkle in his eye, a small detail, a man defecating out of a window on the left in the painting. G builds up a kind of multi-faceted story, which is life, and which in fact corresponds to the brain structuring the act of knowing, with the idea that the brain works by linking stories together. What incredible intuition G had!

"I know that G did not construct the different perceptive details at random, unlike certain artists who are always improvising. He searched painstakingly with his imagination for the basic sensations, he wanted to get as close as possible to a perceptive truth or reality, but with a clear idea of what he wanted to transmit and how to do so; this was a characteristic he had. And this corresponds yet again to his very explicit goal of harmonising the imaginative, the unconscious thing, with the rational, conscious thing.

Carta al hombre (Letter to man) is the title G gave to this fresco of different aspects of daily life. The picture has a special relation to Judaism and the kibbutz, but it takes them as the basis of a universal world vision, as we can see from the cross and the references to Cerro. At the same time it evokes some deadly sins that are part of everyday life, which reminds us of Brueghel and H. Bosch and reflects G's reaction to the amazing complexity of life.

"It is incredible how G has managed to represent the expansion of perception –there is no centre to attract the eye– but in spite of the richness of the perceptions involved, the picture does not give an impression of chaos or disorder, and this would seem to be quite an artistic feat.

"In this way this painting manifests the second principle his artistic work is based on. The viewer's first impulse is to be attracted by the painting, and then he stops and takes a more careful look to "read it" with emotion and reflection. Thus we get back to G's constant attempts to attain an aesthetic balance between the imaginary (unconscious, emotional) and the rational (conscious) aspects, as the explicit basis of his artistic quest.

"What is precious about the painting is that it can be read in any direction... the eye is free to wander around the painting... and "see" something new, something different each time. And in some way this dynamism prompts us to constantly reconstruct our own perception of the painting. We read *Carta al hombre* (Letter to man), and we read it again from time to time, in a process of reconstructing our own perception.

"G bequeaths a letter to us, his letter to Man, which is his own story about the complexity and the richness of life, like his personal message to humanity, but there is no specific message, which is a temptation so many people fall into."

It was a period of great changes. Gurvich himself notes[42] that he appealed to imagination, adventure, intuition, simultaneity; he wanted to know the infinite, he spoke of poetic waves, he talked about routes within him, he wrote about marches from nothingness to creation, he dreamt of going beyond the limits, he went for what is deep, what is mysterious, and he sought the inner pulse of the things vibrating in his soul.

In addition to this he explored new languages in ceramics and achieved remarkable expressions that he soon developed and continued in a long series in Cerro. His first ceramic sculptures, which he did in Israel, are very original. Guillermo Fernández[43] explains, "He created a whole assembly system for the clay sheets. In Israel, Gurvich started sculptural ceramics with folded modelled clay, and he did many things with it." So when he returned to Uruguay he had resources that were not found there.

His great ceramic production phase was in Cerro. In those ceramic sculptures of figures he demonstrated his overflowing imagination. There are different themes, different subject matter, and he included motifs with Jewish content. He produced a series of human figures with Jewish and Torres García –like symbols on their bodies. He did figures from the kibbutz with the typical hat and with painted lines. In these representations he paid homage to primitive art, outlining and geometrising, and he addressed himself to a great purification. He constructed human figures with *menorot*, legs that fly in the air, *chaverim* from the *kibbutz*, ladders to the sky, the awassi ewe, and a series of small points that mark another path of his work, filling all of the surface area.

Another line of expression was very varied figures covered in symbols. He created complex, heterogeneous pieces. He made them with rolls and

Composition
c. 1970
pottery
15 x 12 x 20 cm

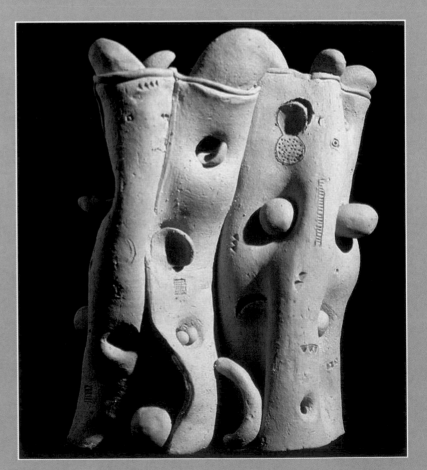

Tower
c. 1970
pottery
23 x 17 x 6 cm

The musicians
c. 1968
pottery
20 x 30 cm

Symbolic abstraction
c. 1969
pottery
24 x 20 cm

Universal woman
1970
pottery
35 x 21 cm

Universal being
c. 1965
pottery
11 x 10 x 3 cm

glued on minute, overlapping shapes, sticking them with slip, and he generated convex and concave forms. Some have Judaic and kibbutz symbols on the outside, which creates a three dimensional effect, and on others these symbols are in cavities.

He also constructed thin planimetric sheets that allude to generic structures of universal man or universal woman, and inside these he placed various shapes in relief. In some cases he worked the outside surface with dots and short lines in strips as if he is suggesting skin, but the inner surface is very smooth and full of protrusions arranged on the base of the horizontal areas that contain them. It is like a drawing on damp clay and there are a number of incisions alternating with the reliefs: zigzag lines, straight lines, a triangle, a bird, a fish, the profile of a face.

The reliefs predominate; there are hands, arms, torsos, eyes, leaves, a Hebrew candelabrum, two ladders, the Ten Commandments. The ladders have seven rungs: they link the terrestrial world with the celestial world. There are thin figures of different subjects that include kibbutz and Jewish themes. Gurvich used clay rollers to make these fine figures with so little volume that the air can penetrate. They are very ethereal.

He made sculptures in the shape of cylindrical towers and hollow truncated cones, with inserted and incised figures and with Jewish and kibbutz symbols that emerge like symbols of life.

Totó recalls,[44] "The reason for the third trip (to Israel) was to say goodbye to his mother, who was already very ill." Totó, who had recently lost her mother, encouraged him to go.[45] "He thought it was his duty: he had to comply with the farewell rite and help her to leave. And he had always been the favourite, the one that had always been there, helping financially, maintaining the household." Totó knew that if he was not there when his mother died he would feel awful afterwards. In fact, Gurvich had psychosomatic illnesses on the trip; in Spain he was in bed with a combination of complaints that the doctor diagnosed as metaphysical anguish. Totó explains, "The religious part of our lives as Jews is leaving forever, the person who taught us to prepare the festivals, to observe the traditions, she is slipping away. That was what Gurvich felt, but in fact his father died first, unexpectedly, from lung edema. He died in his arms, on the kibbutz. He was never the same after those losses. He loved both of them very dearly."

He began to retrieve more memories. Totó recalls, "One of them that stuck in his mind forever was his grandfather, who was murdered by the Nazis. And this is a figure he paints or does in ceramics, it appears in all the religious drawings, tempera pictures and paintings he did afterwards."[46]

In his work from his third trip to Israel there was a religious and symbolic dimension to his representations of the kibbutz. Gurvich added elements from biblical times, and with the pogroms in mind and memories of his grandfather he included figures from the ghettos and the shtetl such as elderly men with long beards. At the same time he used Jewish symbols, ladders going up to the heavens, into a context in which they inter-mingle with human beings and ascending bodies, floating and walking through the air. In his folders of sketches there are numerous studies, some of them water-coloured, of the sacrifice of Isaac, the hand of God touching Man, Adam and Eve newly created, the expulsion from Para-dise, and, to quote Masaccio, "Everything in the context of the bucolic life of the kibbutz."

In his production and his preparatory drawings we find recurring themes like Moses and the Tablets with the Commandments, festivals, ritual meals and tables prepared for the Sabbath. Gurvich brings togeth-er scenes from the *shtetl* with "The blind leading the blind" in a whole in which we find a fiddler, a woman in a small house lighting the candles of *Shabbat* with the characteristic position of her hands in prayer, and religious figures, mothers mourning for their dead children, the *shofar*[47], the village carts.

One of Gurvich's friends was the painter and sculptor Naftali Bezem,[48] a German who had lived in Israel since he was fourteen and whose work is metaphysical and includes the essential myths of Judaism, the *Shabbat* and allusions to suffering. This might have been one more influence that prompted Gurvich to examine Jewish subject matter in depth. This was something that Eva Kaufman experienced as well. She was an artist from Tucuman living in Tel Aviv, she became friends with Gurvich on his first trip to Israel and they had close contact and worked together. Through

In memory of my father
4.iv.1970
oil on wood
21 x 40 cm

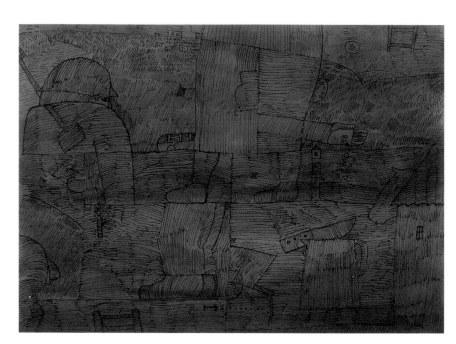

Kibbutz
1964
watercolour, ink on paper
16.5 x 21.5 cm

Bezem and Eva he acquired a greater knowledge of Israeli art, and he imbibed still more on his visits to galleries. He was also in contact with other artists like Mordecai Ardon (1896-1992), who painted some subjects that were very dear to Gurvich.

In that period, Gurvich's range of colours expanded and the fantasy element in his work loomed larger. The psychoanalyst Esther Shajar[49] comments, "I see in his paintings the bustle of life on the kibbutz. I found his exhibition at the Katz Gallery fascinating. I did not know him; I met him at a party in Eva Kaufmans'. I found, and find, something in his art that I have not found in anyone since. He spoke of his paintings in a special way: in the middle of a meeting full of people he spoke with passion, with spontaneity, to a complete stranger, and that fascinated me, it got me thinking. And in time I saw how his works grow; that it was not just a first impression. They have come into my family, and I see the legacy of ancient Egypt, French elements, kibbutz life, constructivism, the Torres García style, the Jewish content, art deco, the golden rule, Paul Klee, a landscape of Ramot Menashé, mornings on the kibbutz with everybody in a hurry to get to work, a whole world."[50]

In a kibbutz scene from his third trip the composition is made up of three vertical sections using intense blues, reds and whites. It is very imaginative. In the foreground there is a *chaver* with a red face who is watching, life emerges from an egg, a humanised tree walks with a leg, a woman is escaping from the scene, a man and a woman are joined at the face, there is a ladder crossing the image and the *menorah* hangs in space. A woman with a blue face and red and blue hands lights the Sabbath candles, and in the centre of the composition there are geometric prisms and figures interconnected with the figurative elements. Different time frames and different places coexist in a same space in a mysterious and magical way.

Gurvich deliberately did not respect the usual coordinates of space and time, and in his painting there are no codes, no inside or outside. These images are dominated by diversification, simultaneity, malleability, mobility, combined and compound beings, and by what is unstable and plural. The imagination takes flight. This is one more proof that Gurvich won his freedom.[51]

Gurvich created a whole area of drawings on cement outside the children home (Beit Ieladim) in the kibbutz Ramot Menashé. He also made art dedicated for children such as paintings on board, painted toys, tapestry, musical boxes. He illustrated stories such as "Hevda the Goat" written in Hebrew.

In this way he followed the legacy of his master Torres Garcia that gave importance to public art and also created for children and at the same time he believed in the cultural and aesthetic politics of the Kibbutz Movement Hakibbutz Haartzi Hashomer that wanted to give a elevetad cultural life to his members and had a remarkable cultural and artistic activity.

Kibbutz child
c. 1964
tempera on paper
33 x 46 cm

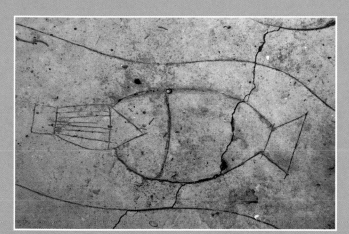

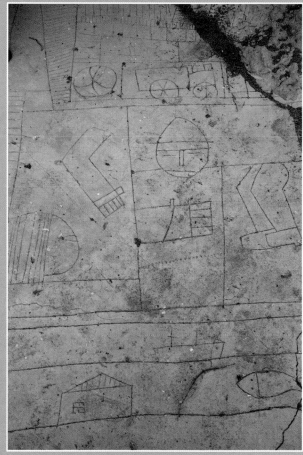

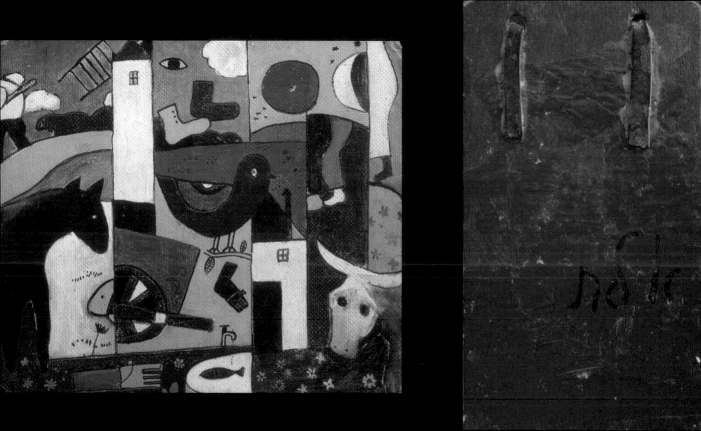

There is a little goat in our stable and her name is Hedva / She is all white, pure white
/ White from her ear to her tail / And only her nose, red.
All the children know Hedva's mother / She is Haviva, the goat of the stable
/ And she is also all white / from her tail to her goatee.

On the same night that Hedva was born, the stable was dark and there was a big storm outside.
/ And Hedva the little goat, frightened and shaking, clung to her mother.
The torrential downpour knocked on the roof. / And a bolt of thunder - Crack-boom!-/ Suddenly casts its white light / And there is noise and fear in the stable!
And Hedva, so fearful, was scared! / "Bah Bah, mama-mama!" / She whines and cries. / Then Bibi licks her head
/ And Hedva suckles in silence.

Winter passed and summer arrived / And Hedva grew a lot! / On her little head horns grew.
/ One on each side, two in total.
She no longer whines or cries at night. / Because it is not nice for a little goat of her age to cry.
/ She lies down comfortably alongside sheep and deer.
She anxiously waits for morning to come / And the shepherd begins to call out: / Brrr-brrr! come, come!
/ Come out the whole flock! / And Hedva jumps for joy.

And what do you think - who is the first on the hill with the flock? / Right! It's Hedva excited / Small and wildly mischievous.
There is a little goat in our stable and her name is Hedva / She is all white, pure white
/ White from her ear to her tail / And only her nose, red.

The Ramot Menashé kibbutz
1956
oil on cardboard
50 x 70 cm

Kibbutz
Homage to Brueghel
1956
oil on cardboard
70 x 100 cm

Sower in night scene
1957
oil on canvas
41.5 x 50 cm

Homage to work on the Kibbutz
1959
oil on canvas
62 x 83 cm

Kibbutz composition with egg
1960
oil on canvas
40 x 52 cm

Sower of stars
c. 1964
oil on cardboard
85 x 108 cm

Rhythms
1968
oil on board
40 x 32 cm

Kibbutz
1968
gouache on cardboard
35 x 50 cm

Kibbutz composition

1970

tempera on paper

25 x 34 cm

Composition of man in red
1966
oil on canvas
57 x 73 cm

Composition with clock
1966
oil with *collage* on canvas
49.5 x 64.5 cm

Kibbutz tree
1966
tempera series on paper
54 x 94 cm

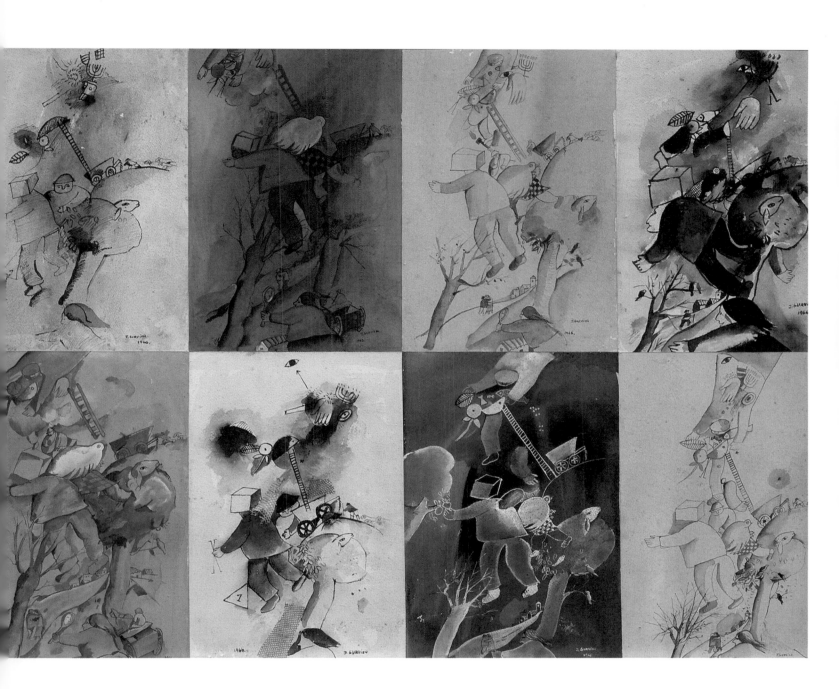

Collage composition
1966
tempera, fabrics on paper
34 x 24 cm

Menorah, couple and flowers on the Kibbutz
c. 1966
mixed technique on paper
52 x 36 cm

World of images in spiral
1966
oil on canvas
55.5 x 75.5 cm

Fantasy world
1966
tempera on paper
34 x 48 cm

Kibbutz scene
1966
watercolour on paper
35 x 50 cm

Figures on pink background
1967
collage, gouache on cardboard
35 x 51 cm

Cosmic world
1966
gouache on paper
31 x 40 cm

Fantasy world in pure colours
1967
oil on wood
120 x 161 cm

Fantasy world with black background
1966
oil on canvas
60 x 80 cm

World of images and figures
1966
oil on canvas
59 x 79 cm

Fantasy world
1966
tempera on paper
35 x 52 cm

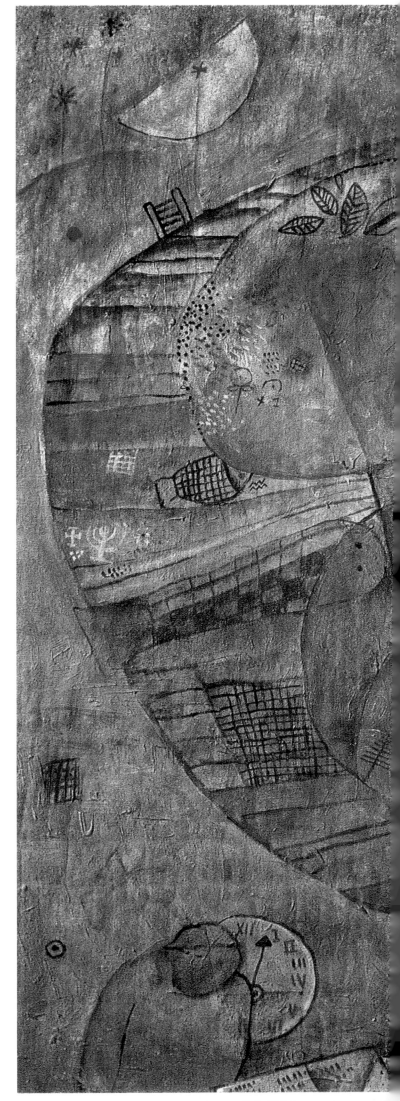

Cosmos with spiral
1966
oil on canvas
60 x 51 cm

Cosmos and kibbutz
1966
mixed technique on paper
60 x 70 cm

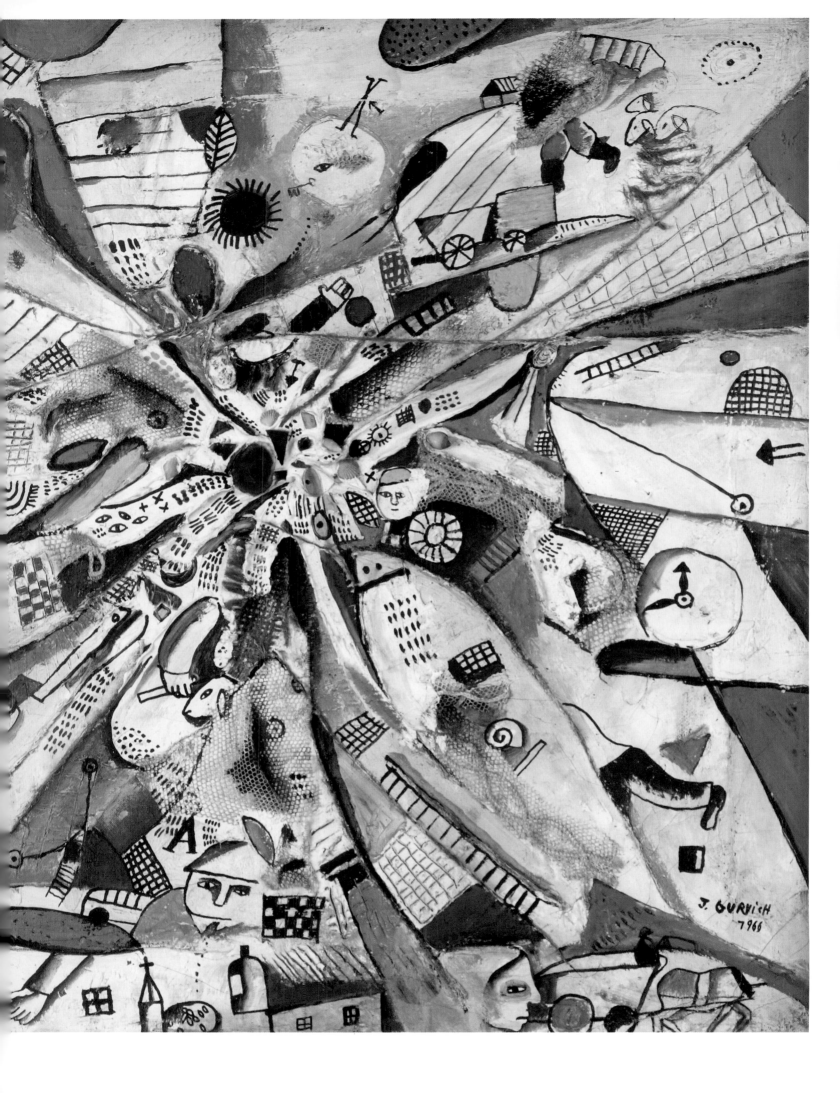

198

Kibbutz composition with couple
1966
oil on canvas
60 x 80 cm

Kibbutz composition
1966
oil on canvas
57 x 76 cm

Chaver and chavera
(couple)
1966
oil on hessian
126 x 91 cm

The kibbutz world
1970
tempera on card
49 x 61 cm

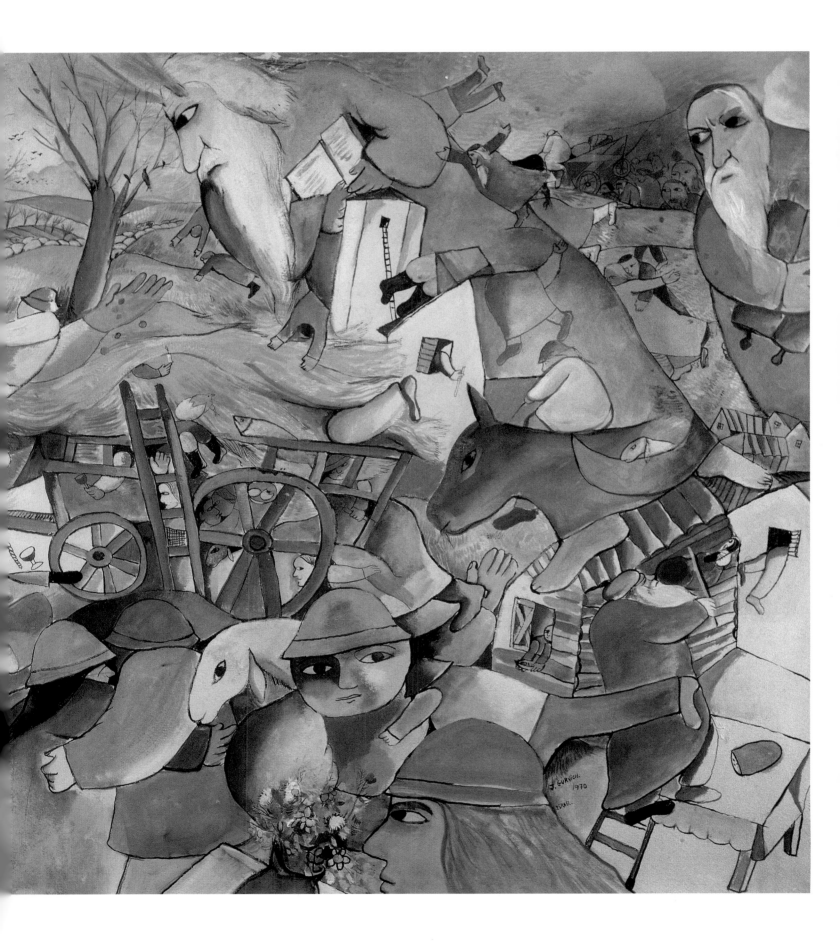

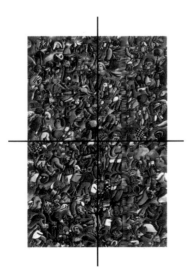

Letter to man
1967
oil on canvas
155 x 101 cm

(developed on following pages)

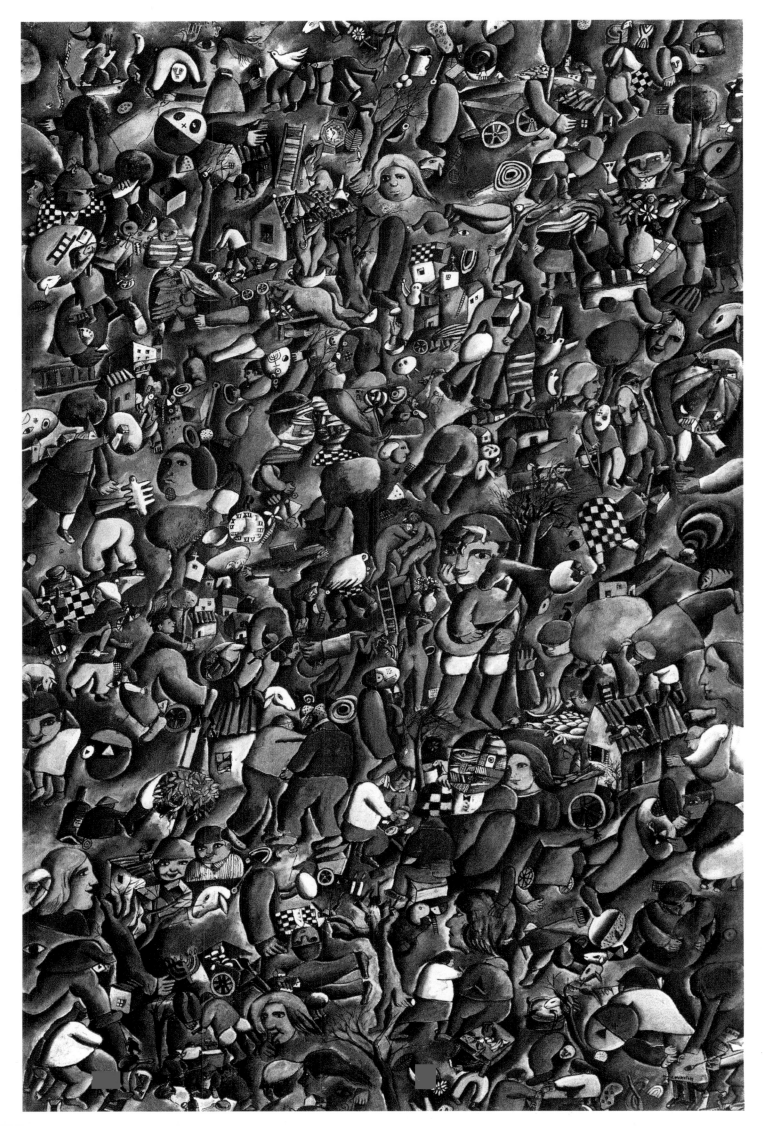

Kibbutz Ramot Menashé
1970
oil on board
78 X 38 cm

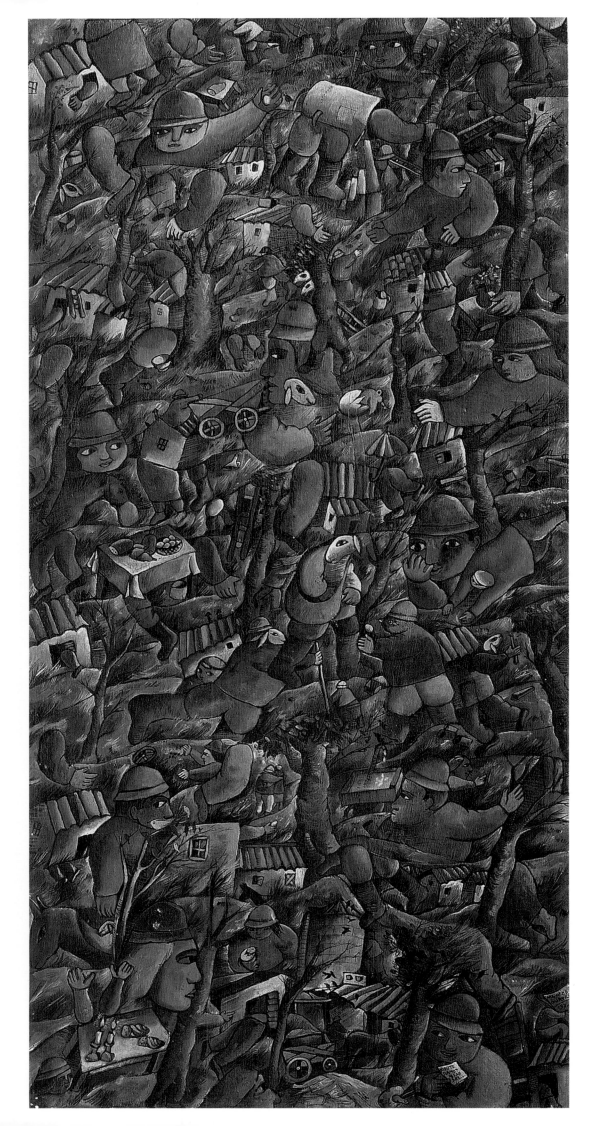

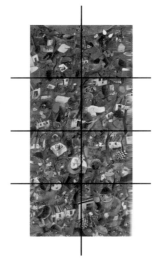

Homage to Ramot Menashé Kibbutz
1970
oil on wood
248 x 125 cm

(developed on following pages)

Kibbutz and Shabbat

c. 1973

oil on canvas

101 x 126 cm

Composition with religious symbols
at Ramot Menashé
1973
oil on canvas
84 X 103 cm

Kibbutz and Shabbat
in vertical composition
c. 1969
acrylic, Indian ink on wood
32 x 42.5 cm

End notes

1   The kibbutz movement went through
     many changes, many different stages,
     and depending on the type of commune
     there were more distinct changes in some
     kibbutzim as of 1969. Those changes were
     accentuated in 1977 and were especially
     intensified after 1985. Today the kibbutzim
     exist, they have even had a revival, but
     under new conditions – they are no longer
     the Socialist commune that Gurvich
     experienced. See: Eliezer Ben-Rafael,
     Crisis and Transformation: The Kibbutz
     at Century's End, S U N Y Series in Israeli
     Studies, New York, State University of New
     York Press, 1997; Ernest Krausz (editor),
     Sociology of the Kibbutz, Studies of Israeli
     Society, New Jersey, Transaction Publishers,
     1983.
2   In Ernest Krausz, Sociology of the Kibbutz,
     op. cit.
3   Ibidem.
4   The adult population always had a role in
     the community's governance, but naturally
     reality beat idealism and more qualified
     leaders and administrators came to the
     fore.
5   Author's interview with Totó.
6   Galia Bar Or, "Universal and International:
     Art in the Kibbutz in the First Decade",
     Contemporary Israeli Art Fund, published
     by Artist a non-profit organization based
     in New York and Tel Aviv , http://www.
     artisrael.org/feature/press/universal-and-
     international-art-in-the-kibbutz-in-the-first-
     decade
7   Nigro was a student of Guvrich's in the
     period of most changes, from 1967 to 1969.
     He got to know him well as he spent entire
     days, from Monday to Friday, from 8 a.m.
     to 7 p.m., at Gurvich's house/workshop
     in Cerro, for classes and to be the artist's
     assistant. He sent me texts on Gurvich
     in June 2003, written in 1983. In Página
     12, in an article entitled 'José Gurvich: an
     imaginary space' Nigro tells of his first
     encounter with Gurvich in April 1966, and
     how he saw him conceive and paint his
     compositions from that year until 1969.
     Adolfo Nigro, "José Gurvich: un espacio
     imaginario", Buenos Aires, Pagina 12, p. 7. I
     also interviewed him many times.
8   Mordecai Bar-Lev and Yuval Dror,
     "Education for Work in the Kibbutz as
     a Means Towards Personal, Social, and
     Learning Fulfilment", Journal of Moral
     Education, New York, Routledge, vol. 24,
     no. 3, September 1995, pp. 259-272; Judith
     Buber Agassi, "The Israeli Experience in
     the Democratization of Work", Sociology
     of Work and Occupations, vol. 1, no. 1,
     Tel Aviv, Tel Aviv University, February 1974;

     Richard Sosis, Bradley J. Ruffle, "Life,
     Ideology, Religion, and the Evolution of
     Cooperation: Field Experiments on Israeli
     Kibbutzim", Socioeconomic Aspects of
     Human Behavioral Ecology, Research in
     Economic Anthropology, Oxford, Elsevier
     Ltd., Near, H., 1992, edited by Michael
     Avard, vol. 23, 2004, pp. 89-117.
9   Work was an end in itself; the human spirit
     was more holistic, creative and productive.
     Human beings were linked intimately with
     nature, and thanks to manual and rural
     work a new way of being Jewish was born.
10   At the same time he also left his legacy,
     with the importance he gave to agricultural
     work as a source of spiritual health that
     legitimized the possession of the land.
11   Work was preached and practiced, and
     education gave work a central role from
     pre-school onwards. In this type of kibbutz
     there were no hired workers (although this
     did spread after the end of the sixties and
     later on expanded considerably). Ideological
     motivation was very important.
12   To be able to support oneself from one's
     own manual labour is a great virtue; this
     was a characteristic of devout peolple in
     ancient Israel. In this way, human beings
     deserve all the honours and goods of
     this world and of the world to come. It
     is written, "When you feed yourselves off
     the fruit of your effort, you are happy and
     blessed." (Psalms, 128:2). Happy in this
     world and blessed in that to come, which
     is all good. Extracted from Mishneh Torah.
     Rabbi Moshe ben Maimon.
13   Antonio Machado, "Proverbios y cantares",
     Campos de Castilla, Madrid, Ediciones El
     País, S.L., 2003.
14   Author's interview with Totó, 2009.
15   Author's interview with Vera Jordan,
     Montevideo, 2009.
16   Tzena was the period of rationing and
     shortages while the country was growing.
     Those were hard times, and they lasted
     from 1949 to 1959.
17   Interview with Vera Jordan, Montevideo,
     2009.
18   Interview with Naftali Bezem, Zurich,
     March 2009.
19   Interview with Eva Kaufman, Israel, March
     2009.
20   Visit to the Ramot Menashé kibbutz,
     March 2009 by Martin Gurvich, Alicia
     Haber, Alfredo Rowinski (photographer)
     and Juan Lucas Pezzino. The interviews
     with Chaverim at the Ramot Menashé
     kibbutz in March 2009 include Boris
     and Maia Blinde, Pinjas "Pancho" Goetz
     (Chilean), Abraham and Manya Diamant
     (Polish: she is an Auschwitz survivor),
     Moshe Landeker (Yekee, Chilean, widower
     of Miriam, José Gurvich's sister), Nitza

Shapira (Chilean, born Mendoza, Argentina, married Efra, Hungarian), Bat Ami and Ari Goldstein (Uruguayan: he was an electrician), Eugenio Rosen and Lía Malinoff (Uruguayan: he was an awassi shepherd).

21 Visit to the Ramot Menashé kibbutz, March 2009. Interview with Boris and Maia Blinde.
22 Author's interview with Totó, 2009.
23 Letter written by Gurvich.
24 Alicia Haber, El mundo íntimo del artista, op. cit., p. 77.
25 Letter written by Gurvich, Gurvich archives.
26 Muki Tsur has lived at the Ein Gev kibbutz since 1956. He is an expert on the history and life stories of the kibbutzian and pioneer movement. He was secretary of the kibbutzian movement and is professor at Bima, the kibbutzian Judaism University in the Jordan Valley.
27 Letter written by Gurvich, Gurvich archives.
28 The Talmud is a fundamental text in Judaism. It contains discussions, contributions and studies by rabbis about law, ethics, customs and history. It consists of the Mishnah and the Gemara.
29 Gershom Sholem, "The Curious History of the Six Pointed Star: How the "Magen David" became the Jewish Symbol, New York, Commentary, 8, 1949, pp. 243-251.
30 Ibidem.
31 Dances in Hebrew.
32 There was no tradition in the sense that all traditions were from the Diaspora. The people had to resort to a combination of Hasidic, Balkan, Russian, Arabic and Yemeni elements and subjects that mattered at that time like the ideals of the return to the land, the days of the Bible, love for the nation, knowledge of their landscape, symbolic fruit like the pomegranate, the desert that turned into a garden, and Israeli productivity.
33 Dance, the strongest influence was the school of Rudolf con Laban, expression dance, Ausdruckstanz, a modern movement developed in central Europe between the two World Wars that reached Israel with dancers and choreographers emigrating from Germany. Von Laban believed that dance had to serve society, workers and the proletariat, and reach the people through the development of folklore. It had to have relatively simple steps so that everyone could take part. Gertrud Kraus, his assistant, immigrated into Israel and was the guru of modern dance in the years of the Ishuv and later of the creation of the State.

Israel was an ideal laboratory because in Europe folklore already existed but in Israel it had to be created from scratch. The most suitable scenario was the kibbutz because it maintained direct contact with the land, and festivals there were celebrated in a communal manner. It was quite an autarkic framework without external influences and open to experimentation. The theme of work could be naturally integrated, as could Socialist ideals, without any thought of marketing or the box office. Ilse Dubon and Rivka Sturman were very famous choreographers of the founding dances.
34 Jazeira.
35 Author's interview with Totó 2009.
36 'Butt' in Yiddish.
37 Author's interview with Totó, 2009.
38 Proximidades (Report by Daniel Rovira Ahlers, author, on the TV program "Protagonista" and published in Tres magazine, no. 156, Montevideo, 5 February, 1999).
39 "Jorge Damiani, Magia, sueño y libertad", in Daniel Rovira Ahlers, Proximidades, Testimonios sobre José Gurvich, op. cit, p. 122.
40 Writings of Gurvich, in Alicia Haber, El mundo íntimo del artista, op. cit.
41 Writings of Gurvich. Family collection, undated and no page.
42 Antonio Machado, "Proverbios y cantares" (Campos de Castilla), op. cit. Poesías completas, Madrid, Espasa-Calpe, 1933.
43 Writings of Gurvich, in Alicia Haber, El mundo íntimo del artista, op. cit.
44 Interview with Guillermo Fernández by Santiago Tavella, 2003, cited in the book by Alicia Haber and Cecilia de Torres, José Gurvich: murales, esculturas y objetos, Montevideo, Gurvich Foundation, 2003.
45 Interview with Totó, 2009.
46 Ibidem.
47 Ibidem.
48 The shofar is a ram's horn used at the Jewish New Year festival, Rosh Hashanah, and the Day of Atonement, Yom Kippur, for religious purposes at the synagogue.
49 Interviewed in Zurich, March 2009.
50 Interviewed in Jerusalem, March 2009.
51 Ibidem.
52 See: Alicia Haber, José Gurvich: un canto a la vida, op. cit.

3. Echoes of spirituality: mother, tradition and Israel

3

Echoes of spirituality:
mother, tradition and Israel

Totó recalls that "...after receiving a letter from Miriam saying their mother was terminally ill, he did his first tempera paintings of explicitly Jewish subjects with religious scenes."[1] Gurvich received the news of his mother's incurable cancer in August 1969. He was in Cerro, and according to Totó he immediately locked himself in his workshop and began the tempera series of scenes from Genesis like Sarah's pregnancy, Sarah's death, Jacob's dream and the sacrifice of Isaac.[2] "That was his immediate response to that terrible grief, that is how he alleviated it, how he bore it and sublimated it and transformed it into art. It was an offering for someone he loved very much."

The person who had passed on his treasured Judaism to him was about to disappear. When he heard about the fatal illness the first thing that in his grief he said to Totó[3] was, "Here is where my Judaic character leaves." He valued his Judaism so much, and he was proud of how his mother had passed it on to him.[4] And his farewell rite began; he evoked a lifetime through the cathartic act of painting. This was one of the reasons why he embarked on biblical subjects. He was fond of those first paintings that were inspired by the Bible and done in loving praise of his mother and her legacy. He was emotionally very close to those works, and before setting out on a new journey he lovingly wrapped them up in velvet and put them away with special care.[5]

His relationship with his mother was very intense and positive, it was an essential part of his life. Vera Jordan recalls,[6] "The bond he had with his mother was very obvious, he put her on a pedestal, and this could even be seen in his body language. And the feeling was mutual; when he entered the room or when she came into the room they adored each other. He protected her, she was a lovable person and everyone loved her, and they had a unique and in some ways surprising relationship. All his life he had been her companion, he worked from early on helping in the home, he stayed with her when his sister went to Israel, their eyes lit up when they saw each other. Eva Kaufman explains,[7] "The Jewish subjects were becoming increasingly important, and this also had to do with his visits to his mother."

He was preparing to go from New York to Israel to see her because she was seriously ill but he could not go because of a series of official procedures that held him up. He got very upset,[8] he adored his mother,[9]

Shabbat
1970
tempera on paper
45 x 32 cm

and was unable to say goodbye to her. After Jaie's death in 1973, more and more religious references appeared in his art.

Religion had very special, very deep, intimate, affective, emotional, and personal connotations for Gurvich, even though he did not practice. And it was essential to his mother, it was part of their identity and it bound them together. He honoured her with what was so dear to her; he evoked her through rites and beliefs. They had a special affinity but it is impossible to know to what extent her religiosity exerted a spiritual influence on him after she died. Perhaps Gurvich inclined more towards the traditions of his people as an element of continuity.

At any rate, this might be why he started to include stories, miraculous elements and religious figures floating in the kibbutz air in some of his compositions; he was joining together two worlds and making them compatible with each other. He shows us elderly men with long beards from the shtetl, which came from memories of his grandfather and of all the orthodox Jews he saw in his childhood, with their heads covered with kippot (plural of kippah, small ritual cap),[10] and with tallitot (plural of tallit) prayer shawls.

He painted many biblical scenes on his third trip to Israel and later in New York. During his third stay at the kibbutz he produced one of his versions of the sacrifice of Isaac, in oil on wooden board, and he grew fond of that piece and never wanted to sell it. It is now at the Gurvich Museum in Montevideo. He also addressed himself to the subject of Jacob's dream, again on wooden board. He collected those boards during his walks on the kibbutz, and he prepared them for painting. In New York he continued with this subject.

Another influential factor in his progressive commitment to religious scenes was the mere fact of being in Israel and on the kibbutz, where everything is done in an open and clear way, collectively, in accordance with the people's wishes, in a national way, and this attitude was shared by the whole population. The Sabbath and the festivals were the kibbutz rest days, and the Bible was a part of everyday life there.[11]

There was also his friendship with the Israeli artist Bezem and with Eva Kaufman. Eva says, "The relationship with Bezem and his art was linked to these themes. Judaism was very alive, the ground was favourable and the subjects arose naturally. None of us were religious, but in Israel it is something you live naturally."

The wealth of Judaic culture that Gurvich had accumulated in his life up to then emerged, memories of Jiezna (Yezne, in Yiddish), memories of his grandfather, his experiences in the immigrant neighbourhood in Montevideo and the religious customs at the homes of his childhood friends. And besides this there was everything else he had absorbed, things that are inexplicable, that cannot be verbalized, that are atavistic.

Plan for a cosmic monument
c. 1962
ink on paper
14.5 x 22.5 cm

Jacob's dream, details

Just a few examples of pictures with religious or biblical subject matter are *El sacrificio de Isaac* (The sacrifice of Isaac, 1969), *El sacrificio de Isaac* (The sacrifice of Isaac, 1970), *El embarazo de Sara* (Sarah's pregnancy, 1969), *La muerte de Sara* (Sarah's death 1969), *El sueño de Jacob* (Jacob's dream, 1969), *La muerte de Abel* (Abel's death, 1973), *Cain y Abel* (Cain and Abel, 1973), *Sucot* (Sukkot, 1973), *Shavuot* (1973), *Purim* (1973), *Pésaj* (1973), many versions of the Shabbat, *Qué pesado ser judío* (It is hard to be a Jew), many representations of Hannukah, Adam and Eve, and many paintings of the creation.

Gurvich chose the biblical scenes he was most interested in, and his choice shows many aspects of the man he was. Very often there is a main subject, but at the same time these is a kind of summary of several key elements of Judaism. In Jacob's dream, for example, he painted images of Moses, of a mother lighting Shabbat candles, a Star of David, a Menorah and the tree of life, and he added still more themes on the painted board with the same name. And in The Sacrifice of Isaac he included several stories from Genesis. In numerous compositions he condensed many subjects, times and spaces into one single space.

Of all his significant paintings with traditional Jewish subject matter just six were done on commission, and that happened only when he was in New York. Some people have taken those six as a paradigm of his work on explicitly Jewish themes and believe he did all his other pieces for clients, galleries or on request. This is not true. There are dozens of pictures with Jewish themes, and he did most of them spontaneously and in a fever of inspiration.

Gurvich always dealt with Jewish subjects in ways linked to the Ramot Menashé kibbutz. This was a position he adopted; to place everything related to Judaism in a kibbutz framework, to show it as it is practiced on the kibbutz, and this was a new way of experiencing Judaism, it was a secular, socialist interpretation in a rural context. This was a personal decision, an original preference, and as such it was idiosyncratic. Instead of presenting these subjects in the framework of the Diaspora he chose to do so in a place that was dearer to him, and this shows the extent to which the kibbutz and the new forms of the festivals dazzled him, and the extent to which he imbibed the messages of the new State.

Despite this great secular influence and the fact that Gurvich was not a religious man, his work with biblical themes conveys very considerable spirituality, a belief in something superior to man, a higher reality, elements that go beyond the terrestrial. While he includes references to Michelangelo (the divine hand touching a man's hand), and there are ascending ladders and angels, these should not necessarily be interpreted as the expression someone who practices a religion. But they do have mystical connotations, allusions to incorporeal elements, to what is ethereal, invisible, evidence of another world or of a spiritual aspiration. Totó[12] says, "He had to go through that process; he had to go back to Judaism to assimilate it."

Some Jews believe that God is a necessary fiction, but for reasons of their own identity they have strong connections with festivals, the Shabbat and certain rites. The experience of the English thinker, philosopher, and historian Isaiah Berlin is interesting in this respect because it is shared by many of us and it was typical of Gurvich. Berlin was not a religious person, he said he was deaf to religion, that he could not experience the divine or understand the word of God, but he went to the synagogue every once in a while to identify himself with the traditions of his ancestors, and he liked the ceremonies of the temple because they were manifestations of a profound human experience.

In his own way, Gurvich let those spiritual aspects resonate. He had a spiritual impetus; he made a spiritual itinerary, as can be seen in his production from 1969 on. His friend and kibbutz companion Vera Jordan comments,[13] "Judaism was important for him. It was revived on the kibbutz, he heard those stories every day, and even though he was not a religious person he bore the Bible in mind because it was taught there, it was a constant source of history, of identity, and this went beyond a belief in God. And besides, in Israel at that time the Bible featured very strongly, it was in song lyrics and in the history of the place, the geography, the very name of the place where the kibbutz is located. It was all very fresh and real, and the festivals were held with complete naturalness. There was no need to go and study it or go to a synagogue, or to convert and become a religious person, it was part of normal life. Hannukah was and is very exciting, the procession with torches on the hills at sunset, it was very stirring and he liked it very much. Pesach was a very special night, and he did an outstanding mural of that scene."

Shabbat

According to Ahad Ha'am,[14] "The Jews have kept the Shabbat, but it is mainly the Shabbat that has preserved the Jews." The Shabbat started appearing in Gurvich's work as of 1969. Often it is part of a whole, but there are also compositions that deal specifically with the lighting of the candles on Erev Shabbat (the eve of the Sabbath). 'Shabbat' in biblical Hebrew means to cease, to stop or to finish, although generally it is used in the sense of 'to rest'. It evokes the moment God finished creating the Universe, and for religious people it is a day dedicated to God and to rest. It represents the pact between God and the children of Israel (Exodus xx: 8-11), and biblical law is observed because that is one of the commandments. Motherhood is praised in Judaism through

The Shabbat kiss
1967
plaster
39 x 28.5 cm

Shabbat
c. 1970
pottery
16 x 10 x 10 cm

Shabbat
c. 1970
pottery
20 x 40 x 20 cm

Memory of my mother
c. 1970
watercolour on paper
29 x 21 cm

the blessing of the candles of the Shabbat, and it is a task, a commandment, a female mitzvah *par excellence*.

In one of the artist's most moving paintings, a picture he gave to his sister, there is a caption, "For Miriam, in memory of our mother". The main figure is in the middle of the Ramot Menashé kibbutz, it is hypertrophied and it dominates the place like a great presence in Gurvich's life. And there is also an everyday detail, a shepherd with his sheep going about his task, which is a reference to Gurvich himself and his work on the kibbutz.

In another composition, the table for the Shabbat is flying and kibbutz figures stick out from underneath. One of them is holding the Torah scrolls, another a ritual wine glass, and below them life in the kibbutz still pulses, the shepherd guides his sheep, couples love each other, men work, the trees bloom and life goes on, all of which reflects Gurvich's vision of life.

He painted these scenes with a sense of dedication because one of his most treasured experiences was taking part on the Shabbat prepared by his mother. He always carried that image with him since his earliest childhood. Totó tells us that they always took part in festivals when they were on the kibbutz, as his mother always celebrated Shabbat throughout her life and whatever the circumstances. Eva Kaufman recalls that "... she kept on with these practices on the kibbutz, even when she was very ill, which was very touching. She overcame her terrible pain and continued with what she considered essential as a Jewish woman, as a mother. She prepared cholent, a meal that is slow-cooked overnight and complies with Sabbath law, and on the eve of Shabbat she set the table, the challahs,[15] the candelabra, and with the handkerchief she did the candle blessing.[16]... The matter of women and the Sabbath candles became an obsession when he visited his mother."[17]

Gurvich also knew other Shabbat ceremonies from his early life in the Barrio Sur neighbourhood, where he was often invited to his friends' homes for the celebrations. The Shabbat was a fundamental part of his life.

It is virtually impossible for a Jew to forget the Erev Shabbat in his childhood home, even if afterwards, in adult life, he decides to be secular or to leave his Jewish roots behind and assimilate. A secular, Uruguayan contemporary of Gurvich's remembers those experiences in an orthodox family, "As early as Friday morning the wife and mother begin with the preparations for the whole house for Saturday's "family celebration of the feast" by cleaning and putting everything in order, setting up of the special utensils, the different preparations for the night and for the whole following day, so as to have the minimum to do on the day itself (water and food on heaters, the rule about turning on and off the lights) because not-doing was an essential part of the ritual. Nice shawls that were usually embroidered and had been passed down in the family, are placed over the furniture, which is not used, so the entire house is transformed and takes on a truly festival look.

"At night that same Friday, the husband returns from the synagogue and his wife has set a pretty table with the best tablecloth, the best set of dishes and the challah. And immediately the husband sings a song in honour of his wife, thanking her for her work and her welcome. The dinner brings the whole family together in an atmosphere of rejoicing, it includes the traditional rites, blessings, songs, and prayers, and at the end all the members of the family take part in the Shabbat chants.

The festive atmosphere of joy clearly "cuts" the monotony of the weekly routine, and it is truly contagious. In this way, once a week, a pause for family celebration is introduced and, like the silences that are part of music, it breaks and transforms the routine and brings in a pause for happiness.

The Shabbat has deep family content and that is how Gurvich always experienced it with his mother. The family gathers together on Friday at sunset when the festival begins, and there is a supper, carefully prepared and set out on a well-dressed table with its candelabra. The lighting of the candles has particular importance for women, who recite a blessing, then the Kiddush (sanctification over wine) takes place and everybody eats a piece of braided bread, challah, made specially for that day. After that there is a sacred time of reflection and then leisure, creation, song, and prayer. The family share in a time of happiness, pleasure, conversation and meditation. This holy festival creates a sense of community, warmth, family, shared food, identification with culture, delight, spirituality, and the home. And it involves many spiritual values, which is why many secular Jews take part. Not even the Marxist kibbutzim can set aside something that is so bound up with Judaism.

Family and community participation are of fundamental importance because they are associated with a person's very identity.

The Shabbat generates a pause, a time for the spiritual and the creative, a time to study, it fosters intellectual and emotional elevation, it helps to free people from routine concerns and the material world, it brings tranquillity and happiness. It is a day of liberation from all the worries and all the routine tasks that tie people down. All the traditional elements highlight the significance of the bond between keeping Saturday and memory, Zakhor, and whenever there is an allusion to Shabbat in the interpretations the words 'remember' and 'recall' are used, and this entails an act of remembering that helps perpetuate the creation of the world throughout the generations and allows a continuous renovation of the experience.

Shabbat
c. 1970
watercolour on paper
22 x 15 cm

Blessing the candles
c. 1969
pastel on paper
47 x 31 cm

Gurvich's commitment to Judaism was a way of preserving the memory of his mother, his creator. She bore him and she passed on Judaism to him and stimulated him to renew the experience. His painting of the Shabbat helped him to preserve this in himself, and also showed everybody else one of his people's essential festivals.

The *Shabbat* is deeply embedded in national imagery in Israel, and it now plays a key role in secular as well as religious life in the country. It is so important that it is a holiday in the full sense of the word; there is no public transport, no trade, no studying, nothing but the most essential services. Secular Israelis, who are the majority, devote the time to leisure, and religious Israelis keep the day in accordance with tradition. It is a deep-rooted custom. Totó[18] recalls that at Ramot Menashé the *Shabbat* was prepared in the communal dining hall, and that at a certain moment the two candles were lit and the whole ceremony began. Gurvich and his family went first to his parents' house to take part in the *Shabbat* in the most traditional way, and then attended the collective *Shabbat* celebrations

Other weighty factors that influenced Gurvich's approach to the Shabbat in his painting were Bezem's art and his friendship with Eva Kaufman, even though all three of them were lay persons. Eva Kaufman explains, "The relationship with Bezem and his art also have their link. I started to get in touch with these subjects, canopies, table cloths, chuppah, and something happened among the three of us, though in very different ways."[19]

Bereshit: In the beginning

At a certain point in 1966 Gurvich started to paint subjects from Genesis with his new idiosyncratic language. In his notes and sketches we find, in his own handwriting and under the title of Genesis, the first verses of the Tanakh (Pentateuch) illustrated with Torres García-like[20] symbols. He was very interested in this subject, Genesis images appear as details in some of his larger compositions, not only in oil paintings but also in drawings, tempera pictures and ceramics.

Some pieces with a Genesis theme have no explicit title but the counterpoised celestial and terrestrial images are there, linked by a figure or by ladders, sometimes as the main motif and sometimes as a secondary scene in one of his heterogeneous compositions. He shows an earthly world in the lower area and a celestial realm at the top, and the two are consistently linked by ladders or by a divine hand reaching down to touch the hand of man, which is of course an inter-textual reference to Michelangelo's Sistine Chapel. The earthly world is dynamic, mobile, unstable, hectic, vertiginous, throbbing and in full gestation, and the celestial domain is calm. There

Shabbat in the shtetl
1970
pencil on paper
6.5 x 10 cm

Kibbutz composition

1970

watercolour, ink on paper

18 x 24 cm

The creation
1969
oil, ink on canvas
41 x 30 cm

are religious symbols in the pieces, like the Tablets of the Commandments or omnipresent eyes.

This question of the origin of all things is a link between the artist
and his teacher JTG and the Torres García Workshop, but on the kibbutz
the motif acquires special meaning, and that is why he works with
such zeal to present it. And he does this is a variety of ways, in different
versions that are unlike each other.

The original Hebrew name for Genesis in the Bible is Bereshit, which means "in the beginning", and it has acquired special connotations
in the Promised Land today because this is the key location in the Bible
and the place the Jews would return to. The idea of creation has been
explicitly linked to the birth of the State of Israel and the building of a
new country, and like the kibbutz this new State grew in a barren and
abandoned land, and neglected and infertile spaces were recovered and
given life.

At Ramot Menashé he painted an enormous board called *Homenaje
al kibbutz* (Homage to the kibbutz) for the community dining hall, and
he wrote Bereshit in Hebrew in the upper part of the scene, thus combining the Bible story with the concrete reality of the kibbutz. He also
wrote "Let there be light". In the original meaning of the biblical text
it is emphasized that the act of construction is linked to the improvement of the world, the submission of the forces of nature, the domes-
tication of animals, the growing of vegetables and the exploitation of
natural wealth, and all this is what was happening on the kibbutz.[21]

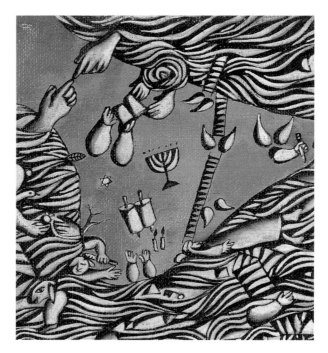

The creation, detail

On the sixth day

The universal, cosmic, eternal and essential human being is a subject
Gurvich developed in a number of compositions including paintings,
drawings and ceramics, and this has connections with Torres García.
Gurvich created dominant, preponderant, hypertrophied figures, and
there is a contrast between microcosm and macrocosm because many
tiny vibrant dynamic figures pulse within the larger ones. So we have
the idea that man is the epitome of the universe.

This is an old notion that comes from Greek philosophers such as
Pythagoras, Plato and Aristotle and from the Stoics. It has appeared
in Jewish literature since ancient times in texts by Philo, Saadia Gaon,
Shabtai Donolo, Abraham Ibn Gabirol, Moses ibn Ezra and Judah Hale-
vi. It is a dominant theme in the Kabbalah and it has various exponents
in Western and Eastern thinking. According to biblical literature, man
was created on the sixth day and he is different from everything else,
and in the Torah it was only in this case, the case of man, that what
God intended with his creation was enunciated. When God made man
he completed the task, which indicates that man is a superior being

Universal woman
c. 1968
oil, *collage* on wood
54 x 39 cm

Cosmic man in pure colours
1967
oil on cardboard
57 x 48 cm

and has dominion over the animals and nature. He is a unique being. For that reason, according to the Torah, if someone destroys a single person he destroys the entire world, and someone who saves a single person saves a whole world.

Gurvich stressed that human beings are pre-eminent. They are essential and their existence persists and carries with it the seeds of creation, and the artist always shows this in the framework of the kibbutz. This location is an entity unto itself, it forms a separate world, a complete world, and by using this as his setting he is sending a clearly humanist message. He puts forward in visual form the metaphysical relationship between human beings and the rest of nature, that each person is a universe in miniature, and this is why it is so difficult to separate the two. His figures are surfaces, and historical and symbolic facts are etched into them, they have content, they are made of palimpsests, and the physical landscape is built up of such fragments.

A lonely heart is not a heart

Another aspect of Gurvich's work was that he extolled love and saw the couple, two people in a loving relationship, as very significant in reinforcing life. This is evident not only in his art but in his writings. He cited Antonio Machado on the subject of love, which the poet regarded as being important in a spiritual way. When Gurvich read Machado's poetry he quivered with excitement because he agreed so much with what the writer was saying about love.

Cosmic couple, detail

> Do pay attention:
> a lonely heart
> is not a heart.

Pareja cósmica (Cosmic couple, 1966) is an excellent example of that commitment to love. The picture shows a universal couple, an inheritance from the Torres García approach, and it has echoes of the first couple, Adam and Eve. The two bodies fit together indissolubly in a symbiotic embrace. They are an ideal couple, beyond any real, normal couple in the world. The image expresses the will to fuse, Julia Kristeva calls this the "desire for fusion",[22] and also the ecstasy, the state of being out of oneself. Love unites the separated, subjective beings, it connects the two worlds. These are loving bodies, and if they were not they would be nothing. So they merge, they draw together, they unite and clasp each other to form a single being. These are images full of life, people who are inseparable and amalgamated. The intensity of love sustains the union and thus adds to the cosmos and unifies the world. The couple are flanked and inhabited by hundreds of micro images, they are filled with symbols and figures from the active and tumultuous real world. In Jewish society the couple is a basic building block, a mainstay, and it is consecrated.

Bodies are channels of life and communication, and in them the collective, the cosmic, the terrestrial and the intimate all come together. The two figures mix into each other and life flows harmoniously through them. The figures are persons, they are private, but because of love they become a space shared by two people, and this serves all of mankind. Some outstanding examples of this image in Gurvich's work are *Pareja besándose* (Couple kissing, 1965), *Pareja* (Couple, 1966), *Pareja con rayitas en B/N* (Couple with black and white stripes, 1966), *Pareja construida en rayitas talladas* (Couple made of carved stripes c. 1965), *Pareja cósmica* (Cosmic couple, 1966), *Pareja y Universo* (Couple and Universe, 1967), *Pareja construida en B/N* (Couple in black and white, 1968) and *Javer y Javerá* (Chaver and chavera, 1970).

Cain and Abel, detail

Sarah, our mother[23]

Two of the tempera paintings Gurvich did in Cerro are dedicated to the matriarch Sarah and they deal with two aspects, pregnancy and death. The scene of death is soul-stirring. Sarah's body in her simple white clothes is lying in state on the ground, in the open air, with Abraham next to her, shattered by pain. The artist emphasises the terrible loss of this great symbol of maternity. In this way Gurvich paid homage to his mother through the legendary mother of the Jewish people, the matriarch, Sarah Imeinu.

The story goes that Sarah "our mother" was a pioneer alongside Abraham when they settled in Canaan. She is an essential figure in the sphere of the Jewish family and her symbolic role is crucially important in Judaism. She longed with all her being for a son although she was sterile, and when she was ninety she finally conceived and gave birth. In fact, the part of the Torah which tells of this matriarch is entitled "The life of Sarah", "Haye Sarah",[24] and it was written to perpetuate her memory, her actions and her contributions.

When Gurvich tackled the subject of Sarah in his art he immortalized his mother.

Since World War II, the pain surrounding Sarah's death has been re-interpreted as a reaction to the Holocaust because the story is linked to Akedah, the so-called "sacrifice of Isaac". Sarah is the representation of the mother who suffers for her son, the mother who dies for her son because it was suffering that killed Sarah – she believed her son was dead. And many children died and many mothers cried and died during Shoah (the Holocaust). Other artists have used this image, like

Cain and Abel
1973
oil on canvas
105 x 80 cm

Mordecai Ardon in 1947, an atheist painter who was inspired by biblical subjects because of their strong metaphorical charge.

The ancient patriarch

According to the story of Genesis, Jacob dreamt[25] of a ladder with angels that came down and ascended, and then God promised him he would protect his descendants, give them a land and allow them to spread, and he made a pact not to abandon him and to bring him back from exile. In the place where Jacob had this dream he laid the founding stone of the temple and he became the patriarch, the father of all the Jews, the first Jew.

This subject attracted Gurvich, he painted it twice, in tempera and then on board, and he repeated it as a detail in other works too. It is a key story in Judaism. Great masters of Jewish thought have interpreted the dream in various ways and it is still fertile ground for exegesis. It recurs again and again in the history of painting and there are many previous works depicting it that Gurvich may have known about since he was an educated man and had travelled around Europe and visited many galleries. This story is part of the history of art, and the subject has attracted many authors.[26]

Gurvich's composition on board *Sueño de Jacob* (Jacob's dream, 1970) is quite outstanding. The land, Jacob and the heavens form a tripartite space with the three elements related to each other. Jacob is in the middle, he is united to the land and separated from the sky, but the three components of the painting are linked by ladders. There are sacred and ritual objects and biblical allusions floating around the three central areas and there are angels going up and down the ladders: there are many ways to gain access to heaven.

Jacob's eyes are closed, which indicates he is asleep, and dreams inhabit his brain. A key subject here is the capacity to know, to gain access to knowledge, and Jacob dreams because he wants to know. There is a higher, mystical, metaphysical knowledge above us, and we aspire to it and ascend to it, and perhaps we may reach it through sleep and dreams. The ladder, which Gurvich had already used in numerous works, is a basic symbol of ascent in the biblical story. It links the terrestrial to the spiritual, it alludes to the efforts of human beings to rise and to use their capacity to reach nobler and more spiritual planes of being. This is the ladder of knowledge; it shows that it is possible for human beings to struggle and reach more sublime heights, to climb up the rungs.

The ladders that link earth and heaven reflect the duality of the world, with its transcendent sphere and its immanent dimension. Also, with their rungs, they indicate the inevitable union of people,

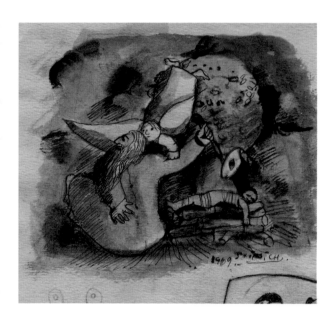

Several plans, deatil of the Akedah

256

people are continuous, they go one after the other and each element is an integral part of a whole.

The angels are spirits that can soar above the world while human beings remain earthbound and are "the feet of the world", the ones keeping the foundations, the solid base. Many eyes watch from a sky in which, next to the traditional Jewish symbols, there are others with clear Torres García roots such as the gold rule (an allusion to Gurvich's teacher Joaquin Torres García), the key and elemental geometric shapes, which is another nod to constructive universalism.

Jacob is an allegory for the earthly world and in the painting he actually contains it, he has within him a pulsing symbolic reality of rural work, of ceremonial rites and fraternity among humankind. However, his body is also associated with transcendence; the trunk of the tree of life comes out from his bowels, and the hands with the Torah, angels and a ladder emanate from him.

In the lower part of the picture, Gurvich shows the kibbutz world and daily life, and they are pouring into the exaggerated body of Jacob and intermingling there with the ritualistic and the religious. This hypertrophied sleeping figure, populated with human beings, animals and objects, reminds us of land that is worked, there are undulating furrows that shape the body. Big figures and small beings are in counterpoise, they are intermingled with animals and objects from daily life, and the normal relations of scale are ignored. The organic whole throbs with life. There is a juxtaposition of scenes and figures, and the dread of emptiness - the horror vacui - is paramount.

Gurvich was very interested in Jacob, in that story so laden with meaning, and he also identified with him because they were both shepherds. There are sheep and flocks in various parts of the composition. There are numerous indications of the ancient patriarch's work, this man who was the founder of his people, the tribes of Israel.

Akedah[27]

In Genesis[28] it says that to test Abraham God told him to sacrifice Isaac, the son who had been born to him in his old age. He made him take Isaac and bind him on Mount Moriah. Abraham was in anguish but he obeyed, he tied up his son and when he was on the point of killing him an angel intervened and told him to sacrifice a ram instead. This legend is known as Akedah (the binding of Isaac). Gurvich did two tempera paintings of this subject and one board, and he also included elements of it as details in other works, which shows what an impact it had on him, just as the stark horror of the story has shocked generations of religious and secular Jewish and gentile readers.

The work on board is extremely dramatic. Abraham, distorted by grief, completely dominates the composition. He is the main figure and his pain and his enormous tears are the most striking feature. He is flushed, he is holding a knife, and he is looking at a great divine eye as he raises his beseeching hand, while the defenceless Isaac is lying helpless and seems to accept his fate. Abraham is not looking at his son or at the angel, he is awaiting the word of God.

The topos in the history of the painting is the dialogue with the angel, but Gurvich adopts a different focus, he concentrates on the suffering of the father, on Abraham and his tragedy, although the angel is already there and is already grabbing his arm to stop him killing his son. Abraham's body is filled with symbols, it houses angels announcing Sarah's pregnancy, and so in this scene the artist is echoing another theme –the suffering that killed Sarah– which further underlines just how terrible God's command is. There are beseeching hands like in desperate prayer that perhaps call to mind Picasso's Guernica, and rabbinical figures with candles looking for the light and the way. There are ladders to heaven, angel's wings, and references to Jacob's dream and to the burning bush. The picture amounts to a compendium of various very meaningful episodes in Genesis. The composition undulates and this makes the scene sway, and there is a cataclysmic atmosphere with earthly colours, the land trembles, everything moves, the skies turn red, the winter tree is in agony and nature itself shakes in the face of this tragedy. Gurvich seems to be protesting against the terrible drama that the father is suffering, and he seems to express the pain of the sacrifice the Jewish people have had to make since they came into being, and also to connote more recent themes. Gurvich was a man of peace, but it was a stark fact that Israel was a military state, young people have to join the army, and since the country was founded they have fought to protect their homeland and many died doing so. And the chaverim of the kibbutz have always made their contribution, sometimes tragic, to this national struggle to survive.

This story has inspired many works in the history of art,[29] great masters have tackled the subject and there have been many interpretations. And it is still an enigma and a cause for controversy.

The Akedah is always present in Jewish life because it is explicitly remembered and given great importance at Rosh Hashana, the New Year. That festival is a time for reflection, for introspection, new directions, remorse, renewal, and there is the sound of the shofar as a moral alarm. During the prayers of Zichronot (remembrance), the second day of Rosh Hashanah, God is asked to remember the Akedah, to keep his promises, the oath, the pact, to be compassionate and protect his people. The sounds of the shofar also hark back to the fact that a ram was taken and put in Isaac's place. The story reminds the Jews that God

The sacrifice of Isaac
1970
oil on wood
63 x 56 cm

stopped the sacrifice and that in fact ne never told Abraham to kill his son because his aim was not to sacrifice Isaac but to test Abraham's faith. The story marks the end of an era, that of ritual killing, and now the Jews do not kill in the name of God. In addition to this, the Akedah is considered a paradigm of the Jewish ordeal as it reflects the fact that the people are always ready to sacrifice in the name of God.

The story has many other interpretations. For some exegetes it proves the possibility of repentance, evil can be eliminated, and it is never too late to mend our errors and repent. Abraham did not kill, he did not hurry, he thought about it and he knew how to listen to that other voice. He was given a fresh opportunity to better himself and to develop self-control.[30]

According to some interpretations, the experience of Isaac and Abraham teaches us that we can attain a deeper understanding of humanity and its relation to God. Abraham can be praised for obeying God, but it is to God's credit that he did not accept that immoral tribute. Judaism is considered an ethical religion and it would not allow ethical considerations to be suspended even to obey God. The trial of Akedah is interpreted as the choice between blind obedience and the moral dimension. Abraham held his hand, and the terror on the mountain did not end in murder. Abraham might be an example of love of God and of free will, and the story may imply that obedience to God and correct human decisions are compatible.

For a thinker as important as the French philosopher Emmanuel Lévinas, Abraham signifies an ethical attitude because he is a good listener to the second voice, because he does not doubt that it is the word of God –although it comes through an angel– because he takes his time and does not act immediately, he stands at a distance from obedience, he is receptive. He says to the angel that he is there and shows he is open to listen and to answer, so the ethical dimension is not suspended. Lévinas does not agree with the philosopher Søren Kierkegaard who, in Fear and Trembling,[31] considers Abraham a knight of faith who is ready to suspend ethical considerations and is prepared to do an immoral and unthinkable deed in order to obey God.

The French psychologist and semiologist Julia Kristeva[32] has another explanation, "The Akedah is the "dignity in the difference" and marks an alliance, a bond of trust, that Abraham loves God but this bond does not exclude other ties because Abraham was able to save his son and obey God at the same time. He could love as a father and also love God."

Since the Holocaust the biblical account also has other obvious connotations. The writer, essayist, theologian, poet, professor, Nobel Prize winner and Holocaust survivor Elie Wiesel, who is a believer but allows himself to question divinity, considers that God made a mistake when he demanded that sacrifice. Isaac was left traumatised because he was almost killed, he was obsessed with fear, he never forgot the experience, it destroyed his youth, he was marked until the end of time, and Wiesel compares him to a survivor of the Holocaust. Wiesel himself could never forget what happened to him as a near-victim of genocide. He considers himself a new Isaac, he believes that the survivors of the Holocaust are Isaac. Wiesel points out that Isaac is not a pre-figuration of the crucifixion of Jesus, which is what some Christians believe, because the act never took place, God did not abandon his son. In Jewish tradition, death cannot be used to glorify God. Each man is an end in himself, a living eternity, no one can sacrifice another human being, not even for God. Truth must always emerge from life, never from death.[33]

According to other modern interpretations, Abraham was at fault in a moral sense because he did not question God's command or rebel, and still other commentators maintain that God would never demand such a demonstration of faith.

From the post-Holocaust perspective the Akedah is important because it is in a way unintelligible, and for religious people it means accepting God's will even if we do not understand, even if it does not make sense. For secular people the story has to do with the will to continue in spite of everything. The Akedah is a symbol of perseverance in identity, of keeping faith in life even when facing the worst. The Akedah, like the Holocaust and the birth of the State of Israel, is an integral part of the modern Jewish identity. It is one of the paradigm images in Israeli society.

Yet its connotations have varied over time. For many, in the early years of the country, it was a symbol of the existence of Israel in the modern world, of the sacrifice the Zionists made to create the State, of people giving their blood and that of their children so that Israel could be born and survive. Abraham and Isaac suffered, and now Israeli fathers and sons were paying the price of their love for their mother country. Many writers and thinkers have linked the Akedah with what was going on in Israel, as a way to understand and experience and the parent-child and child-parent relation. Moshe Shamir, an outstanding writer and a leader in the founders' generation, called the Akedah "the story of our generation". Other writers have dealt with it intensely, like Haim Gouri, who coined the stirring phrase "They were born with a knife in their hearts."[34]

In Israeli literature from the early decades of the country, Isaac is often seen as an active hero, the paradigm of the Zionist pioneer, because he discharged his responsibility and faced his destiny, he offered his life so the country could be re-born.[35] But on the other hand there are authors who take a pessimistic view and deny that parents have the right to sacrifice their children for the benefit of future generations, and they do not want God to test parents ever again. The famous writer A. B. Yehoshua considers that the biblical story is like "A black bird flying over our history".[36]

Gurvich's painting has been interpreted in many ways and it is part of this ongoing debate, and in fact it is helping to keep this important subject alive.

Joséphine Balken,[37] who collaborated on this book, has another conception of this painting's symbolism. Her understanding directly derives "...from being as close as possible to the biblical story and not imposing interpretations, so as not to force the meaning out of the context in which it was written, so that it can really preserve all its force and its intrinsic richness as a symbol."

As regards Isaac's mother Sarah, "The biblical account shows the pain and suffering of a mother as a universal symbol for all time, and it should not be taken as an allegory of the Holocaust, which cannot be compared with anything. It should simply be taken as the description of the pain of a mother who represents all the mothers in all spaces and all times, faced with the suffering and death of her children, in any spatial, temporal or cultural context.'

The annunciation of Sarah, detail

With regard to Sarah's pain, she has this to say, "Moreover, Sarah was too old, when she gave birth to Isaac she was ninety, and after so many years of infertility God gave her that gift. Is their attachment to the son they were so many years longing for greater than their love of God? Sarah is distraught when confronted with this command from God, how is can such a demand be possible? She cannot understand it. There is no greater anguish and suffering than a confrontation with the unknown, the incomprehensible, and Sarah, at her age, could not endure such strong emotions."

As to the Akedah itself Balken comments, "God's demand seems to go against the Ten Commandments themselves. How is it possible to accept such a contradiction? Perhaps it is true, as the Danish philosopher Kierkegaard said, that "faith is a leap into the absurd..." and that life is full of contradictions, even in our everyday routines, and we should learn to live with them.

"When we analyze Gurvich's painting from this point of view we find incomprehension at the inherent contradiction in God's mysterious will when he demands such terrible obedience. And bear in mind that Gurvich did his version of the sacrifice of Isaac on one of his trips to Israel, when he was on the kibbutz, which is a secular Jewish community.

"I find it difficult not to focus on the visual and aesthetic virtues of the painting, the harmony of shapes and colours, and especially on the impact of the very strong emotional expression in the figure of Abra-

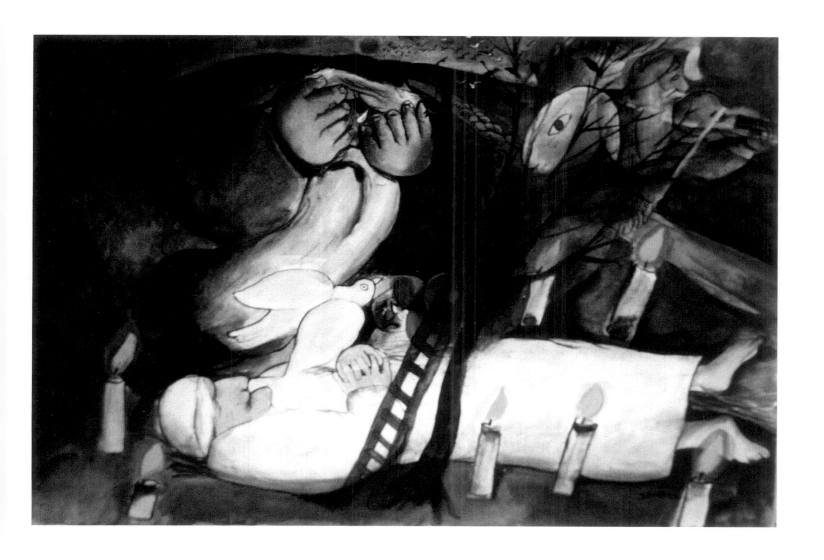

The death of Sarah
1969
tempera on paper
32.5 x 46.5 cm

ham, which almost seems to embody the principles of expressionist painting.

"The main focus is Abraham's all-too-human reaction to this distressing and desperate situation; he is imploring God and crying out his incomprehension and his pain. At the same time there is a sign of rebelliousness in him as regards God's command, it is there in his face, his gaze is averted from Isaac who is about to be sacrificed, sideways and upwards, which shows how desperately he needs an explanation and an answer from God. The stormy sky with its dark greys accentuates even more this outpouring of emotion.

"Abraham holds the knife in his left hand over the body of Isaac, who can barely be distinguished, he hardly has form, he is tied to a stack of logs. There is an angel holding Abraham's arm ever so gently so as to stop him committing this act, but the angel too is looking away in the same direction. Gurvich has managed to grasp and communicate the emotional power of the situation.

"The painting admirably transmits the emotional complexity and intensity of the event through Abraham's stance and the emotions in his face. He is imploring, crying out desperately, but even in this despair there is strength and determination mingled with his very human pain as a father, and there is an air of challenge about him, or perhaps even rebellion against God's command. And what does this angel sent by God seem to presage? Is Abraham also crying because he is disappointed in his God?

"The focus of the painting is obviously the complex and difficult relationship between Abraham and God, who, in line with Hebraic regulations, is not depicted. To one side there is the vague head of an animal, it might be a lamb, and according to tradition this is a symbol of atonement. In the whole picture it is the only thing that is looking at Isaac."

Dream of Jacob and Apollo XI (1969), detail

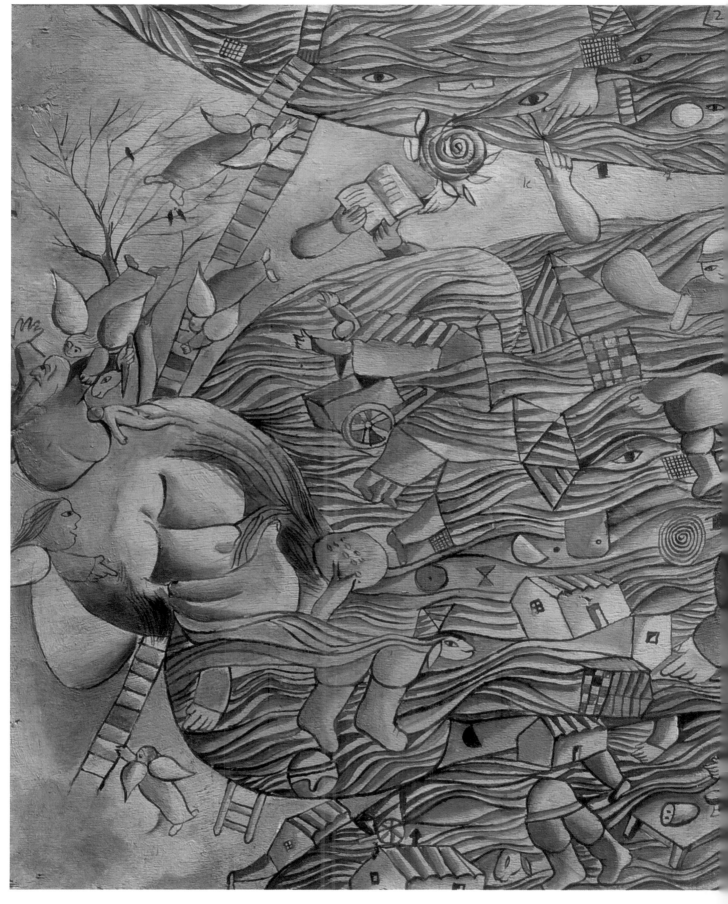

Jacob's dream
1970
oil on wood
34 x 60 cm

A fight born from envy

Gurvich painted Cain and Abel on the kibbutz in a winter atmosphere. The world is turned upside down, it is disturbed, black birds are flying over, ominous clouds cover the sky, a huge, black eye –is it God, or ethics, or goodness?– watches from the celestial sphere and the angel is already holding the dying Abel. Gurvich implanted some verses by Machado here:

The envy of virtue
made Cain a criminal
Glory to Cain! Nowadays vice
is the most envied thing[38]

Antonio Machado repeatedly deals with the theme of Cain. In *La tierra de Alvargonzález* he wrote:

Much of Cain's blood
the peasant people have
and in the rural home
envy started fight

And in Proverbios y cantares (Campos de Castilla):

VI
What men call
virtue, justice and goodness
one half is envy
and the other is not charity

Some modern commentators on the Cain and Abel story are pro-Cain, and this started with Byron. This romantic poet found in Cain conceptions of seduction, exile, alienation, evil and the outsider. Coleridge and Baudelaire were fascinated with the character and transformed him into a victim of injustice and resentment.[39]

Gurvich, on the other hand, adhered to the traditional version and interpretation. He chose a biblical text about which there are varying points of view,[40] and the story itself is still very moving when it appears in pictures, books, cinema or television programmes. He cared very much about his painting of Cain and Abel and he hung it above his marriage bed.[41] There was something ethical in his motivation to tackle this startling story, the first murder, the first criminal, the first fratricidal act. He thought that envy, evil, greed, jealousy, selfishness, aggressiveness, and the confrontation between brothers were detri-

Composition for Jewish festival (Moses and the Torah), detail

Sketch for a monument (Moses receiving the Torah)

n.d.

pencil on paper

25 x 35 cm

mental to the world. And he was interested in Abel, the first innocent victim of evil, the first martyr.

According to the Torah, the act of only one murderer, of just one, threatens the existence of the whole Universe, so Abel took on a whole new significance in post-Holocaust culture and became a symbol of injustice: the good are innocent victims.

The French philosopher and theologian André Neher deals with the subject of the confrontation between brothers, the fratricidal struggle, and considers that the most important message of this biblical story is man's marvellous capacity for fraternity. The brothers should talk to each other, communication is essential, but one of them never talks and that is why their relationship fails. That is one of the teachings of the story. In addition to this, it makes people think about different kinds of coexistence and that there must be fraternity in the sphere of possessions. Each brother should give the other what he owns, and each brother should be able to have at his disposal everything the other has.[42]

The Torah and Moses

Gurvich drew on the beautiful myth of how God gave Moses the Ten Commandments and the Torah on Mount Sinai. Torah is a Hebrew word that means teaching, instruction and law, and it consists of the five books of the Pentateuch, namely Genesis, Exodus, Leviticus, Numbers and Deuteronomy (Bereshit, Shemot, Vayikra, Bamidbar, and Devarim).

In one Gurvich version of this event, the divine hands reach down from the celestial sphere towards Moses' hands, then the hands of Moses emerge with the book already facing the people, and his head and feet crop out among other symbols like an ascending ladder and a key of wisdom. Other versions are synthetic and feature the whole body of Moses, the sphere and the menorah, in an interesting layout that plays games with superimposed layers.

Festivals

When Gurvich was on the kibbutz, and also in Cerro and then in New York, he did scenes of Jewish celebrations. He started during his second trip to Israel and went deeper into this subject matter in New York. Most of these works came from an inner motivation and he painted with no other purpose than to express his own subjective vision. He did them in a spontaneous way, for himself, and responding to his own interests. Thus the whole cycle of Jewish biblical subjects and various festivals came from deep within himself. As regards the paintings he was commissioned to produce, and there were only six, he was given the subject but not instructed as to how he should approach it. He was completely free to do them as he chose, and he chose to take the kibbutz as the setting. This is understandable. No one who lived on a kibbutz in those heroic years could ever forget those images.

Aspects of life that in the Diaspora demand dedication and personal or family effort, or entail becoming a member of a synagogue, are present on the socialist kibbutz in a completely natural way, in a communal and secular way. Gurvich shows the origin, the common destiny and the indestructible nature of the community and of time itself. The artist celebrates that eternal present, which amounts to imposing order on chaos.

The Hanukkah festival celebrates the victory of the Maccabees over the Seleucids, who at one time dominated ancient Israel. A handful of men defended their faith and their people against a powerful overlord. For religious people, it is the celebration of the inauguration of the Temple after it was desecrated by the Seleucids. According to the religious account, there was a miracle when they re-dedicated the Temple: there was only enough sacred oil to light the candles for one day, but God intervened and it lasted for eight days. For this reason the celebration takes place over eight days and is known as the Festival of Lights. The lights of the Hanukia, the special candelabrum, are lit.

It became an important national festival in Israel, but it also had secular interpretations that did not allude to any miracles or divine intervention. Under Labour governments in the country and on the socialist kibbutz, the emphasis was on victory and the joyful celebration of a community festival. The underlying messages were of liberation from foreign domination, of the way the few can defeat the many, and the light of triumphant heroism, all of which were essential and unifying elements in Israel. Hanukkah extols the courage of the Macabees, it stresses personal sacrifice and the active struggle for the nation, the Jewish people's desire and will to survive and have an autonomous homeland. And the chalutzim, the pioneers, were seen as the new Macabees.

Hanukkah is a very joyful and lively event; there are special meals, songs for the occasion, gifts for the children and a number of important rites. People play with the Sevivon, which is a teetotum or spinning top. This has four faces, each with a letter from the Hebrew alphabet that taken together form Nes Gadol Hayah Sham, "A great miracle happened there". It symbolizes adaptability, happiness, the miraculous and changing destiny. But in the kibbutz socialist tradition, the spinning top only has connotations of play.

The most moving part of this festival on the kibbutz is the open air torchlight procession. For people who participated in this during

Hanukkah, detail
(Martin on his father's shoulders in the procession)

Festival at the kibbutz (Hanukkah)
c. 1966
oil on canvas
50 x 60 cm

Hanukkah, detail

the first decades of the State, when group celebrations were essential, it was an unforgettable experience. The whole community took part including the children, it as at night and they carried torches up to the high tower and sang songs, and when they looked down the lights of the kibbutz took on a whole array of meanings.[43] On his first stay in the country, Gurvich went to this festival alone, and later he went with his family. Totó, who went at Ramot Menashé, says,[44] "It is amazing what you feel." She remembers that you first went to the Holocaust square, a small square with flowers, a little lake and a monument with the names of the extermination camps, and the people remembered and paid homage to those who lost their lives in the genocide. Then the joyful procession began, and people participated in everything with great enthusiasm. In a tempera composition in greys and yellows, Gurvich himself appears with Martín on his shoulders. There were also special meals, which Gurvich painted in warm scenes, and games with the spinning top, the dreidel that Totó[45] remembers very well. She[46] says that Hanukkah was a subject that came from Gurvich's very soul, it was something deeply rooted inside him and it made him feel more than ever that he belonged.

Gurvich painted Hanukkah many times and did several versions in tempera, first in the kibbutz and later in Cerro and New York, and it also appears as a detail in many other of his works. In the *Jánuca* he painted in Cerro in 1966 a hypertrophied couple predominate and there two *chaverim* from the kibbutz, dressed in work clothes, who are flying over Ramot Menashé. Gurvich seems to be saying that without the union of man and woman no celebration is possible, it is the essential couple that gives meaning and dignity to the occasion, and like so many of his painting, this is a tribute to love. The man and woman are inhabited by figures, by a microcosm that subtly rise in their clothes. Beneath them we see the kibbutz in full activity, and a chaver in the foreground looks straight out at the viewer, which connects the celebration with the current situation of the person looking in. The beautiful landscape of the hills of Menashé is represented in an almost naturalistic style but the rest of the composition is imaginary. For Gurvich, Hanukkah is an ascetic, rural, secular, communal celebration, in which the chaverim in the torchlight procession come up from every road towards the water tower where the great Hanukia is lit.

Pesach is the most popular of all the Jewish festivals. It celebrates the mythical liberation from slavery in Egypt and the legend of the exodus of the Hebrew people, led by Moses, to the Promised Land. *Pesach* means 'to miss out'. According to the legend, God sent the ten plagues to Egypt but he passed over the Jewish houses so the plagues did not fall on them. This festival is also called the celebration of the *matzot* (unleavened bread), since in the desert that is all the Hebrews had to

Hanukkah, detail

Sketch for *Pesach*

c. 1973

watercolour on paper

9 x 14 cm

eat. It celebrates unity and the start of freedom, and it takes place at the beginning of spring so in that sense it also alludes to renovation and to all aspects of awakening. Memory is an essential element since the Jews remember they were slaves and they freed themselves, and they have a duty to pass on this knowledge to future generations and to meditate on the subjects of slavery and freedom. This is what underlies the *Seder*, a dinner, in which the dishes are served in a precise order and a leader reads the *Haggadah*, the account of what happened. The festival lasts seven days. On the evening of the *Seder*, children receive special attention, they are encouraged to listen to the story and actively take part in the celebration with questions, games and songs. *Pesach* embodies the notion that the Jews were not born to be slaves, but by extension it applies to other peoples and their need for freedom. Like every festival, it has religious and lay interpretations. The secular orientation was very intense in the early years of Israel and the story of the *Pesach* stressed the fact that it was men and not divine intervention that worked miracles, and how people can overcome difficulties with courage and bravery.

On Zionist Socialist *kibbutzim* like Ramot Menashé the secular, agricultural and community aspects came to the fore and the message was socialist and nationalist. Festivals were tremendously important on the kibbutz, and it was hard work to make all the preparations. Like other special days, *Pesach* became a cultural event with concerts, dances, folk and classical music, choral singings and poems by new authors. The *kibbutznikim* (members of the kibbutz) revolutionised the literature of the *Haggadah*,[47] and this was studied by the expert Muki Tsur.[48] New *Haggadot*[49] were written; between 1930 and 1960, some five hundred *kibbutz Haggadot* were produced. Secular *kibbutz*im were conscious that they had to generate a different collective memory, and this process meant taking aspects from tradition and making innovations around them. What was stressed was a thirst for life, a positive spirit, a love for awakening, a world in which there should be no more servitude, and the construction of a moral society: this was the message these people were committed to. They would rewrite the *Haggadah* and thus emphasise their own ideals and their new Jewish identity, and celebrate national freedom, socialist ideals and the dignity of work.[50]

Gurvich took part in many *Pesach* celebrations on the kibbutz, and he later painted them from memory. *Pesach* deserved many compositions, and elements of it appeared in other paintings. In order to paint *Pésaj* and other festivals in New York on commission, he had to study more religion, and he researched the life of his co-religionists and their customs and rituals. The picture he did in New York shows the story but locates it in an imaginary context, there are scenes from the Exodus and there are religious figures like Moses, the avenging angel, and the prophet Elijah in some kind of bubble. Gurvich included a table with ritual food, the ciborium for the prophet Elijah, the hand-washing rite and the scene of Moses carrying the *Torah*. The most important element is the *chaverim* at the ascetic table, the *chavera* with the ordinary apron, and the enormous *kibbutz* couple. Everyday life features strongly with the usual common figure looking out of the composition, eating a piece of *matzah*[51], the unleavened bread. And there is a boy, who is Gurvich's son Martín. In this painting we feel it is a people's festival and the everyday, natural, habitual things are interconnected with miraculous stories. He painted different kinds of ceremonial food, which not only have profound symbolic meanings but also awaken memories so they are very significant for non-religious Jews as well. Each is a symbol of an aspect of slavery and the liberation of the Israelites.[52]

Shavuot, another of his canvases, has more religious images than the other festivals, and there is a reason for this. This festival celebrates the handing over of the *Torah* on Mount Sinai, and Gurvich gave power and eminence to the traditional image by including angels. Moses is shown twice: receiving the Ten Commandments and then carrying them. He is a powerful, potent, amazing being who leads, and rays emanate from a light blue and yellowish resplendent sphere, an allusion to the burning bush. A secular interpretation of these events would stress agriculture: it is the feast of the first fruit, the *Bikkurim*, a celebration of the spring harvest, and on the kibbutz the celebration centres on the fertility of the soil, work, the harvest and the growth of the community. The message is that the Promised Land is fertile thanks to hard work.

Gurvich immersed himself in the non-religious aspects of the festivals, but later on, when he did *Shavuot* in New York, it was the traditional story that predominated.

Another Gurvich subject was *Purim* which literally means a draw or raffle. It is a people's festival commemorating the liberation of the Jews from the evil schemes of Haman the prime minister of Persian King Ahasuerus, who is believed to be King Xerxes I of Persia (486-465 BC). The story goes that Esther, the king's Jewish wife, interceded for her community and saved them from being killed. It is a joyful event with fancy dress costumes and readings from the *Book of Esther*. Whenever anyone says 'Haman' people shake rattles to show symbolically they reject men who plan to slaughter their people. The rattle is a toy but it became a kind of weapon, a sign of protest and a metaphor for liberation. People give gifts to their loved ones and friends to strengthen the bonds between them, and they make donations to the needy to signify social solidarity and the importance of making other people happy. *Purim* is very significant because it shows that Jews were able to evade a catastrophe, to avoid extermination, to survive as a people, to achieve salvation, and that tyrants are punished. Moreover, this was

Pesach
1973
oil on canvas
127 x 91 cm

Sketch for Jewish festival
(Pesach)
C. 1973
watercolour on paper
9 x 14 cm

El angel exterminador
sketch for Jewish festival (Pesach)
C. 1973
watercolour on paper
9 x 14 cm

Sketch for Jewish festival (Pesach)
C. 1973
watercolour on paper
9 x 14.5 cm

Shavuot
1973
oil on canvas
102 x 91.5 cm

Purim
1973
oil on canvas
91 x 122 cm

the start of the time of light and joy, rejoicing and honours, which were highly-valued messages throughout the long history of pogroms and persecution and even more so after the *Shoah*. *Purim* is hope. It embodies a wealth of religious meanings but it can be celebrated in a secular way, and one of the forms this takes in Israel is children's fancy dress parades through the streets. The folklore is very rich, there are numerous songs, tales, funny stories, jokes, mimicry and all kinds of amusing performances.

Another Gurvich theme was *Sucot* (Sukkot), the Feast of Huts, the Feast of Tabernacles. This commemorates the forty years the Hebrews survived in the desert after the exodus from Egypt and before they arrived in the Promised Land. It is a seven-day festival, but in the Jewish Diaspora it lasts eight days. Gurvich shows the humble, provisional

Sukkot
1973
oil on canvas
91.5 x 122 cm

Sukkot (unfinished)
c. 1973
oil on canvas
90 x 121 cm

dwellings called Sukkah (booth or hut) as a symbol of the people's hard life in the desert. And the Sukkah has wider connotations as well; it is poor, it is exposed, it is temporary, and it symbolizes fragility and all that is contingent in human existence. This is why people read the book of Kohelet and focus on the words "Vanity of vanities, all is vanity", which expresses the idea that what matters most is not material things but moral qualities. Life in this world is like a provisional hut, a Sukkah, and the real values are those that have to do with the spirit of the people of Israel. The fragility of the Sukkah also alludes to the vicissitudes of Jewish life in the Diaspora. During the seven days of the festival, Jews leave their homes and move to Sukkot (plural of Sukkah), and in Gurvich's painting the chaverim are sitting in the Sukkah. This humble dwelling emphasizes the idea of social equality and that people do things to help their fellow men, the idea of charity. In the Sukkah Gurvich paints, the roof is made of branches, leaves and shoots from the land, but it cannot be too dense because people must be able to look through and see the stars. This construction also relates to the importance of all that is natural, underlying, egalitarian and modest; aspects that were highly valued on the kibbutz. Sukkot is joyful because it is the major agricultural festival, it signals the end of the fruit harvest and the farming year in Israel. This is another weighty element in kibbutz society and it is shown in Gurvich's work. The religious background is that the souls of our ancestors and the people's leaders are invited: Abraham, Isaac, Jacob, Joseph, Moses, Aaron and David. Other people are invited to join in the celebration and what is stressed is the concept of peace. Sukkot reminds practising Jews that God protected the Hebrews in their years of wandering, that it was the desert that built the spiritual image of the Jewish people, and how they received the Torah there from the hands of God. Naturally, Gurvich includes religious elements: the two great figures with shawls that are flying over the kibbutz.

Gurvich saw at first hand how festivals were very important in Israel and on the kibbutz, they pervaded national imagery and started to play a key role in not only religious and also secular life. And they have come to mark the Israeli calendar: there are numerous holidays. On many festival days there is no school, a lot of shops close or are open for only a few hours, most Israelis take days off and those who are religious go to the synagogue.

Gurvich was there at an opportune time to develop the iconography of these festivals and to devote himself to those subjects. Socialist Zionism, which was the force that founded the State of Israel and formed its governments in those early years, is a movement with close ties to Jewish traditions,[53] but with a secular perspective. Gurvich grasped religious symbols which had been brought to the fore to unify the people.

This was religion expressed in a different way, traditions reinterpreted, and he used religious images but often without their divine connotations.[54]

In Israel at that time, religious elements were given a different value and transformed, and festivals became secular and nationalist, they served as unifying elements in a Zionist socialist society. This was not just a matter of party political ideologies or policies, it involved active participation and creative work or the part of thinkers, musicians, writers, members of the kibbutz, intellectuals, artists and various sectors of the population. There were State guidelines, but it was a collective stance. As Liebman and Don Yehiya have said,[55] it was Statism as a civil religion.

Collective rituals were significant for their values that bound people together, values linked to history, tradition, the land and the country, and even though these came from a religious tradition the religious aspect was not paramount. And Gurvich was exposed to all of this, especially through his kibbutz experiences.

Festivals were celebrated in a very particular way, mainly in the early decades, and Gurvich witnessed this. It was a different way of commemorating them, it was from a lay perspective, in a communal form, in a special rural framework and on Israeli land. Those experiences left an indelible mark on a galut (of the Diaspora) Jew, as Gurvich was. The festivals acquired new characteristics, in all senses. They were occasions to introduce new folk dances, new songs, to have processions with special choreographies and costumes, and many professional artists became involved in raising these events to new cultural heights.[56]

Gurvich was immersed in this world and he took an interest in many aspects of it because of the messages they transmitted and their significance as elements in identity. They were stories that captivated and affected him because they spoke of life experiences, and while they dealt with universal ideas they also bound him closer to his people and his mother.

284

(on following pages)
The creation on the Kibbutz
1969
oil on canvas
58 x 78

The creation
1968
tempera on paper
35 x 53 cm

The creation
1970
watercolour, ink on paper
18 x 24 cm

The creation in orange
1973
oil on canvas
45 x 59 cm

Construction composition
1962
painted and carved wood
50 x 27 cm

Astral man
1966
oil on canvas
162 x 100 cm

Cosmic man in New York
1970
tempera on paper
59 x 48.8 cm

The creation
c. 1969
pottery
26 x 27 x 1 cm

Figure worked with pricker
n.d.
terracotta
26 cm

Universal woman
c. 1970
pottery
26 x 22 x 2 cm

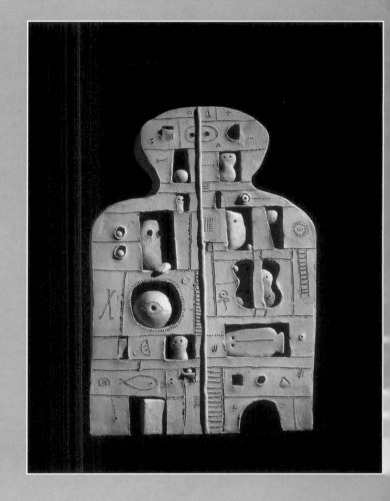

Spatial form
c. 1969
pottery
34 x 23 x 27 cm

Constructed man
c. 1968
pottery
33 x 21.5 x 4.5 cm

Cosmic man
c. 1968
painted pottery
22 x 8 x 4 cm

Kibbutz figure
n.d.
terracotta
28 cm

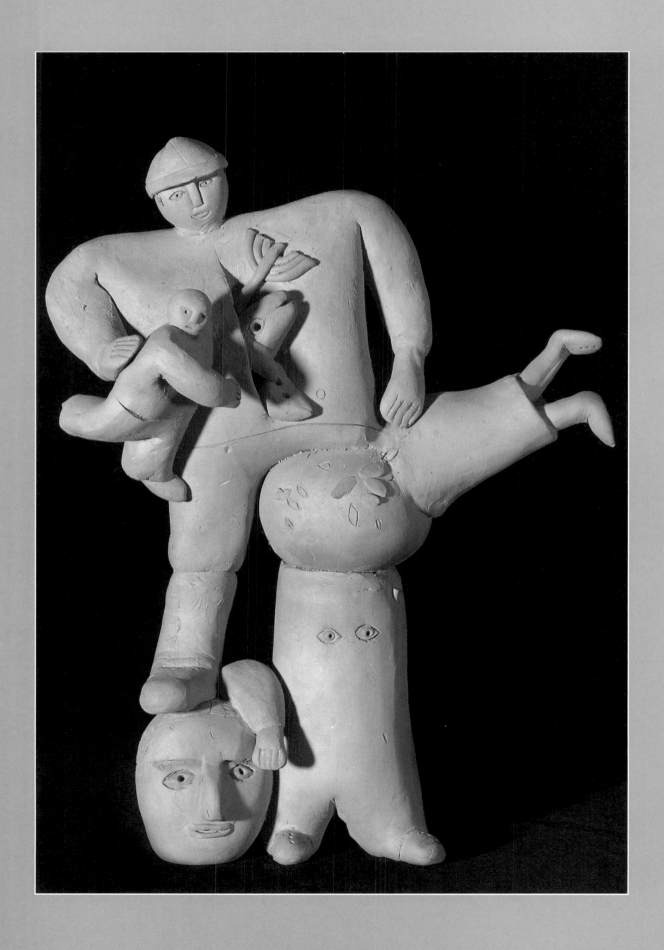

Couple in relief
1965
oil on plaster
34 x 26,5 cm

Universal couple with Menorah
(piece in Jerusalem, in restoration)
c. 1965
oil on wood and plaster
99 x 60 cm

Cosmic couple
1966
oil on canvas
148 x 88 cm

(on previous pages, at left)
Collage couple
c. 1965
oil on wood
46.5 x 38 cm

(on previous pages, at right)
Couple constructed in stripes
1965
oil on incised wood
39 x 24 cm

Astral couple (unfinished)
c. 1966
oil on canvas
160 x 100 cm

Kibkutz
1970
oil on wood
38 x 30 cm

Couple in pure colours
1968
tempera on card
34 x 49.5 cm

Couple
1970
tempera on paper
48 x 60 cm

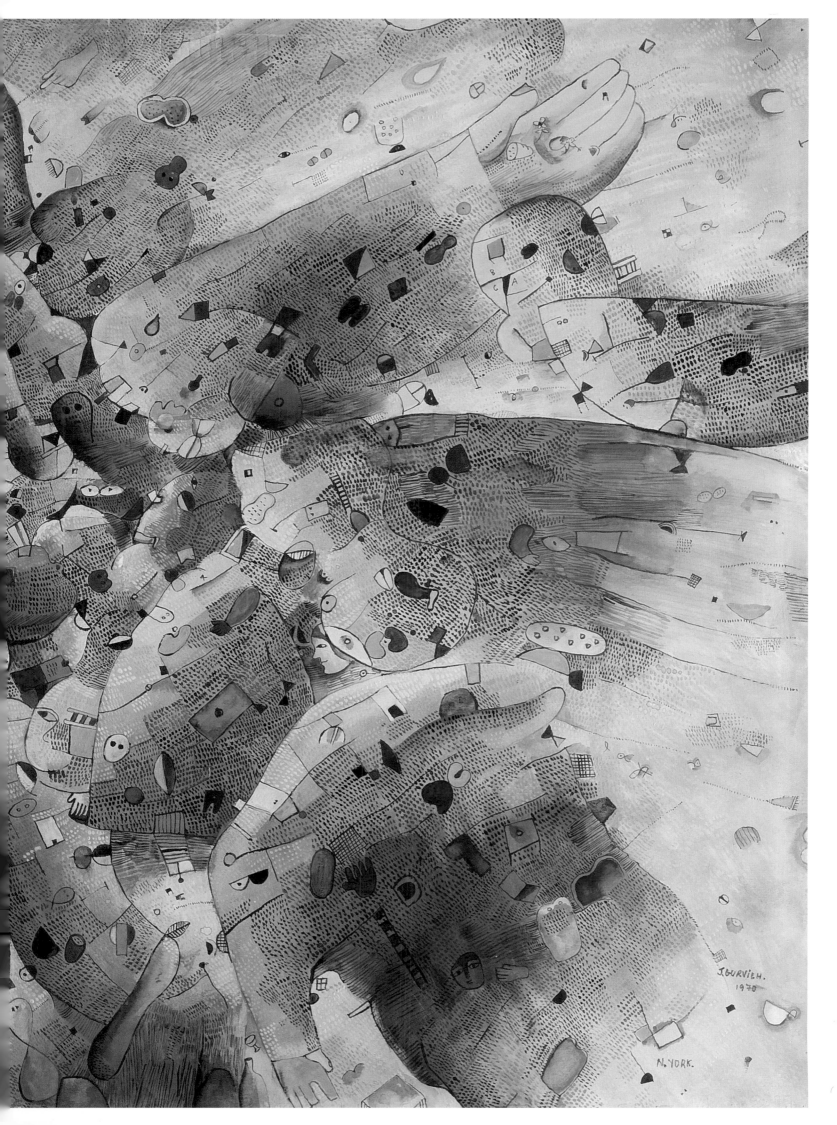

Cosmic couple in black and white
1974
oil on canvas
123 x 92 cm

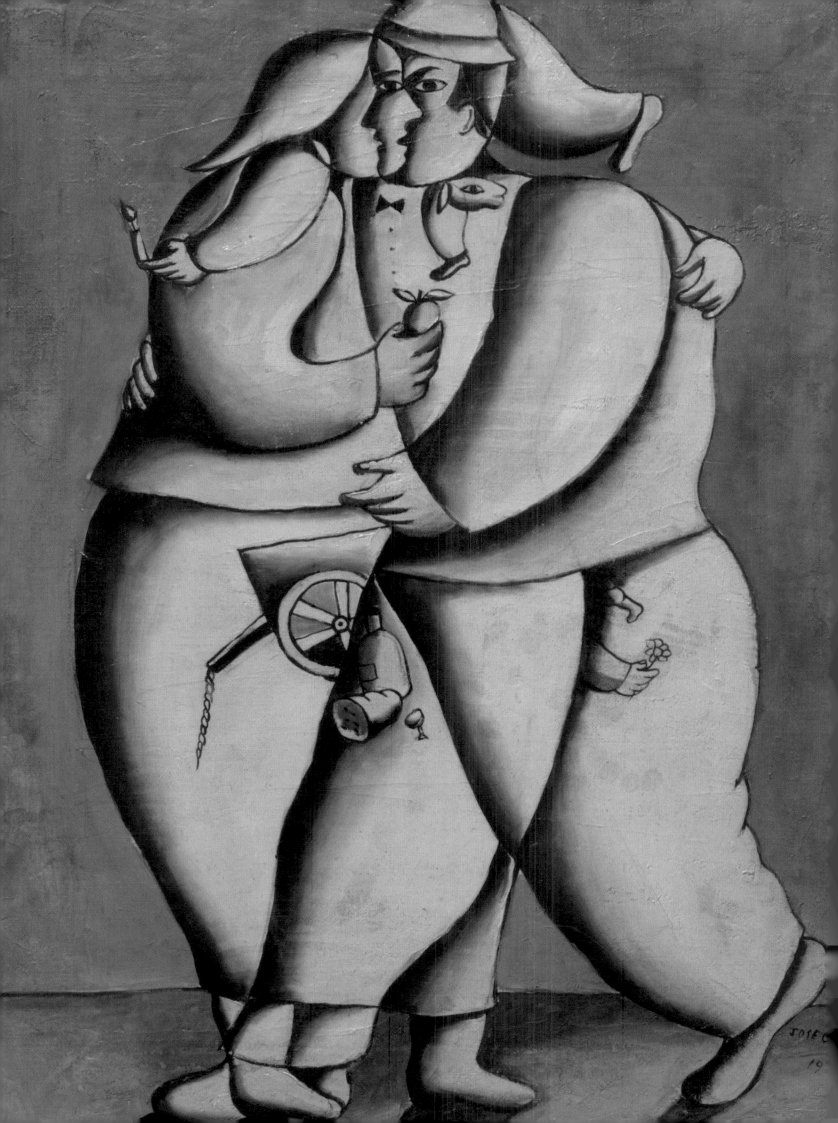

(on previous pages, at left)
Couple in black and white
1974
oil on canvas
44 x 36 cm

(on previous pages, at right)
Couple in turquoise
1974
oil on canvas
46 x 35.5 cm

Couple constructed in black and white
1974
oil on canvas
44 x 35 cm

Couple kissing
1965
tempera on paper
34 x 49 cm

Chaver and chavera and the hills of Menashé

1970

watercolour on paper

22 x 32 cm

Couple
1967
oil, tempera on paper
39 x 49 cm

Couple 1
c. 1968
sculpted and painted plaster
35 x 49 cm

Couple nearly kissing
c. 1966
tempera on paper
35 x 50 cm

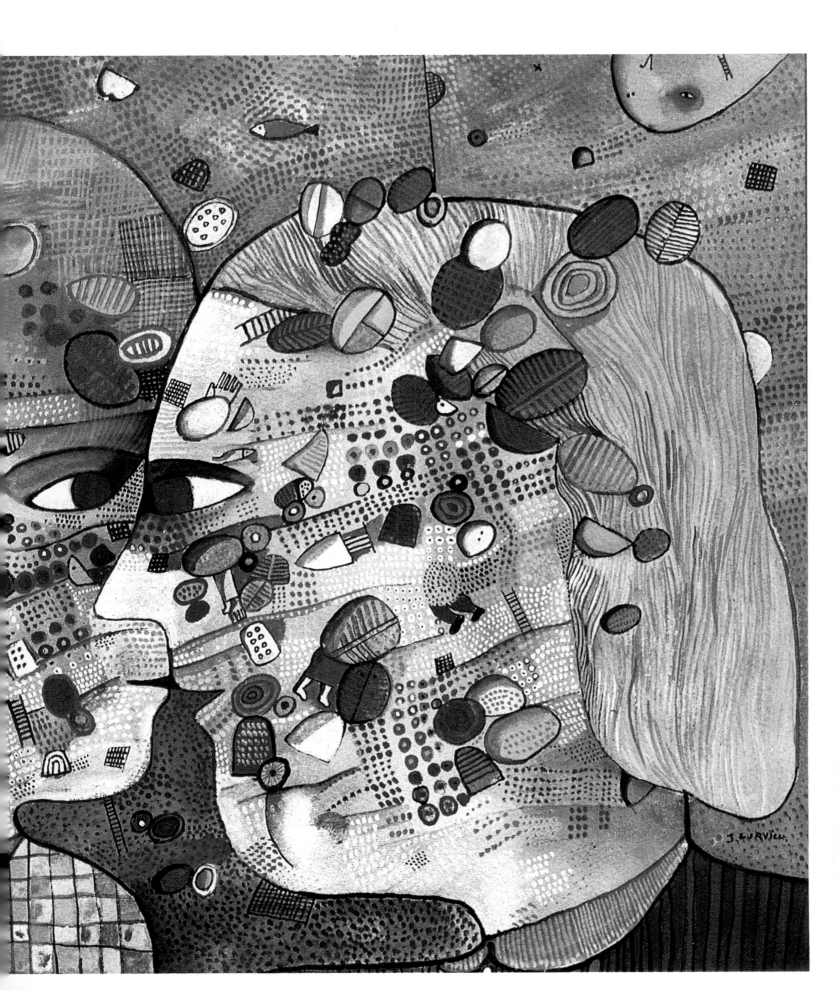

330

Couple with stripes
1966
oil on canvas
58 x 73 cm

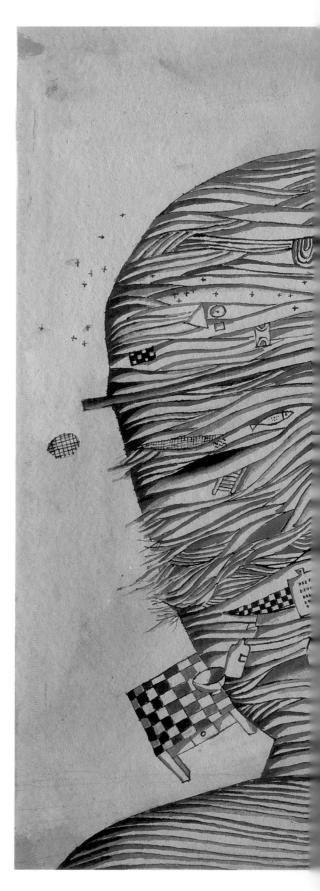

Couple with stripes in black and white
1966
tempera on paper
34 x 48 cm

Couple
1966
tempera on paper
32 x 45 cm

Couple
1966
tempera on paper
33 x 46 cm

Couple
1965
oil on plaster and wood
69 x 58 x 10 cm

Embrace
c. 1968
painted pottery
18 x 17 x 11 cm

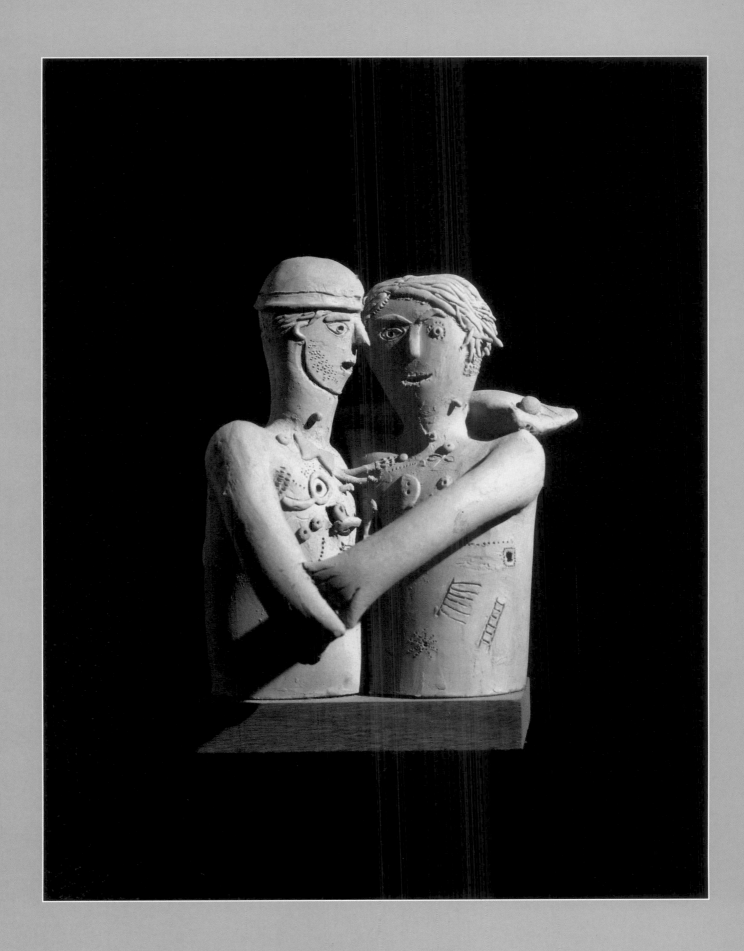

Composed couple
c. 1969
pottery
27 x 16 x 7 cm

Fertility
c. 1970
pottery
35 x 10 x 8 cm

Totem
n.d.
terracotta
48.5 cm

The death of Abel
1973
oil on canvas
75 x 60 cm

Sarah and Abraham
1970
oil on wood
48 x 70 cm

The annunciation of Sarah
1972
tempera on paper
30.5 x 45 cm

The sacrifice of Isaac
1970
tempera on paper
60 x 48 cm

The sacrifice of Isaac
1969
tempera on paper
47 x 34 cm

Dream of Jacob and Apollo XI
1969
tempera
63 x 49 cm

Jacob's dream
1969
tempera on paper
34 x 48 cm

Hanukkah
1966
oil on wood
120 x 160 cm

Hanukkah
1967
oil on canvas
59 x 79 cm

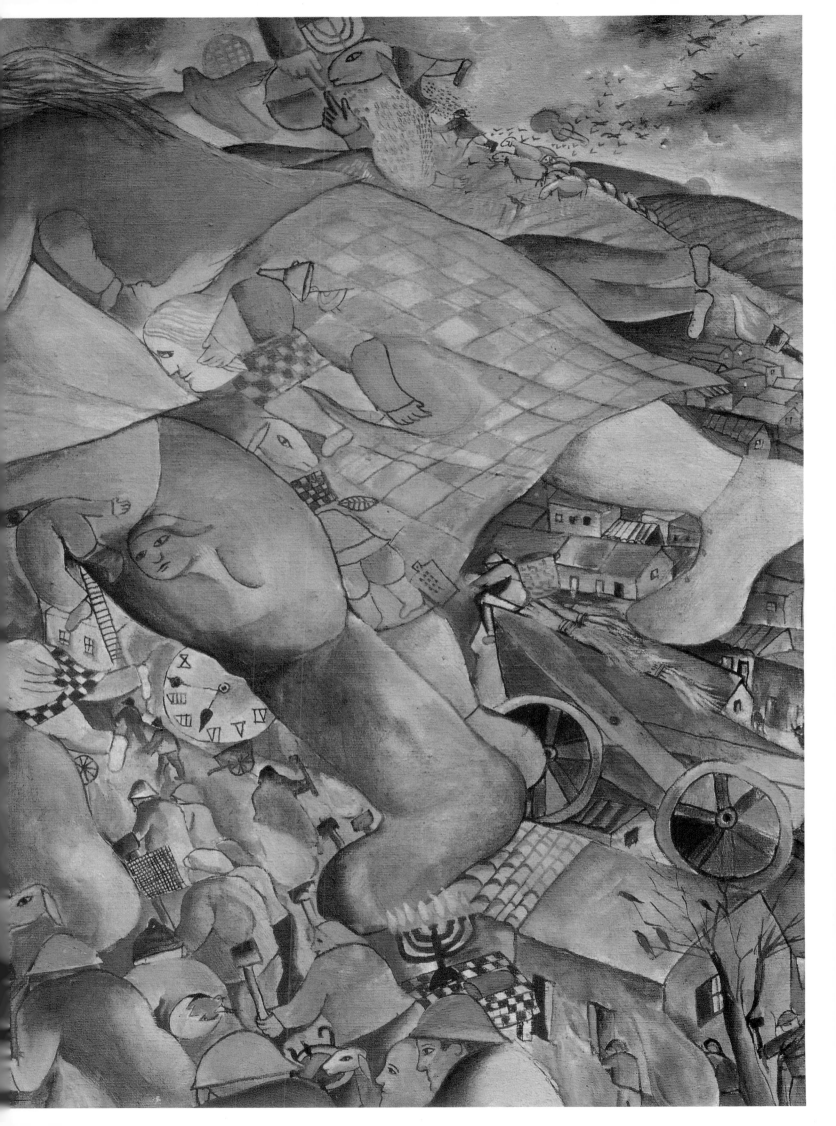

Hanukkah
1973
oil on canvas
81 x 101 cm

Hanukkah
1969
oil on canvas
58 x 78.5 cm

362

Hanukkah
1964
tempera on card
34 x 47 cm

Shabbat
1973
oil on canvas
74 x 59 cm

Shtetl (scene of *the Shabbat*)

1970

watercolour on paper

18 x 24 cm

Shabbat
1973
oil on canvas
102 x 81 cm

Evocation of Shabbat in the shtetl
watercolour on paper
1970
24.5 x 33 cm

Shabbat
1974
oil on canvas
45 x 34 cm

Torah
c. 1969
watercolour, ink on paper
25 x 35 cm

Evocation of Yezne at Ramot Menashé
1969
oil on canvas
50 x 61 cm

End notes

1 Author's interview with Totó, 2009.
2 Ibidem.
3 Ibidem.
4 Ibidem.
5 Ibidem.
6 Author's interview with Vera Jordan in Montevideo, 2009.
7 Author's interview with Eva Kaufman in Israel, March 2009.
8 Author's interview with Totó and numerous interviews with friends of Gurvich, 2009.
9 Author's interview with Totó, 2009.
10 Cap used by religious followers as a sign of devotion and respect for God, who to them is above human beings.
11 Yuval Dror, Bible teaching in the schools of the Labour and the Kibbutz movements, 1921-1953, Tel Aviv, School of Education, Tel Aviv University.
12 Author's interview with Totó, 2009.
13 Author's interview with Vera Jordan, Montevideo, 2009.
14 Ahad Haam, Hebrew name of Asher Zvi Hirsch Ginsberg (1856-1927), thinker and essayist, secular Jew and founder of cultural Zionism.
15 Festival braided bread.
16 Author's interview with Totó, 2009.
17 Author's interview with Vera Kaufman, March 2009.
18 Author's interview with Totó, 2009.
19 Author's interview with Eva Kaufman, March 2009.
20 Alicia Haber, El mundo íntimo del artista, op. cit., p. 78.
21 Nejama Leibowitz Parashat Bereshit, "In the Image of God". Taken from: Reflections on the Parashah, Prof. Nejama Leibovitz, Jerusalem, published by the Department of Religious Education and Culture for the Diaspora, part of the World Zionist Organization, 1986, pp. 9-13.
22 Julia Kristeva, Historias de Amor, Mexico, Siglo Veintiuno Editores, 1987.
23 See Menahem Mendel Bronfman, Chayei Sarah, Ramat Gan, University Parashat Hashavua Study Center Torah Bar-Ilan, November 22, 2008, http://biu.ac.il/JH/Parasha/eng/chaye/bron.html
Rabbi Lina Zerbarini, New Haven, Joseph Slifka Center for Jewish Life at Yale, 2006, Hillel: The Foundation for Jewish Campus Life, http://www.hillel.org/jewish/archives/bereshit/chayeisarah/2006_chayeisarah.htm
Where Was Sarah?, Rabbi Avi Weinstein, Hillel's Joseph Meyerhoff Center for Jewish Learning, http://www.myjewishlearning.com/texts/Bible/Weekly_Torah_Portion/chayeisarah_hillel5759.html
Rabbi Reuven H. Taff, Additional commentaries and text studies on Parshat Chayei Sarah at MyJewishLearning.com. http://www.myjewishlearning.com/texts/Bible/Weekly_Torah_Portion/chayeisarah_hillel5759.shtml
24 Genesis, 23:2.
25 Genesis, 28:10-22.
26 Works on Jacob's Dream: Representation of the Doura Europos 245 synagogue, Jacob's cream on the ladder reaching the heavens, Via Latina, Catacombs, Roma c. 300-400 B.C., The ladder of the divine rise, Saint Catherine's Monastery, Sinai 12th century, Jacob's dream 1639 by Jose de Ribera, Jacob's Dream, by Bartholome Esteban Murillo 1660 and 1665, Jacob's Dream, Harmerszoon van Rijn Rembrandt, Jacob's Dream, Sir Edward Burne-Jones, 1897, Jacob's Ladder, William Blake, 1808. Helen Frankenthaler, Jacob's Ladder, 1957, Jacob's Dream Marc Chagall (many versions).
27 Akedah: the Sacrifice of Isaac is known by this name in Hebrew. It means hindrance.
28 Genesis, 22:1-24, Parashat Vaiera.
29 As in the works The Sacrifice of Isaac by Domenichino 1630, by Giovanni Battista Tiepolo 1726-29, by Caravaggio, by Rembrandt, 1635 and 1636, by Chagall, 1960-1965.
30 Taken from Reflections on the Parashah, Prof. Nejama Leibovitz, Jerusalem, published by the Department of Religious Education and Culture, part of the World Zionist Organization, 1986, pp. 24-32.
31 Søren Kierkegaard, Temor y temblor, Madrid, Tecnos, 1987.
32 Julia Kristeva, "International Forum on Religions" November, Jerusalem, 19-24, 2008. http://www.kristeva.fr/jerusalem.html,
33 Elie Wiesel, Messengers of God: Biblical Portraits and Legends, New York, Random House, 1976.
34 Among others, Uri Zevi Greenberg, Abraham Shlonsky, Yehuda Amichai and Amir Gilboa also use the topos metaphorically.
35 Yael S. Feldman, "The Akedah and the Intellectual Melting Pot of the 1950s", New York University, AIS Association for Israel Studies. Conference, June 2007, Avi Sagi, "The Meaning of the Akedah in Israeli Culture and Jewish Tradition", Israel Studies, 3.1, Indiana, Indiana University Press, spring 1998, Chaim Gouri, "Heritage", in T. Carmi, ed., The Penguin Book of Hebrew Verse. Penguin Books, 1981, p. 565, Yael Feldman, "Isaac or Oedipus? Jewish Tradition and the Israeli Akedah", in Biblical Studies/Cultural Studies, edited by J. Cheryl Exum and Stephen D. Moore, Journal for the Study of the Old Testament Supplementary Series, No. 262, pp. 174-184.

36 This attitude began in the 1960s, in controversial times, when the settlements on the West Bank were first set up. Aryeh Ben-Gurion, a member of the Beit Hashitta kibbutz, writer and creator of new material for Jewish festivals in the kibbutzian framework in the fifties, was shocked that so many of his students were killed in Israel's wars, and the Akedah became a terrible major theme in his life and writings. After his death this material was collected in a book of 72 poems by various authors with paintings by Menashé Kadishman. The authors of this anthology protest in different ways and rebel against the myth.

37 Friend of Gurvich, psychologist and author of a chapter in this book.

38 Antonio Machado, "Proverbios y cantares" (Campos de Castilla), op. cit.

39 Ricardo J. Quiñones, The Changes of Cain: Violence and the Lost Brother in Cain and Abel Literature, New Jersey, Princeton University Press, 1991.

40 Cain and Abel appear over and over again, not only in Filon Ambrosio and Agustin, but also in Dante, the Corpus Cristi drama, in Machiavelli, Shakespeare, Byron, Melville, Wells, Conrad, Hesse, Unamuno, Tournier, Coleridge and Baudelaire. Genesis: A Living Conversation, The First Murder PBS produced and directed by Catherine Tatge; Bill Moyers, executive editor. A production by Public Affairs Television Inc presented on PBS by WNET/New York. With Mr. Moyers, Mandy Patinkin, John Barth, Rebecca Goldstein, Mary Gordon, Oscar Hijuelos, Charles Johnson, Faye Kellerman, Burton L. Visotzky.

41 Interview with Totó, 2009.

42 André Neher, L'existence juive, Paris, Seuil, 1962; 5th re-edition, 1990, pp. 38-42.

43 Other memories of triumph and different heroic acts were recalled, like Masada, the ghetto uprisings such as that in Warsaw, the birth of the State, the work of the unions in the Histradut, the work of the military defence of Palmach and the Haganah, and the suffering in the Holocaust.

44 Interview with Totó, 2009.

45 Idem.

46 Idem.

47 Muki Tsur and Yuval Daniel, editors, "Going Forth in the Month of Spring", The Kibbutz Haggada - Israeli Pesach in the Kibbutz, Jerusalem, 2004, in Hebrew. Muki Tsur, "Pesach in the Land of Israel: Kibbutz Haggadot". Indiana, Indiana University, Israel Studies, July 2007, Vol. 12 No. 2, Pages 74-103.

48 Muki Tsur, Pesach in the Land of Israel, op. cit.; Carol Novis, Understanding the

Exodus Personally: The Kibbutz Haggadah, New York, The Jewish Daily Forward April 7, 2006, http://www.forward.com/articles/1215/

49 Haggadah (plural: Haggadot), Muki Tsur, Pesach in the Land of Israel, op. cit.; Carol Novis, Understanding the Exodus Personally, op. cit.

50 Each year, new births, recent events, news from the kibbutz, news of the harvests, the arrival of new chaverim, messages against oppression, the Holocaust, songs of World War II partisans and the history of the birth of Israel were added to the account. They highlighted new fruit. Also they introduced illustrations by top Israeli artists and poetry by Hebrew authors like Bialik, Tchernikowsky, Lamdan, Rachel, S. Shalom, Shlonsky and Ben Amitai, Penn.

51 Flat bread made without yeast that is eaten during the Passover.

52 These include Charoset (apple, nuts, sugar, rub [syrup extracted from dates] and raisin mix) which represent the mud with which the Jews made bricks when they were slaves, and crushed nuts are added, which recall the stones that they added to the mix, and red wine to the rub, in memory of the blood that was spilt and the children that were sacrificed, evoking the clay used by Jewish people to build the pyramids and palaces. Maror (bitter herbs) recalls the bitterness. Karpas (parsley, potato, radish, celery) that is submerged in salt water recalls the tears shed in Egypt. Chazeret (lettuce) represents the affliction and transition from slavery to freedom as it is somewhat bitter but later its taste is pleasant. The salt water represents the tears shed in the times of slavery. There's also a glass of wine on the table, placed there for Elijah the prophet, who – according to the story – shall bring peace to all nations.

53 Eliezer Ben-Rafael, "Las etnicidades judías en Israel", Araucaria, Revista Iberoamericana de Filosofía, Política y Humanidades, Seville, vol. 10, no. 19, 2008, pp. 99-111.

54 Charles Liebman and Eliezer Don-Yehiya, Civil Religion in Israel, op. cit.

55 Idem.

56 This way of celebrating was a creation of the pioneers and it started before the establishment of the State, like many other inaugural Israeli elements. There were many important choreographers before the foundation of the State and during the first decades, and they invented the dances and festivals for the group feasts. One of them was Yardena Cohen, who eliminated the division between performers and audience,

transforming the festival into a group participation event in which all the members of the kibbutz joined the dance. She used Biblical stories from a secular perspective and re-named fundamental elements inherent to the people. She included numerous references to nature, organized everything outdoors, and added the history of the kibbutz region and topography. The choreography followed the guidelines of the new dance school of Isadora Duncan and Rudolf von Laban (Ausdruckstanz), which marked a trend for the future. With that spirit, she organized and directed numerous kibbutz festivals that were presented in many kibbutzim around the country. Other choreographers followed her lead and also brought in Biblical texts (in a modern way) and organized commemorative parades for "The Song of Songs", "The Book of Ruth", "Spring" and "Genesis". There was a sort of competition among the kibbutzim because they wanted to stand out in the organization of the festivals. The spirit of those festivals spread around Israel in those times; it was contagious and left its mark on the whole population.

4. Hard freedom, tough happiness

4

Hard freedom,
tough happiness

In his art Gurvich did not refer to anti-Semitism or the *Shoah* in any methodical way, he did not particularly focus on these subjects, but they are there in the figure of Jesus, the image of the stigmata, and his paintings of the pogroms, the attacks on Jewish populations in the *shtetls*. These were at their height at the end of the 19th century and beginning of the 20th, particularly in Russia and Eastern Europe. He also dealt with the persecution of Jews in vaster scenes in his kibbutz compositions and in those connected with the common saying, "It is hard to be a Jew".

Yezne

Totó explains, "Gurvich bore the mark of Lithuanian anti-Semitism. He knew that when they left Lithuania the situation of the Jews there was very difficult, and in the town where they lived it was unbearable, it was a ghetto, there were no jobs. The image of his grandfather was etched in his memory and he recalls it in every religious person in the drawings, tempera compositions and paintings he subsequently did."[1] Gurvich did not have good memories of Jieznas, called Yezne[2] in *Yiddish*, the *shtetl* where he was born and lived until he was five, when his family was forced to emigrate. He had a terrible reaction to the words Jieznas or Lithuania.

The situation in Lithuania became extremely hard for the Jews in the period between the two World Wars and Gurvich and his family were very affected by anti-Semitism. There was an atmosphere of discrimination, his parents had to endure awful experiences, and when they left they took the memory with them.

In the *shtetl* they lived in poverty and the threat of pogroms and persecution hung over their heads. The whole context was frightening. There were pogroms in Lithuania, anti-Semitism was in the air at that time and it drove the Gurvich family and millions of other Jews into exile, not only from Lithuania but from other parts of Eastern Europe.

They fled from exclusion, oppression, hardship, deprivation and anti-Semitism, and when they left they were burdened down with trauma, bittersweet feelings, the spectre of persecution, and the anguish that was such a feature of those eventful journeys, but they also had dreams of freedom, dignity and progress, passed on in Jewish families orally and in written form from generation to generation. The children assimilated those life experiences in many different ways. In some of Gurvich's compositions we find *shtetls* in danger. In *Composición del kibutz* (Composition of the kibbutz, 1966) there is a winter scene which combines Ramot Menashé, Yezne and *Hannukah* celebrations, and Gurvich includes the pain of the pogroms with the mother crying at the coffin of her children, *shtetl* images and Lithuanian soldiers, all in an oppressive atmosphere.

Lithuania was a very painful example, and even today and for a long time to come it is and will be traumatic for all Jews. It is impossible to forget. Today that land is in different countries, part in Lithuania, part in Belorussia and part in Russia, but in its heyday it was one of the most distinguished Jewish communities in Europe. The *litvaks* or Jewish Lithuanians had schools, study centres, thinkers, important synagogues and *yeshivot*,[3] and the region had been pre-eminent in Jewish culture since the 17th century. People from that community became famous all over the world not only in the sphere of religion but also on a secular level, and in the 20th century there were many outstanding *litvaks*. They had rabbis who were highly regarded for their interpretations of the *Talmud*, and the figure that stands out among them was Rabbi Elijah ben Solomon (1720-1797), known as Vilna Gaon. He was a renowned spiritual leader and a rabbinical authority, he was a leader in analytical and intellectual aspects of the movement known as *Mitnagdim*, which led the traditionalist rational religious school and opposed Hasidim.[4] In more modern times there were world famous thinkers and scientists, and also ideological leaders of the workers' movements in Lithuania. Vilna (Wilna) was known as the "Jerusalem of Europe". This community thrived for six hundred years in a climate of relative tolerance and peaceful coexistence.

But the situation changed completely at the start of the 20th century, in the period leading up to Lithuania's independence, and it worsened in the inter-war years. Anti-Semitism in Lithuania stemmed from various political, nationalist and religious factors.[5] The underlying anti-Semitism of the Lithuanians was partly based on Christian doctrine whereby people who were not baptised did not have a soul, so in a sense they were not real people, and this belief came to the fore in times of crisis. And it was political difficulties and nationalism that gave rise to that crisis.

Lithuania yearned to win its independence from Russia, but this was a complicated and traumatic process that involved a real war of independence, invasions by Germany and Russia, clashes with Poland and with what was then the Soviet Union. Not only was

Kibbutz composition (1966), detail (memories of Jieznas)

K bbuts composition (1966), detail (evocations of persecutions)

the country invaded many times but it had trouble with minority groups within its borders as well. Its internal situation became very unstable and there was war, internal fighting and civil disturbance in this fragile democracy. Radical nationalist organizations came into being and there was fanatical Catholicism, both of which were very negative factors with regard to the situation of the Jews. The policy of *Lithuanisation* (Lithuania for the Lithuanians) led to the Jews being marginalised and excluded from normal life. Gurvich's parents themselves were victims of this, for example, when he was born they were not allowed to give him the name they wanted and had to choose a Lithuanian name instead: Zusmanas.

Another factor that aggravated the situation was the stance of the Lithuanian Catholic Church. Most of the Catholic clergy pronounced themselves nationalist, anti-Semitic, anti-Orthodox, and anti-Polish, and with few exceptions they were against every ethnic or religious minority. The most important newspapers in Lithuania carried on a violent anti-Semitic campaign.

The Lithuanian Guard Union, which was formed in 1919, blamed the Jews for all Lithuania's evils, encouraged Judeophobia and urged everyone to despise and harass them. In 1930, anti-Semitism extended to the *Lumpenproletariat*, the working class, peasants, university students, civil servants and journalists. Even schoolchildren handed out pamphlets against the Jews,[6] and their lives were made impossible. The campaign against them featured all the old stereotypes: the exploiter, the murderer of Christ, the capitalist, the Bolshevik. There was a rising tide of pogroms, killings and oppression, and they were humiliated in many ways in an onslaught to erode their dignity.[7] This was the day-to-day situation and the climate that drove the Gurvich family to emigrate.

Shoah

The *Shoah* brought yet more grief and unbearable suffering. Totó remembers that on one occasion "...the family was in Cerro watching television. Gurvich liked to stop work in the evening and he was interested in some television programmes. That day they showed a film about the Warsaw Ghetto, it was extremely cruel, it was the whole history of the ghetto including the final slaughter and the victims left helpless and in isolation. When the programme finished Gurvich was pale, he stood up from the armchair my mother had given us, and although usually he never went to his workshop at night he locked himself in and spent almost the whole night alone. At four o'clock in the morning he woke me up and said, "It's done. I got rid of the rage."[8]

In 1969 that documentary on the Warsaw Ghetto uprising and its final destruction caused him a lot of pain. It was the biggest and also the first urban rebellion in Nazi-occupied Europe. Seven hundred and fifty badly-equipped resistance fighters clashed with a German Army bent on destroying the ghetto and sending the Jews to concentration camps. The Hashomer Hatzair group, under the leadership of the young Mordechai Anielewicz, attempted to save the almost sixty thousand Jews still living there at that time.

On 18 January 1943, Heinrich Himmler, the supreme commander of the SS (SS Reichsführer), gave orders for the ghetto to be destroyed and its population moved out. The operation started on April 19, 1943, the night of the Jewish Passover (Easter), but the attackers came up against Jewish resistance and had to fight. The Germans had overwhelming military and numerical superiority, they killed Anielewicz and many members of the resistance and utterly destroyed the ghetto, but the surviving Jews went on fighting for almost another month until they were finally defeated on May 16, 1943. This meant the mass deportation of thousands of Jews, who were subsequently murdered in the gas chambers.

Gurvich's response was to paint a pogrom. He did burning buildings, dying figures, a Jew crucified like Jesus, and an elderly religious man killed and bloody, with the Star of David to identify him, in the middle of a scene of fright and terror that is set in a *shtetl*. Mothers cry out in desperation, corpses scattered on the ground, the coffin of a child to symbolize the many children who died, and there is another religious figure who holds his head, unable to comprehend how this could be happening. It is a distressing scene of destruction and pain. People are fleeing in terror as the chaos caused by the persecution spreads. People are fleeing, people are fleeing.

Gurvich painted what usually happened in pogroms in the *shtetls*: the ordeal, the suffering and the being alone, but curiously he left out the resistance, the rebellious struggle, the new spirit of the Jews who were rising up in the Zionist movements, or the spirit of those who refused to die passively, which is what happened in other parts of Europe. From the ashes of the Warsaw ghetto and the body of Mordechai Anielewicz there emerged a message that has never faded, the call to protect yourself, to fight for your rights, to fight for freedom and for life. The uprising inspired acts of resistance in other ghettos such as those in Bialystok and Minsk, and in extermination camps like Treblinka and Sobibor. From that time on it stood as a symbol of the Jewish capacity to resist, the idea of fighting to the death, and the fact that many Jews had reacted dynamically and met persecution and anti-Semitism with force. Perhaps Gurvich did not show this because what struck him most deeply was the end result, the defeat, the annihilation.

Pogrom, detail

It was inevitable that the *Shoah* would loom large in Gurvich's life. He lost some of his family, and almost everyone from his home town disappeared. Totó says, "The Nazis in the Holocaust virtually wiped out the whole family that was left behind in Lithuania."[9] Vila[10], a frequent visitor to Gurvich's parents' house, says, "... and there was the question of the Holocaust. Everything had been lost in Lithuania, all the news from there was bad." The stories came one after the other; there were awful accounts of what refugee Jews had to go through on their troubled journeys to escape, and the survivors who reached Montevideo told their terrible tales. In the Hashomer Haitzar everybody talked about the tragedy. In Ramot Menashé, there is a square dedicated to the *Shoah*, and there were European Jews who had survived the death camps and the ghettos. Gurvich had a friend who had survived, a painter called Bezem, and he told the ghastly story of persecution, loss and suffering. His parents were killed in Auschwitz.

In those early years in Israel the Holocaust was a burning issue that aroused great interest because survivors were arriving all the time, and it had happened so recently and people's memories were still fresh. There was also a boom in books about the concentration camps, Auschwitz in particular, by Yehiel Feiner, also known as Yehiel Dinur, who signed his works Ka-Tzetnik 135633. He described the sadism of the Nazis in a horribly raw way.[11] From the mid-1950s and during the 1960s his books sold by the million, especially *Bet ha-bubot* (The House of Dolls, 1955). In those years his horrific stories fed the need the Jewish State and Israelis had to overcome the stereotype of the victimized Jew and to be strong and proud. This must never happen again, not ever. Never again would they be led passively to extermination. When Gurvich got together with his cousins in New York they told him what had actually happened to his relatives and friends, how they had been murdered, and what had happened all over his native land.

What came to light about Lithuania was dreadful. It was a special case in the *Shoah*. It was under Soviet rule, and when it was invaded by the Nazi Germans the Lithuanians received them as saviours and blamed the Jews for collaborating with the USSR. The stereotype of the Jews included the idea that they were agents of the KGB, and this was one of the reasons the Lithuanians played a key role in annihilating them. The murders began in 1941, before the Nazi invasion and the Soviets withdrawal, they were perpetrated by Lithuanians, and in the subsequent massing killings Lithuanians played a leading role. The bloody hand of the assassin was Lithuanian, the motivation behind the act was Lithuanian, and they worked with particular ferocity. When the Germans arrived on 3 July 1941, Lithuanians had already killed 40,000 Jews in just twelve days. Some of the things that happened were utterly horrific, like the massacre in the Lietükis garage in Kaunas (Kovno), which shocked the whole world. They did it in daylight, in front of women and children as if it was a show, and while playing harmonicas, clapping and singing the Lithuanian national anthem, they beat Jews to death with sticks and iron bars, and drowned them with hoses forced down their throats. This slaughter has been thoroughly documented with testimony and photographs, and it was reported at the Nuremberg Trials.

In 1941, detachments of the *Einsatzgruppen* (German mobile killing units), along with their Lithuanian henchmen, began shooting men, women, old people and children in the forests, rigid with cold in the depths of winter. The Nazis and Lithuanians executed the children first, in front of their parents, and forced the parents to dig the graves that are now, tragically, very well known. By November the murderers had almost finished their appalling task. This kind of slaughter, which was quite common in Eastern Europe, is known as "the *Shoah* by bullets".[12]

This hit Gurvich very hard, it was so close to home, and story of what happened in his own village was horrifying. In Jieznas almost the whole Jewish population disappeared during that fateful year and the Lithuanians actively collaborated. The head of the rural district made a list of Jews and their properties, and Lithuanian police officers and Nazi sympathizers carried out the arrests and many of the killings. There were mass detentions and shootings. Several dozens of people met their deaths in Prienai and Alytus, in the Forest of Vidzgiris. They were compelled to dig their own graves. Those who survived, some women, children and elderly people, were locked up in the town hall and the synagogue. The men were driven to the lake to dig a trench, and on the following day soldiers who were mostly Lithuanian ordered them to undress and massacred them. Afterwards, they took the women and children there too, also naked, and shot them dead. Those same pro-Nazi Lithuanians, the notorious members of the Lithuanian Activist Front whose aim was to free the country from communists, Russians and Jews, buried some of them alive. There was a special group among them, identified by their white armbands, whose the only task was to destroy Jews.[13]

There is a wall, a monument to the Holocaust, in the Valley of the Communities of Yad-Vashem in Jerusalem, and on it there is a name carved in stone: Jieznas.

Lithuania has the awful distinction of being the country in which, proportionally, the most killings in the Holocaust took place: 91% of the Jewish community was wiped out. And it was not only Lithuanian Jews who died there, but also refugees from other East European countries. Lithuania has another claim to notoriety: it was where the first general, mass, swift, efficient slaughter of Jewish men, women, and children took place. Ethnic cleansing started there. The transformation from persecution to genocide took place there.

Gurvich, like many other Jews, was never the same after Nazism. This was inevitable. He was a modern Jew of the Holocaust and post-Holocaust era, an accidental survivor, as were most of those who for different reasons managed to emigrate and be saved but lost their families and co-religionists.

The *Shoah* left an indelible mark, as Yehuda Bauer explains, "For the first time in history, people were condemned to death just for being born ...Nothing like this happened anywhere else in the world... The murder of the Jews was aimed not only at German or Polish Jews, or even at European Jews, but at the 17 million Jews living in all the Diasporas in the whole world in 1939. The killing of the Jews was something planned for the whole world, it was universal.[14]

Pogrom, detail

Pogrom, details

The *Shoah* left a terrible scar. It is shocking that hardly any country tried to protect the Jews, although there were some notable exceptions like Denmark, the most outstanding example, Japan in occupied Shanghai, and some other isolated cases like Bulgaria at one time. Even the countries that are deemed more democratic and enlightened failed, their response hovered between silence, negligence and indifference. Switzerland, Sweden, Great Britain, the United States and Canada put restrictions on Jewish immigration and many countries closed their borders altogether. The policy was to let in the smallest possible number of refugees, and exclusion was even stricter for the poor and for people who had no connections. This meant the Jews could not emigrate, and they were condemned to death because they had no way out. There were only a few examples of solidarity and bravery by people, some of whom had nothing to with Judaism who risked their lives to save Jews.

"It is hard to be a Jew"

On his third trip to Israel, Gurvich started with the subject "It is hard to be a Jew", and he subsequently continued with this in New York. He took this slogan from one of his favourite authors, Shalom Aleichem, who created numerous characters that have endured in literature like Tevye, Menajem Mendl, the Fiddler on the Roof, and the mythical *shtetl* Kasrilevke, in which Aleichem described with sensitivity and empathy the tribulations of the Jews in the *shtetls*. "It is hard to be a Jew" is a play inspired in an old saying that was very popular among the Ashkenazis. In Yiddish it is *"iz schwer tzu sein a yid."* It is used ironically with melancholy humour as a metaphor for being a Diaspora Jew. It expresses how difficult it is to go on in the face of the threat of persecution and pogroms (Shalom Aleichem himself was a victim in 1905), of the painful confrontation with intolerance, of the dilemma of being a Jew in the modern world, and it relates to Zionist ideas and socialist universalism. It also embodies the question of whether or not to assimilate, the decision of whether or not to be religious, and within religion which path to choose. It is a difficult challenge to be faithful to traditional values and fit into the modern world as well. As Lévinas said, it is hard kind of freedom, *"Difficile Liberté"*.[15]

The French philosopher and theologian André Neher says that living the life of a Jew is "a tough kind of happiness."[16]. There are many reasons for this, including the unforgettable trauma of genocide. Neher believes that Auschwitz has left such a mark on the Jews that nothing Jewish can be conceived, built, or done without thoughts and action that hark inexorably back to that massacre. We are, and we will always continue to be, contemporary with Auschwitz.[17] The French activist Pierre Goldman,[18] says Auschwitz was always there, and although he never suffered the horrors of Nazism himself he could not escape from it.[19] The French thinker Robert Misrahi says the Holocaust is the absolute point of reference for all possible futures, for all Jewish experience and consciousness. Another French thinker, Luc Rosenzweig, believes that the spectre of Auschwitz is present like an *a priori category* of knowledge. Auschwitz has become a symbol for many Jewish and non-Jewish thinkers. It was the biggest extermination camp; there were two gas chambers and four incinerators and the prisoners were killed *en masse* with a deadly gas called Zyklon B. One million Jews died there, 70,000 Poles and 21,000 gypsies, and there were also 15,000 Russian prisoners of war.

Albert Memmi, a Tunisian-born thinker, novelist, researcher, sociologist and philosopher residing in Paris, is only too painfully aware of the troubled history of Jews and anti-Semitism in the world. He says, "The Jew lives, Judaism endures". In his 1962 book *Portrait of a Jew*, he talks about the burden of being Jewish in an anti-Semitic universe.[20]

Schalom Aleichem's dictum is still relevant today. At the Bronfman Foundation symposium, the Mexican historian Enrique Krauze entitled his paper, "It is still hard to be a Jew" (*Es iz schwer tzu sein a yid*). "It is hard to be a Jew. I believe that these melancholic words from Sholem Aleichem still apply, but it is also important to examine, as a historian, the reasons why this expression came into being."[21] According to Krauze, intolerance and persecution were the norm in the Diaspora. There were exceptions; the Jews lived in peace and tranquillity in medieval Spain, in some periods in the *shtetls* in Poland, when humanist liberalism bloomed in the German Enlightenment and in post-revolutionary France. But at other times and in other places the Jews had to endure awful anti-Semitism, like the pogroms of the Tsarist regime in the 19th and 20th centuries, and those who survived had to resort to radical solutions like emigrating to other parts of Europe, America or Israel. But more terrible than anything that had gone before was the Holocaust, this manifestation of the desire to eliminate the Jewish people. And Krauze adds that anti-Semitism is still a force in the post-war world, albeit disguised behind a new face.

Gurvich knew exactly what anti-Semitism was, from its latent, everyday form to its savage extreme. He knew it from his memories of Lithuania, from the *Shoah*, from what had happened to his family and friends, and even from some events in a tolerant and friendly country like Uruguay. In his early years in this new country there was xenophobia and anti-Semitism, and it increased after the Terra coup

It is hard to be a Jew, detail

d'état[1] in 1933. Uruguay had always welcomed newcomers and kept its doors open but then the Government began to restrict immigration (the laws of 19 July 1932 and 13 October 1936) just when there was a real need, when the Jews were suffering from Nazi persecution. Many ships with European refugees were turned away, among them the Conte Grande, and these dramatic events were chronicled in Yiddish community newspapers like *Folksblat* and *Unzer Fraint* in Montevideo and *D. Presse* and *Idische Tzeitung* in Buenos Aires.

In many cases, Jews managed to enter the country thanks to friendly Uruguayan diplomats who went against official State policy at that time and broke the rules. The whole decade from 1930 to

[1]   1933-1938. Gabriel Terra (873-1942) was elected President 1931, staged a coup d'etat against his own Government in 1933, enacted a new Constitution in 1934 and ruled by dictatorial decree until 1938.

1940 was a time of tension, and the Jewish community in Uruguay, which was already traumatised by what was happening in Europe, was seriously concerned for its own safety. There was anti-Semitic propaganda in the press, in *La Tribuna Popular* for example, and *El Bien Público*.[II] There were some acts of violence, tar bombs against Jewish institutions, there was a marked Nazi influence, there was nationalistic conservative anti-Jewish feeling in various political and social sectors, Germanophile political parties, and explicit Catholic anti-Semitism.

However, those attitudes did not really filter down to the people, and in daily life, at school, in the neighbourhood, with friends and at work, the norm was calm and peaceful coexistence. This was very different from the Jewish experience in Eastern Europe and Germany, and the Jews lived without fear, they integrated into life in Uruguay and came to love the country. In addition, liberal sectors in the traditional parties and the Uruguayan left, and also intellectuals, students and unions, were opposed to any kind of racism or anti-Semitism, and the model of a tolerant country became dominant. Besides this, after recovering from the Terra period, Uruguay aligned itself with the allies.

Gurvich did a series of compositions entitled "It is hard to be a Jew", and quite apart from its artistic merit it is also valid for its content. An enormous elderly man carries the Tablets of the Law (1970), in his other hand he holds a sabbatical table and the tree of life is growing out of him. He is surrounded by symbols: the ladder up to the sky, hands that receive the *Torah* from the celestial sphere, houses that walk, sheep, and the image of Jacob sleeping. The elderly man has Judaism on his shoulders, he looks up to the sky in anguish, he is afflicted, he is a symbol of distress and dismay. There are dramatic elements that show deep uneasiness, suffering, and painful grief caused by what has come to pass, anti-Semitism and above all the *Shoah*. Nevertheless, that elderly man is also a severe, strong and imposing being, and he is not going to give up that easily. He is resilient. He is a giant figure, and although he is serious and solemn, although he is faced with dilemmas and sacrifices, he has an enormous extremely positive heritage full of wisdom, universal legacies like the Bible, ethical monotheism, a specific conception of life, myths, legends and hopes for the future. And he clings to them, he does not let go of the Bible scrolls, he is holding them tight, and in the other hand he is holding the table of the *Shabbat*. Jacob is there, dreaming peacefully with life pulsing inside him. So even though there are horrors, people suffering, and an elderly Jew holds his head in anguish (which features in both the 1974 versions),

II   Uruguayan newspapers founded in the 1870s that disappeared in the second half of the 20th century.

Skecth for pottery
c. 1968
pencil on paper
24 x 18 cm

the legacies survive. It is significant that there is a woman carrying out the *Erev Shabbat* rite and there is the inevitable tree of life, the source of hope. In some sketches Gurvich makes a compendium of Judaism with the scene of the *Akedah*, the tree of life, Jacob's dream, the handing over of the *Torah*, the sabbatical table and candles, the kibbutz world and real scenes of work. It is hard to be a Jew, but it is enriching. That huge figure is also a symbol of resistance and of Gurvich's love for his own identity.

It is difficult to be a Jew, and although it entails an onerous and exhausting heritage, that burden is worthwhile. It is so valuable and it has encouraged generations to survive everything, to continue being Jewish and to ponder on their heritage and revitalize it, which is exactly what Gurvich was doing in his work.

Part of this precious burden is very old, it is in biblical texts, in those scrolls that Gurvich's monumental Jew is holding onto with such force. It is ethical monotheism, the Ten Commandments, Leviticus, the Psalms, the Proverbs and the words of the prophets. It is a heritage not just for the Jews but for the whole human race. As the Christian historian Paul Johnson[22] has pointed out, it contains the concept of equality in the eyes of law, the sanctity of life, the dignity of human beings, personal conscience and individual redemption, social responsibility, love as the basis of justice, the ideals of pacific coexistence between nations, harmony between human beings, respect for others, civil loyalty and so many other principles that constitute the grounds of Western morality. And there is more, the universalism of prophetic thinking, the capacity to choose between good and evil, the faculty of human beings to improve and grow and comprehend the forces which mould our destiny, the value of the family, care and reverence for parents, the ideal of monogamy, and caring for the poor, widows, and orphans. The basic ethical foundations and aims of all this are kindness, compassion and love, honesty and sincerity. Education is important in this heritage, and theft, falsity, perjury and oppression are condemned. All this and much more is in the Bible.

Always

For Gurvich, like for all Jews, the *Shoah* is a crucial component of the post-war Jewish identity; it is a defining experience, a root experience. When he produced his kibbutz work with its Jewish subject matter, he did what the German community in the 19th century used to call *Trotzjudentum*, "Judeity in spite of", "the Judeity of defiance", and in his own way he sang, *we do live*. And besides its artistic value, his work has value as a rejection of the disappearance of Judaism, as steadfast adherence to an identity. Jews keep on creating, Gurvich kept on painting, and his painting is alive. One of the *litvaks* was perpetuating traditions in his own way, in Uruguay, Israel, and New York, and now there is even an art gallery of his work in Montevideo.

After the *Shoah* it became more important than ever to preserve culture, to improve it and enrich it and pass it on, to communicate it and share it, in different places, from different points of view like Gurvich's for example. And it is this that imbues his work with special meaning, it is part of a response that endures. Identity has not been lost, Gurvich did not lose it, and today everyone can share in it, gentiles as well as Jews, and very especially his Uruguayan countrymen.

Pogrom
1969
oil on canvas
50 x 70 cm

It is hard to be a Jew
1970
oil on canvas
79 x 60 cm

It is hard to be a Jew
c. 1970
pottery
26.5 x 16 x 8 cm

It is hard to be a Jew
c. 1970
pottery
26.5 x 16 x 8 cm

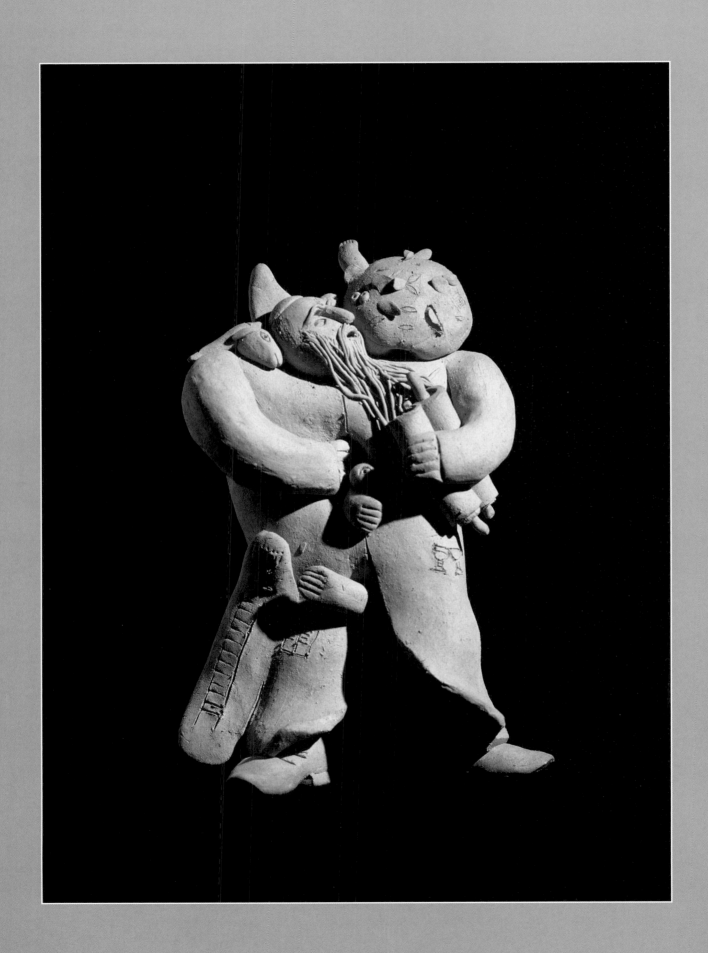

It is hard to be a Jew
1974
oil on canvas
66 x 66 cm

End notes

1   Interview with Totó, 2009.
2   This used to be called "Yetsmev" in the Gurvich family, because of how it sounded. Its name today is Jieznas, Yezne in Yiddish, Ezno in Russian, Iezno in Polish. It is also known as Jezna, Yezna, Yeznas, Eznas, Iyeznas and Eznas.
3   Ieshiva (plural: ieshivot).
4   Hasidism: A religious movement that emerged in the 18th century, founded by Israel Ba'al Shem Tov. It proclaims a personal relationship with God through the heart, feelings and the spirit and happiness.
5   Azriel Shochat, "Lithuania and the Jews", The Holocaust Chapter, Washington, Symposium Presentations, Center for Advanced Holocaust Studies, United States Holocaust Memorial Museum, July 2005; Michael MacQueen, "Lithuanian Collaboration in the "Final Solution: Motivations and Case Studies, Lithuania and the Jews, The Holocaust Chapter, Washington, Symposium Presentations, Center for Advanced Holocaust Studies, United States Holocaust Memorial Museum, July 2005; Marcus Ernst, "The Beginning of Anti-Semitism in Independent Lithuania", Jerusalem, Yad Vashem Studies 2, 7-48. 1958, L E K K E T - World Union of Jewish Studies www.lekket.com. Vygantas Vareikis, Preconditions of Holocaust, Anti-Semitism in Lithuania, 19th century until mid 20th century June 5, 1940, Klaipeda, Lithuania, Department of History, Faculty of Social Sciences, Klaipeda University, http://www.komisija.lt/Files/www.komisija.lt/File/Tyrimu_baze/Naciu%20okupacija/Holokausto%20prelaidos/Eng/Vareikis%20/Research%20y%20V.Vareikis%20(english).pdf
6   In 1939, the Lithuanian Christian Workers Union called on its members and all workers to take up the fight against the Jewish parasites that made their wealth from Lithuanian blood.
7   In 1922, students from the University of Kaunas (Kovno) protested against the presence of Jews in the University. In 1923, violent groups destroyed signs in Yiddish and Russian on businesses and Jewish homes. Anti-Semitic articles by Jokubas Blažinas stimulated attacks on the community. There were more serious incidents in 1929.
8   Interview with Totó, 2009.
9   Idem.
10 Interview with Ernesto Vila, 1999.
11 Born in Sosnowiec, Poland, in 1917, and died in Tel Aviv in 2001. He was a poet and religious activist. He was married and he studied in the Yeshiva. He was a rabbi. He published poems in Yiddish. He was sent to Auschwitz in 1943 and he remained there a year and a half until he escaped in 1945. After his terrible experiences in Auschwitz he was unable to use his own name any more and he called himself Ka-Tzetnik, with the number he had tattooed on his arm. He was no longer able to remember anything except his experiences at the concentration camp and that is why he said he was born at Auschwitz and that his life was only justified if he spoke out about the victims. For him that name was an identity, not a pseudonym. Auschwitz was in all his writings, that was his mission and he was obsessed with it. He wrote about the most terrible cruelty and pain.
12 More is known about this today thanks to the work of a French priest, Father Patrick Desbois, and thanks to an initiative by Cardinals Jean-Marie Lustiger and Jean-Pierre Ricard, and Rabbi Israel Singer. There has been a systematic search to locate the mass graves (more than five hundred have been identified so far), and reports have been compared with accounts by witnesses who are still alive. From 1941 to 1944, almost one and a half million Ukrainian Jews were killed, and the people in Eastern Europe openly took part. There was an exhibition at the Shoa Memorial in Paris from 20 June 2007 to 6 January 2008.
13 International Jewish Cemetery Project, International Association of Jewish Genealogical Societies, Lithuania Jieznas Prenai district, Kaunas County. http://www.iajgs.org/cemetery/lithuania/jieznas-trakai-uezd-vilnius-gubernia.html. Bibliography in Hebrew and Lithuanian, Le-zikharon shel kedoshei kehilat Jezna she-nispu bi-shnat 1941, Jerusalem, 1967, Słownik Geograficzny Królestwa Polskiego (1880-1902), III, pg. 581.
14 Yehuda Bauer, "HaShoa: HaMeyuhad VeHaUniversali", The Holocaust: the Singular and the Universal, Jerusalem, Jinuj LeTarbut BeJevra Rav Tarbutit - Suguiot BeHishtalmuyot Morim, Cultural education in a multicultural society – Issues for the improvement of teachers, Jerusalem, Anthology 9, Hebrew University in Jerusalem, School of Education, Department of Teacher Improvement, 2000, pp. 161-162.
    The 2000 Stockholm International Forum and the 2005 United Nations Resolution determined that because of its unique nature the Holocaust had to be mandatory in school curriculums. Today it features in most European curriculums.
15 Emmanuel Lévinas, Difficile Liberté, LGF, Paris, Livre de Poche, 2003.

16 André Neher, Le dur bonheur d'être juif, Paris, Le Centurion, 1978.

17 These thoughts on Auschwitz were taken from André Neher, Regards sur une tradition, Paris, Bibliophane, pp. 11-13, 1989.

18 Yair Auron, Les juifs d'extrême gauche en mai 68, Paris, Michel Albin, 1998.

19 He was a communist, leader of the new French left-wing, author of Souvenirs obscurs d'un juif polonais né en France, Paris, Seuil, 1975, editor of Les Temps modernes - Libération. He was killed by neo-Nazis on 20 September 1979.

20 Albert Memmi, Portrait of a Jew, New York, A Viking Compass Book, 1971.

21 Enrique Krauze, "It's still hard to be a Jew", Congress organized by The Samuel Bronfman Foundation, June 2008. http://www.thesbf.org/pdf/KrauzePaper+Session%20v4_0.pdf

22 Paul Johnson, A History of the Jews and A History of Christianity, New York, Harper Perennial, 1988.

5. Jesus, the parable of the blind and the deadly sins

The creation in collage
1967
oil, fabrics on
canvas
100 x 162 cm

When the Nazi anti-Semitism began, and then later at the time of the *Shoah*, the figure of Jesus became a significant tool to fight anti-Semitism and denounce Nazism, and Chagall was the leading exponent of this. Starting in 1912 he did a long series of paintings including *Crucifixion Blanche* 1938), *Descente de croix et Crucifixion bleue* (1941), *Crucifixion Jaune, Obsession and Les Crucifiés* (1943), *Résurrection au bord du fleuve* (1947), *Quai de la Tournelle* (1953), *Job* (1975), *L'autoportrait à la pendule* (1946), *Traversée de la Mer Rouge* (1945-55), and then in a triptych he produced during and after the War, *Résistance, Résurrection and Libération* (1937-1953). The crucifixion also appears in *Exode* (1952) and in *Le Sacrifice d'Isaac* (1975).[3] These works, especially those of the 1930s, 40s and 50s, were obviously connected to what was happening in Europe: the destruction of the synagogues in Munich and Nuremberg, Crystal Night in Germany, the deportation of the Jews from Poland and the genocide. Chagall's Jesus is always identifiably Jewish, by his clothes and the symbols around him. In 1977 Chagall explained, "I think Christ symbolises the real Jewish martyrdom. I realised that in 1908 when I painted that image for the first time. I was very influenced by the pogroms. Afterwards, I painted it and drew it in my pictures of ghettos, surrounded by the agony of the Jews, of Jewish mothers suffering, terrified, holding their little children in their arms."

Other Jewish artists have used the image of Jesus as a symbol of the Holocaust: in 1942 Emmanuel Mané-Katz (Paris), in 1942-43 Mark Rothko (New York), in 1945 Abraham Rattner (New York), Josef Foshko (New York), and the Dadaist Marcel Janco (Tel Aviv), in 1982-83 George Segal (New York), and in 1951-53 Mathias Goeritz (Mexico).

But Gurvich's biggest influence was Marc Chagall. Gurvich's image of Jesus evokes the Jewish prophet, a man of the people who walked in the land of Israel preaching a simple religion, a message of humility and above all of love for his fellow man. His real message never had anything to do with being anti-Jewish, but that is what developed in Christian Europe and led to harassment, persecution, expulsion, destruction and death. For centuries.

It is fitting that Jesus should appear in a Jewish context. He was born and lived as a Jew, he was called rabbi, and many thinkers including the famous historian Joseph Klausner in his work *Jesus of Nazareth*, see him as one of the great Jews, an excellent moralist, who fought to bring Judaism back to its original simplicity. He never wanted to become independent or to set up another religion; that was done on the initiative of Saul of Tarsus (Paul of Tarsus), who lived later.

The figure of Jesus in Gurvich's work may also be linked to Antonio Machado, who was a great admirer of Jesus because of his respect for and dedication to his fellow men, among other things. Jesus figures repeatedly in the poet's work, and Gurvich sometimes cited these in his writings: Jesus as the essential you, as the other one who walks with you. For a Jew it is absolutely crucial to recognise other people's right to be different, and Gurvich expressed this through his representations of Jesus and quotes from Machado.

The blind leading the blind

Gurvich greatly admired Brueghel's The Parable of the Blind (1568), it awakened his iconographic passion and he cited it in numerous paintings (*Pogrom, Shtetl, Carta al Hombre*) and echoed it in some other compositions. He was interested in its content, its message, which is one of the reasons why he uses these images in his art. And the parable of the blind leading the blind is now an established part of Western culture and has become a well-known saying.

Gurvich used it to focus on ideas he felt strongly about like the ineptitude, crassness, backwardness and incompetence that come about when people let themselves by led by guides who are inept or unfit. He is sounding an implicit warning against the dangers of following leaders and teachers who do not know, and he is also reprimanding leaders and teachers who believe they know enough to act as guides but who end up taking their disciples to disaster and ruin. There ought to be a conscience examination before someone becomes a leader, if not he is a "blind" master.

The parable is illustrated with teaching in everyday life, with many examples of "blind guides" who are taking people to a tragic end or leading them astray, playing on their poverty of spirit, their ignorance, their vulnerability, their weaknesses, their spiritual, intellectual, or moral "blindness". It is a call to be cautious and to choose your teachers carefully.

Brueghel's main inspiration for this was Jesus's parable (Luke 6:39), but there are precedents in Hebraic texts in the Old Testament. Jesus was a Jew who was well versed in the culture of his time and who knew his Bible, so he was familiar with them, and to understand his teachings we should see them in the light of the Palestinian Judaism of the time. The Hebrews used the idea of blindness in a number of ways. The *Torah* speaks out against false leaders and, metaphorically, against the blindness of mind, of unconsciousness, of lack of wisdom and of ignorance. In Isaiah 56:10, and there are different translations, we read, "His watchmen are blind, they are all without knowledge," or "His watchmen are blind, they all are ignorant," or "His watchmen are blind; they do not know." In Leviticus 19:14, there is an emphatic warning that one should not give bad advice to people who do not understand certain things. This is an interpretation of the phrase, "Thou shalt ... not put a stumbling block before the blind" (*lifnei iver lo*

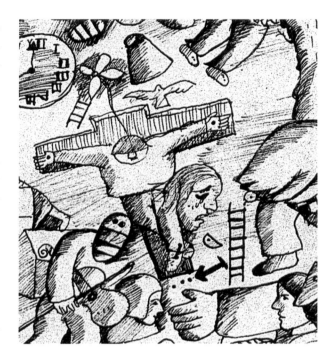

Letter to man (1967), detail

The creation in collage, detail

The creation in collage, detail

Dream on the kibbutz, detail

Forms with perspective, detail

Letter to man, detail

Fantasy world with black background, detail

titten michshol). As a metaphor this can be understood in many ways and contains many lessons. We should not give bad advice to a "blind person" who cannot evaluate a situation because we will send him the wrong way, and nor should we take advantage of his weakness to harm him because he does not have the intellectual, moral or spiritual capacity "to see", to weigh up, to understand, to protect himself, and he may trip up. Bad leaders should not exploit these people or tempt them, they should not take advantage of their position to do them harm, which are subjects the expert Nehama Leibowitz also tackled. These questions are linked to the Jesus parable: he was a Jew of his time.

Bible expert Susana Poch[4] clarifies this point, "There cannot be the slightest doubt that Jesus based his teachings on the knowledge he had of biblical texts, mainly those in which laws and mandates are enunciated and on the books of the Prophets.

The people who researched what Jesus said to write the gospels also used the Bible, mainly the prophet Isaiah, to support and legitimize some important points in his life and teachings. Many prophets, above all Isaiah and Jeremiah, and the books of Exodus, Numbers and Deuteronomy, use blindness in a metaphorical sense with many possible interpretations. In Isaiah 29:9-10, 18 it is used to indicate how bribes stop judges from seeing what is right. In Exodus 23:8 and Deuteronomy 16:19 it may represent deceit, lies, oppression, injustice, imprisonment and prison, in the sense that the blind are fragile and people deprived of their freedom are in the dark.[5] What Jesus says could be interpreted not only with regard to false leaders in general, but also and more specifically to people exercising religious leadership when they should not because they are forbidden to do so. There was debate about whether the blind should be allowed to enter the temple, whether they could discharge all their religious obligations and whether they could be judges. They were exempt from making the three annual pilgrimages to Jerusalem. And there is another sense that could apply to Jesus's words, blind priests were disqualified from carrying out sacrifices of any kind.

At the time of Jesus and approximately until the defeat of Bar Kochba, the notion of a struggle between the forces of light and the forces of darkness was a topos in the literature of the period. Light and darkness represented the forces of good (the Jews) against those of evil (the Roman Empire), and this image was used in a fighting literary genre of which John's Apocalypse has remained as an example in the Christian canon. In this, people on the side of darkness were "blind" to the change (luminous = true) that the arrival of the Messiah promised.

The prophet or *navi* is somebody "called" to speak the word of God (*navi* = calling), somebody who "sees" what others do not (this is what

Mural: The blind
c. 1958
cement
37 x 64 cm
detail

roeh and *joze*, which are synonyms of *navi*, mean). Jesus was not only a teacher and a legitimate heir to the throne, he was a prophet too. He is the only one who sees and is able to transmit his legitimate vision (brightness) to the faithful followers. The others are blind."

Some experts claim that in the *Tanakh* there are other references to blindness as a metaphor for lack of comprehension, like in Isaiah 42:16-21, 56:10, 59:10, 43:8, 29:9, 18, 35:5 and 6:9-10. They suggest there is a precedent in Zephaniah that repeats the image in Isaiah of blindness as punishment 1:17, Numbers 23:8 and Deuteronomy 16:19, 27:18 and 28:29.

At any rate it is clear that the subject fascinated Gurvich not only because of Brueghel's masterpiece but for its moral content, he used it in his work in Cerro and on the kibbutz in Israel, and he was passing on a message highly charged with connotations.

The seven deadly sins

Hieronymus Bosch's *The Seven Deadly sins and The Four Last Things*, *The Garden of Earthly Delights*, and Pieter Brueghel's *The Seven Deadly Sins or The Seven Vices* were also hugely important sources of inspiration for Gurvich. He blended these ideas and images into his Jewish subject matter and he did paintings specifically on the theme of the Seven Deadly Sins.

In many kibbutz context paintings, he syncretically incorporated the theme of the seven deadly sins as inter-textual echoes of the work

Lust, detail

of Brueghel and Bosch as ways to express human weakness. This can be seen in *Carta al Hombre* (Letter to man), *Escena de Kibutz* (Kibbutz scene, 1966), *Composición* (1966), *La lujuria* (Lust, 1966) and *La gula* (Gluttony, 1968).

The theme is essentially Christian and specifically Catholic. The seven deadly sins were codified during the period of the Roman Pope Gregory I (*circa* 540-604), they are lust, gluttony, greed, sloth, anger, envy and pride and they are classified as part of the first teachings of Catholicism. According to this doctrine they are deadly sins in the sense that the punishment for them in eternal damnation, although the sinner may be absolved through the sacrament of penance or forgiven if he is perfectly contrite.

Jews have a different conception of this matter, which can be found in *Pirkei Avot*, the Ethics of our Fathers. There are no seven deadly sins but there are sins that are considered very serious, and three in particular are so serious that it is better to die than commit them, namely murder, immoral sexual acts (especially incest) and idolatry. In addition, there are many acts that are serious transgressions against the numerous commandments and precepts the Jews have to adhere to (*the mitzvot*), which in fact total 613. Nevertheless, action that springs from iniquity, uncontrolled emotions, weaknesses of character, errors caused by the psyche, incorrect moods, ways of being hurtful or undesirable attitudes can be corrected or modified, and people are not commanded to die rather than commit acts of lust, anger, gluttony, greed, sloth, envy or pride.

Judaism is optimistic; there is a route to return to goodness. One of its key notions is that human beings have free will and are able to choose their path in life, and if they make a mistake and stray from the correct way they can repent and return to it. Repentance in Hebrew is *teshuvah*, which literally means return. Transgressions, iniquities and losing one's way are governed by the laws of life (*Halakhah*), and the way back can be achieved through repentance, the Day of Atonement, prayers and above all through one's actions, that is to say charitable work, a return to abiding by the laws, ethically connect conduct and repairing the harm one has done to others. And of course, for religious people, there is another way, through divine mercy; God has 13 merciful attributes.

The concept of the seven deadly sins is of Catholic origin but it has now become part of Western culture and in that sense, although the Jews do not accept these sins from a religious point of view, they are still aware of them and accept them as part of the cultural matrix of our times. This is why Gurvich was attracted to this theme, and of course his perspective was secular.

When he brings this subject into his work, as in *Carta al Hombre* (Letter to man) or other kibbutz scenes, he does not dramatize or condemn human beings. On the contrary, he shows human weaknesses in the whole context of man's reality, of what man's life is, of the complexity of existence, of the wide variety of experiences, of moments of light and darkness, of successes and impediments. And this life panorama includes love, work, life, spirituality, art, dreams, poetry, birth, ladders to ascend, the ability to fly, musical lyricism, childhood innocence, eternal couples, trees of life, and the clock that marks the inevitable passing of time. But there are also mistakes, setbacks, limitations, suffering, difficulties, blindness, false leaders, crucifixions, the ultimate evil of murder, and man's fall into anger, envy, sloth and other excesses.

La lujuria (Lust) is set at night and the symbolic moon is there, as if night were a time that lures us into eroticism and sexual activities, which is a traditional analogy. Gurvich paints unconscious fantasies and the realities of people's sex lives, but this is not a portrayal or representation of life on the kibbutz, rather it is an allusion to matters that involve the whole human race. There are lyrical characters devoted to erotic love-making beneath a colourful sunshade and surrounded by brightly coloured flowers. The artist seems to be portraying the special pleasure of loving sex, and it occupies considerable space in the painting. There are other couples (that may also be sharing love) who have blissfully given themselves up to sexuality. A range of different sexual acts are shown, and from a secular point of view some of these are considered normal behaviour between consenting adults in their life together, while others are considered sexual options (like lesbianism, which is depicted in some areas of the painting). Gurvich also includes acts that are considered unnatural such as sex with animals, with plants and with objects. The landscape is made up of hypertrophied lower limbs and the scene shows desires that stem from the unconscious, and realities too, but the artist does not condemn them. The order of the world does not seem to be altered by desire, fantasies or indulgence in sex, while in contrast there are other acts such as gluttony that do interrupt the harmony, structure or balance of life.

La gula (Gluttony) is a kibbutz scene and Gurvich depicts human beings who have lost their normal restraint and given themselves up to dark desires and all kinds of excesses, which was the exact opposite of what was really going on in that tough environment in those years. So he is not presenting a vision of reality but rather looking into the unconscious mind and attempting to show appetites and desires that people have under control, a potential for abuse and debauchery that is restrained. To achieve this, Gurvich's figures are out of proportion and exaggerated, they are hypertrophied, obese beings in extreme scenarios where they have succum-

Letter to man, detail

bed to overindulgence, and he brings their weaknesses into the light while the world itself is thrown out of kilter by their unrestrained behaviour. However, there are many elements that stand in opposition to this vision of decadence, like the *chaver* kibbutz in the top corner with his violin (a sign of spirituality and possibly a self-portrait by the artist) who is amazed by it, and the face of a distressed woman flying above who observes the scene like an alert witness. There are scenes from the Sabbath that serve as calls for an ethical ethno-religious group to hold fast to its rites, and people may rise above this scenario of uncontrolled appetites by ascending a ladder which invites them up to the celestial realm represented by the sky, which is minimized but is still there. The sheep follow their path as if nothing was going on and the shepherd who goes about his tasks is an appeal to the forces of nature and the value of work. There is also a chick hatching from an egg, a sign of the potential for rebirth and new life, and some *chaverim* continue with their daily work. Gurvich is optimistic and indicates that the world turned upside down, the *mundus inversus*, can be put to rights.

On the canvas of *Los Pecados Capitales* (The Deadly Sins) Gurvich reflects all the sins through what might be called anthropozoomorphic beings that correspond to the animal component in man's nature, his alter ego. According to legends and fables, the excesses, vices and violence of sinners are traditionally attributed to this. There are echoes of the Flemish masters and of Luis Solari, with their moral messages conveyed through anthropo-zoomorphic creations. The being that bursts through overeating is a pig, and the lustful lovers are joyful sensual kittens. Pride is useless, it is the vanity of vanities, and death waits in the mirror. At the end, after all the excesses, death is what will triumph. One day he will come to each of us and take us away in his cart, and Gurvich sets this scene in the perfect place, the winter landscape of Cerro. But he does not regard gluttony, lust or sloth with the same censure, he seems to observe them with a sarcastic smile, with a kind of compassion, with a certain amount of empathy.

Josephine Balken[6] offers her own interpretation on some of these themes, "When we consider the Christian symbols in G's work, even in a framework that is explicitly Jewish, it seems to me that at any given moment he is reflecting his intense immersion in the daily life of his existential surroundings, and this can be seen in his paintings from his stay on the kibbutz and those from Cerro and New York. It is characteristic of Gurvich that he is intensely committed to his surroundings, as can be seen in his series of "spatial" paintings.

"Gurvich constantly draws on elements that make up his reality, but what is extraordinary is his intense ability to transform what is everyday and mundane and take it to a transcendental level, to the spiritual dimension inherent to each one of us. He was a profoundly spiritual being, but was not labelled as such. He was something like a philosopher-artist or an artist-philosopher, just as Machado, could be considered a poet-philosopher or a philosopher-poet. G's spiritual dimension is also revealed in what we love about Brueghel and Bosch, that they present us with a panorama of everyday life with a wide variety of facets, but they transform it.

"In this sense, G's *Carta al hombre* (Letter to Man) paintings must be seen in the light of what he was trying to do, they were Letters *to* Man, he was transmitting his view of the world, of the space-time in which he lived, which was what his predecessors Brueghel and Bosch had done and were far more famous for. In a sense all works of art consciously or unconsciously serve as testimony. Thus G shows daily life with its numerous facets and he includes the Jewish and Christian symbols from his own Western cultural heritage and from the times he lived in. I honestly believe that if G had lived in the present day, he would have also included Muslim symbols because they now constitute part of our everyday reality in the Western world.

"It is clear that G. has strong leanings towards all that is universal. This is a reflection of his philosophical and spiritual convictions and it may also be part of the legacy from his mentor, Joaquin Torres García. But of course G changed this and made it his own. He could not do it any other way, he had to express his individuality through his search for the universal.

"The references to Brueghel, Bosch and even Chagall in his work in no way imply that he was inspired by their themes, but rather that they shared "elective affinities", as Goethe put it, since those painters also started from daily reality and built on it to achieve a spiritual or universal sense. They showed the great diversity of human conduct in their paintings, including the immoderate things and the imbalances stemming from instinct, that go to make up everyday life.

"The Greeks, who were rationalists *par excellence*, had the concept of the sin of Hubris (*hybris*), and it featured in many of their tragedies.

"Any lack of moderation, any excess of an instinct or of a form of human conduct, can be characterized as "sin" because it breaks the balance of life that is so necessary for survival, it is in a sense against ecology. This calls to mind the biological definition of life as a perpetually broken equilibrium, which also evokes the essential characteristic of life that it ends in death, the stopping of the life force that adaptive dynamism has maintained. In some cultures, diseases are considered as ruptures in the natural balance of ecological harmony.

"Another element in G's work, stemming from his position in the space-time flow of life, is the well-known ancient metaphor of the wise monkeys. And yet another is the image of blind men walking in a line as if they are tied to each other. They walk without looking, they follow the leader but cannot see the path, which is a tragic comment on people's inability to find their own paths in life. When you cannot see the world you have no choice but to follow the line.

"And since G was a very sharp and perceptive observer he could see beyond reality, he had a broader and richer perception of the world and this gave him a tremendous ability to diversify themes, styles and materials in his work.

"Einstein once said, "The most beautiful feeling in man is the sense of mystery; it is the origin of all true art, of all true science. He to whom this emotion is a stranger, he who can no longer pause to wonder and stand rapt and in awe is as good as dead. His eyes are closed."

"G was constantly in a state of admiration for the world, he had a feeling for the mystery of life, life was a constant search (the road is made by walking)."

Deadly sins and chaver kibbutz
1966
watercolour, ink on paper
13.5 x 20 cm

The seven deadly sins
1963
oil on cardboard
43 x 54 cm

Composition with deadly sins
1974
oil on cardboard
127 x 66 cm
(details on following pages)

434

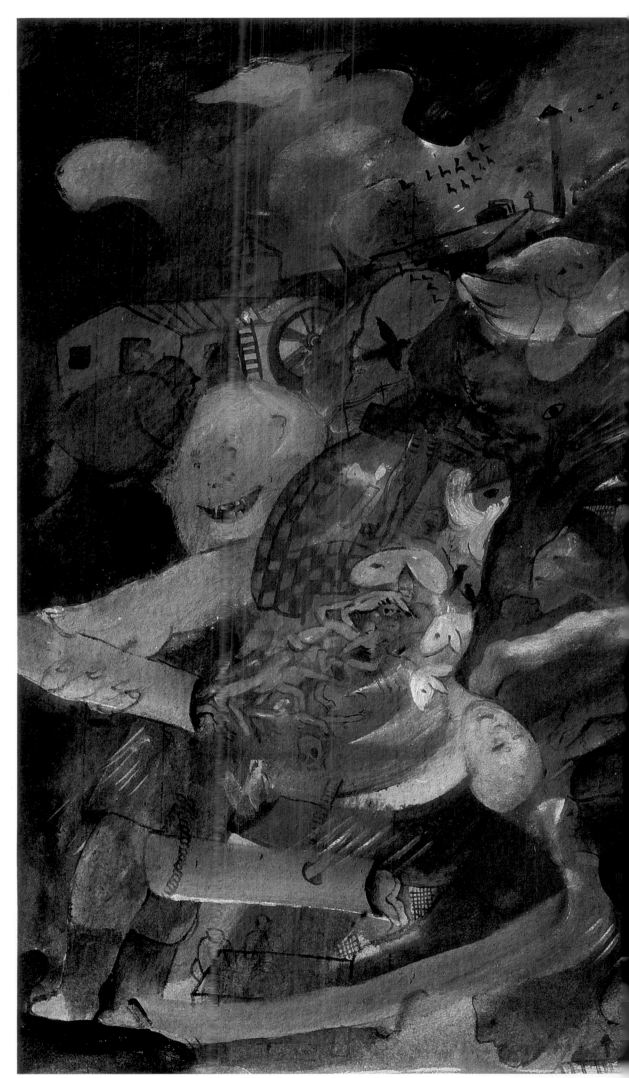

Dream on the Kibbutz
c. 1966
tempera
34 x 48 cm

Composition
1966
oil on canvas
60 x 80 cm
(details on following pages)

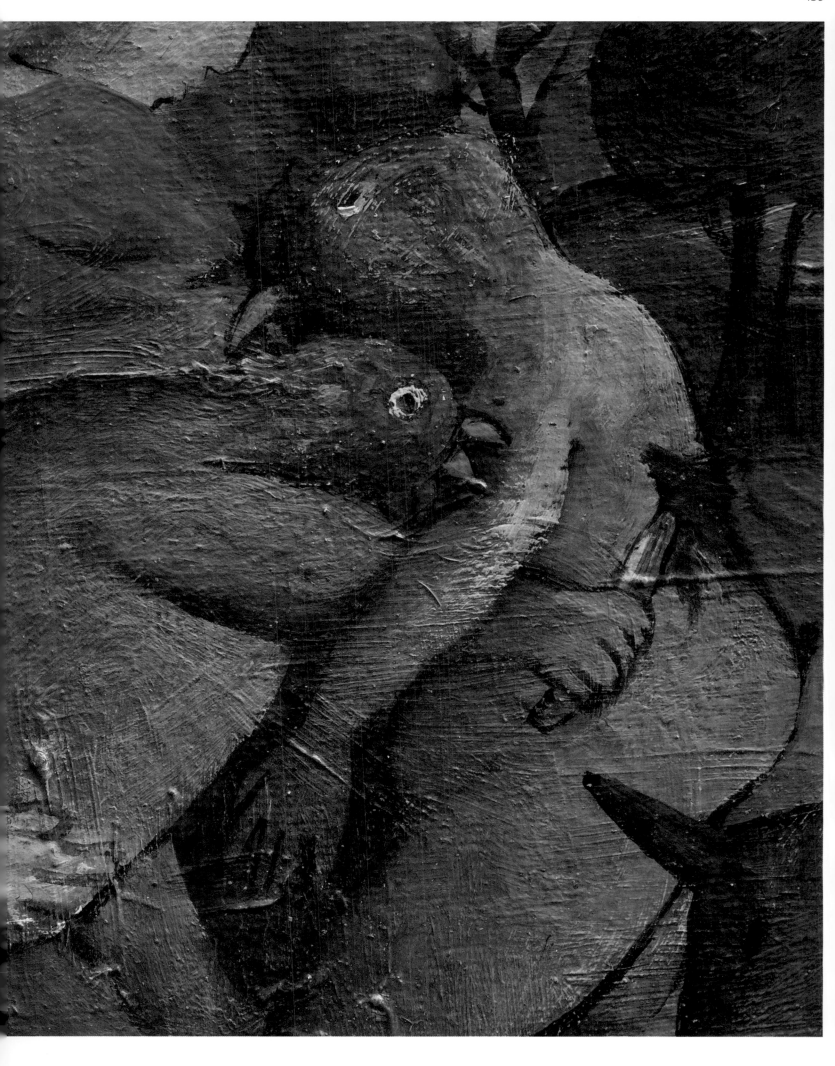

442

Lust
1966
tempera on card
35 x 48 cm
(details on following
pages)

The seven deadly sins
1967
oil on wood
30 x 42 cm

Gluttony
1968
tempera on paper
32.5 x 48 cm

End notes

1 Ziva Amishai-Maises, "The Jewish Jesus", Journal of Jewish Art, vol. 9, 1982, pp. 84-104; Depiction and Interpretation: The Influence of the Holocaust on the Visual Arts, Oxford, Pergamon, 1993, Part 2, Ch. 3, R I.

2 In his letters to his Christian Russian patrons he specifically stated that his intention was to show Christians that they were not following Jesus' doctrines when they persecuted Jews, that when they attacked Jews they were attacking Jesus himself, and that if Jesus were to return he would oppose aggressive Christianity.

3 In January 2010, an unknown work by Chagall came to light, a painting that touched on the same theme, and since then it has been at the London Jewish Museum of Art. It is a gouache from 1945. It has a Russian title that translates as Apocalypse in Lilac, Capriccio, which is in the artist's handwriting. He uses the image of Jesus on the cross as a metaphor for the Nazi persecution of the Jews. He painted it while in exile in New York. It is a brutal and disturbing picture and it shows that the artist already knew many more details of the atrocities that the Germans committed. Chagall's Jesus, like that of Gurvich, wears Jewish clothes and has Stars of David. He is wearing the Tallit, a white shawl with stripes worn by men for praying, which has fringes called taitzit – the strings and knots on it represent the 613 mizvot, the sacred commandments. He also wears the tefili or phylacteries, worn by religious people in their morning prayers

4 Unpublished writings by an Argentine professor who lives in Uruguay, Susana Poch, who kindly allowed them to be used in this publication. Poch is a professor of modern art (University of Buenos Aires). She graduated from the Jewish Masters Seminar. She specialized in Argentine Literature as a teacher at the Faculty of Philosophy and Letters (UBA) under Professor David Viñas. She was a teacher at the Written Expression Workshop for the journalism and advertising degree courses at the UBA Faculty of Communications and the University of Lomas de Zamora. She moved to Uruguay in 1993. In Montevideo she joined a research team led by Doctor Hugo Achugar at the University of the Republic (UDELAR). She is the General Workshop Coordinator and she heads a writing workshop for psychotic patients at the C.I.P.R.E.S. (Center for Investigation in Psychotherapies and Social Rehabilitation) (UDELAR). She has done research into genealogy and family history. She coordinates study groups on literature and critical readings of the Bible. She has published articles and books on many of the subjects that she has worked on.

5 Susan Poch writings: See Numbers: 16:14, Deuteronomy: 27:18 / 28:29 / Jeremiah: 31:7, Isaiah: 6:10 / 42:7, 16-19 / 35:5-6 / 43:8 / 49:9 / 56:10 / 59:9-10 / 61:1, Hosea: 6, Zephaniah: 3:5.

6 Written by Josephine Balken and sent to the author from Switzerland.

6. An open personality and free intelligence

Concentric astral man
1967
oil on canvas
121 x 91 cm

6

An open personality
and free intelligence

In 1966 Gurvich wrote,[1] "I want to open a window in nothingness, in infinite space...". In the mid-sixties he wanted to move away from moderation, circumspection and caution and see what he could win with reckless courage. This meant still working with his experiences in Israel but he brought in absurdity, weirdness, the illusory and the irrational, he was interested in enigmas and mysteries, he went far into the unknown, and he declared his specific intention to look at the world through his soul.[2] He used the eyes of the spirit, of creation and of emotion. He treasured contributions from dreams, fantasy and lyricism, he brought in more spontaneity and surprise, he fully seized his freedom, and although he had periods of doubt and uncertainty, he did this with pleasure. He once said to Totó, "I am balancing on the edge of a knife."[3] And he was successful in this new approach, which can be seen in the changes and innovations in his work.

The production he left as a legacy, the testimony in his writings, the impression he made on his colleagues and pupils, and the memory his family and friends have of him evoke someone who was open to mutation, a porous personality prepared to welcome innovation and make changes, a versatile, inquiring being, who was always making new discoveries. He was permeable, broad-minded, emancipated, anxious, always researching, always in a state of metamorphosis. His *Mundo fantástico con fondo negro* (Fantasy World with black background, 1966) is a portrait of himself with his head down and his palette and brush; he is in full creative fever and we can see his artistic turmoil, we can see he was going through transformations.

The painter Guillermo Fernández[4] remembers Gurvich as being always open to discoveries and full of high-spirits that impelled him to constantly search and explore. Fernández says the artist was surprising with his intelligent grasp of what was new and different. He was extremely versatile, he constantly brought in new colours, and he had an amazing capacity to transmute poor materials that he just picked up into works of art. And he had a very extensive repertoire, he had a passion for innovation, he could perceive and understand new languages in art and this meant he could draw on traditions other than those that he found in the work of Torres García, like the legacy of Chagall, Brueghel, Bosch, El Greco and Goya. He questioned the art of other masters and extracted answers that he could use in his own compositions. Fernández defined him as "A curious eye that could handle four thousand systems at the same time."

According to the painter Ernesto Vila,[5] Gurvich wanted to create a new aesthetic map in line with his inquiring, open-minded, eager nature and his ability to metabolize contributions from a wide range of sources. He was the very antithesis of dogmatic, Vila[6] explains, he operated mainly by intuition, by imagination, and he was a researcher, committed to freedom and infused with spontaneity. Vila[7] was stunned that he was so receptive to other aesthetic influences, so open to surprises, to what was atypical and alive. Vila[8] says Gurvich admired many artists whose work was quite unlike the TTG,[1] such as Washington Barcala, Américo Spósito, José Cúneo, Bosch, Brueghel, Miró, Klee, Chagall, Francis Bacon and Luis Solari.

His pupil Adolfo Nigro[9] recalls, "One day he said to me, "Tomorrow, wake up blue". I had shown him some of my work with a central white canvas, and Gurvich pointed out that colours were repeated, they were all the same, they were monotonous. This caused an argument, but he insisted I should break up the order. He said, "Throw shapes in all directions, change, do not be the same... paint in green, in red...". He insisted that I should not repeat myself, that I had to vary my visual solutions. He pushed me to modify reality. In Gurvich's opinion, reality ought to be created in painting. When he said "painting" he meant all the possibilities of visual arts, not only painting. When he told me "you must wake up blue", he meant "be free".

"One afternoon I was showing him my latest drawings, and what did Gurvich say? "Don't bring me so many drawings. Just do one, but put your whole life into it". And, holding the drawing in his hands, he went on, "Tear, stain, rub, soil scrape, perforate, but bring this paper to life". And he finished by saying, "A work of art is a world - put your life into it".

"Gurvich's visual language is extremely varied; he dives into space and fills it up with images released from all contingent connections. Up in the air in his dreams these images combine, and they have to combine so they can convey an energy that is ancient and at the same time very modern. He invents, he imagines his images, they precede his visual thought, they originate in reality but they do not reproduce it. Gurvich takes possession of his images until he touches their intimate essence, their substance, the other possible worlds they embody. These are images that descend from the unconscious and emerge as concrete shapes, and in so doing they become more magnificent.

"He works with small shapes that make up great extensions of colour. Sometimes these are the shapes of figures or objects in the world around us, and sometimes they are pure geometric currents. Gurvich activates the life of the land itself, its roots and its fruits, its dreams, collective dreams, the dreams of all men, and these emerge from the very centre of the artist's being and feed back all that energy into us. In his work, he unites cosmos and microcosm, man and the universe."

---

1   TTG stands for Taller Torres García (Torres García Workshop).

Figures on white
c. 1968
fresco
63.5 x 35.5 cm

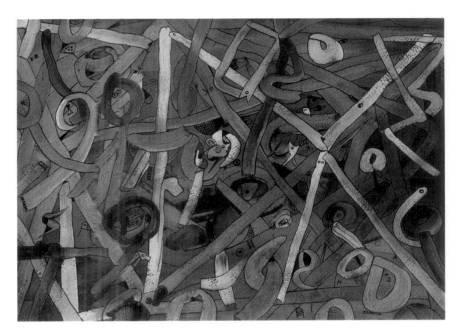

NA + 1
1967
tempera on paper
35 x 50 cm

Nigro goes on, "The Torres García Workshop was unforgettable. Gurvich read Antonio Machado to us. His experience as a shepherd on the kibbutz was crucial in the development of his work, as was his trip to Greece, whose light and whose colours he subsequently reflected in a large number of tempera paintings. We had tea and sometimes, in the evening, he played the flute.

"I remember another day, at dusk, after we had finished work, he told Drangosch and me that what would remain forever, as an example etched in our memories, was his capacity, his enormous capacity for work. He created as if he was talking, as if he was breathing, with his hands and his whole body moving freely, and with great faith in man, in nature and in the arts. He said again and again that we had to travel. That occasionally, every year or two, it was necessary to leave. That it did you good, it meant revitalizing yourself, it meant struggling against the routine of things learned.

"In those years we talked with Gurvich about so many things! He was a great talker. He moved his hands when he spoke, and now and then nodded his head. Always restless. He was interested in everything... books and movies of the time. He even wanted to know how egg tempera was made. This profound restlessness drove him to investigate things, to get deep into the unknown."

Nigro recalls how Gurvich considered it essential to seek out a variety of sources of training. He thought that the task was never finished and that we had to speculate about what was infinite. He believed that metamorphosis was indispensable, and he sought different ways, different quests and new explorations. He drifted away from theoretical limitations. He talked a lot about the dizzy whirl he was immersed in during the 1960s. He wanted to free himself. Nigro describes how he moved away from theories and canons, and chose the path of hard work, discipline, reality, fantasy and personal experience. He was very excited at novel experiences, he was very interested in seeing what happened in other territories that were not like Torres García, and this is why he went to exhibitions at the Enrique Gómez gallery, an *avant garde* artist of the time. And he was always referring to three "books", indispensable works of reference, Bruegel, Bosch, and Miró. Nigro[10] thinks Gurvich often felt that in Montevideo he did not have people who thought the way he did, he needed to see other things, and even though Torres García had enriched him and that message was important, there were other stimularts to be found, other possibilities. According to his pupils, his wife and some friends and colleagues,[11] the TTG was a phase, and Gurvich wanted to find other ways to go, other touchstones of creative stimulus. Nigro[12] remembers the way he urged his pupils to search for different sources in the history of art, he encouraged them to invent, to use many colours, to experiment with tearing, dirtying, breaking and activating surfaces, and to p ay with materials, always with a daring and lively spirit.

In one of his notebooks Gurvich wrote, "Imagination bursts, it runs frenzied through endless corridors, extracting the absurd. I'm on the brink of a silence and a void, and from it I take (by force, from leaving reason behind) a weird world. And through this I come to know, from the abundance of anguish and joy, of voices that have echoes, shapes, colours, feelings, wherever this physical experience leads... Fantasy is in disrepute, but (I yearn) to lean out into the great silence or emptiness and extract the voices yet not heard! How much imagination do I need? Then comes the work, then begins the conflict between invention and harmony, and I start putting the voices coming and going in order, grasping them, distinguishing them from the echoes...and creation starts. Creative imagination, get to work – I trust you... There is no need to see everything our eyes see, we should use them for what our soul wants to see[13].

"I have broken almost every rule," Gurvich wrote "...to find the infinite and free space...I have released the hidden energies of my spirit and I'm going along as if I had a toy in my hand. The doors of the imagination. In the beginning I leaned fearfully...then I went through...the dark night, a silence... and I started to walk in boundless space, and a new music started to emerge, new worlds appear".[14]

My voice is a chant. It is not enough for me to name all the things I have seen, perceived or imagined, I have to sing them, I feel I must transform them into melody, into song. "My art" is not a realistic testimony, it is lyrical, it is a tale, it is something I must tell, and I must invent the melody so it becomes a story told with colours and shapes. My art is pure fantasy, I want to make spiritual reality, an imperceptible, subtle reality."[15]

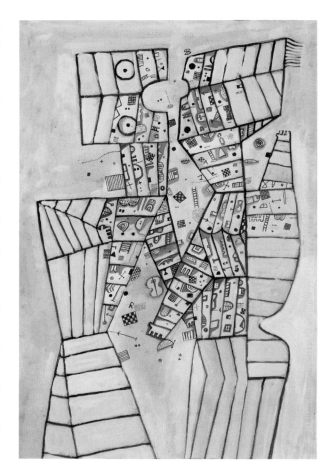

Constructed couple
c. 1966
ink, tempera on paper
50 x 34.5 cm

Kibbutz
c. 1966
tempera, watercolour on cardboard
35 x 49 cm

In the 1960s, Gurvich created, thought and wrote. In his writings, he shows how important it is to search within oneself for that heartbeat. He thought the keys to the doors to infinity are a concept, limits and intuition. Intuition is what imagines, it is the unlimited thing. He said he wanted "...to catch spontaneity in the shape, I want to open a window to nothingness, to infinite space... to give life millimetre by millimetre". He wanted to give himself over to giddiness and experimentation, to go through the doors, to let his imagination explode. His leitmotiv was "Reason shall not set limits". He thought that freedom entails an intuitive, lyrical, loving, spiritual adventure. He was interested in the subtle vibration of the soul.

In the catalogue for Gurvich's exhibition at the Comisión Nacional de Bellas Artes (National Fine Arts Commission) in May 1967, he said, "Pure play and invention go together, they are almost juxtaposed. The images in my paintings are purely poetic. Their origin: they are experiential and they come from artwork. My intention: free creative play. The man and the things are seen from inside outside. My greatest pleasure is the creative game where the freedom of the image and the freedom of space emerge. Freedom of the image creates spontaneity since there is no rational watchfulness to stop me from speculating. It is then that the free space becomes an infinite place of possibilities. Thus, I am weaving this experience with immense pleasure. If there is a free spirit, there is necessarily a free space.

"Art does not reveal the truth, it is not committed to reality, art is an invention of man and man expresses himself through it. Expression is feeling given form, and intuition is the way to get to the feeling, where reason is left out.

"I have certain paintings that were insp red by the contemplation of a ripe fruit... Contemplating deeply, identifyirg myself, living that full image of a peach or a tomato, I began to convey the golden or reddish fullness of that fruit in my painting. Fullness and intensity; that was the answer. I gave up reasoning so as to completely feel every millimetre of the canvas, to fill each artistic instant with life and rhythm in a free and infinite space of possibilities. Shapes appear spontaneously, without categories, without watchfulness, solitarily free, and colour explodes like a ripe summer fruit, and an intense and silent black isolates the shapes so their colours can sound without any rivalry, without obligaticns. They appear, shape by shape, and together they sing a song I had hidden inside me for so long.

"Concepts limit us but intuition frees us. On the verge of a concept, leaning over the edge, adventure opened up before me, and the thirst for adventure came from a pressing inner neej. In my adventure, everything was possible because I imagined everythirg. In order to find life I had to dive into the free space with just one hope: to find my own voice in the dark depths of that space. It was then that imagination ran frenzied through endless corridors, extracting an undreamed-of world, a world of adventure in which I rowed full of anguish and joy, full of voices singing the "always yet" song with echoes, shapes, colours and feelings."[16]

Nevertheless, Gurvich did not leave behind plastic construction and order; he generated dialectical relations between imagination, free creative play, discipline, fantasy, immediacy, institution, irrationality, rationality, order and rules. He worked with shape and rhythm, he took pains with details, and he always sought to preserve the whole. And he did not leave behind the important legacy of Joaquin Torres García (1874-1949), which included searching for what is essential, valuing our ancestral heritage and exploring our origins. He shared with his teacher an interest in the social and public ramifications of art, the importance of symbols, synthetic representations of the daily world, the expression of 'universality in the temporality of objects" while keeping one eye on the cosmic dimension.

Two other images that occur frequently in Gurvich's iconography are the universal man and the essential couple. He did many compositions that show how much he valued handicrafts and he kept to modest organic materials, just as Torres García had done. When his work broke free from Torres García aesthetics he continued using some of his teacher's symbols, including the golden rule, the ladder, and the numbers 1, 2 and 3, as can be seen in his 1960s and 1970s compositions. Torres García was a key teacher for Gurvich after they first came into contact in 1944, and this was intensified when Gurvich definitively joined the TTG in 1945. He was a very active member of this group, he taught in it and he took part in its most outstanding activities until it finally closed. Gurvich came away with a very marked Torres García style, but at a certain point later on he started

Rhythms of the kibbutz, detail
1966
tempera on paper
35.5 x 51 cm

Composition with ladder
c. 1965
mixed technique on kitchen board
40.5 x 24 x 7.5 cm

to explore other paths of expression and established an own language, iconography and subject matter.

When the artist, with his unusual questing nature, came into contact with the kibbutz and the spirit of Israel, this triggered new lan-

guages in his art. The Israel context was a laboratory for experiments, for unprecedented and original subjects, and new paths opened up in every direction every day.

At that time Israel was being born and different and original aspects were emerging constantly. There were new initiatives in nearly every field of human endeavour, inventions born of necessity in almost all areas. The feeling of inaugurating something momentous was in the air, that was the *zeigeist*, the spirit of the times. The watchword was innovation, and new creations were produced, new procedures were discovered, and dynamism and vitality were endemic. The Israelis were persistent, and the new pioneers planned and built and geared everything to growth.

The country was in the process of transforming, modernising and progressing in great haste, and the people were committed to drastic change and innovation. One prominent example of this was the kibbutz movement, a completely revolutionary concept that was utterly without precedent. The kibbutz initiative was adaptable to all circumstances, it was by nature flexible, it developed over time, it turned to a kind of industrialization when it had to, and at the end of the 1960s it underwent far-reaching changes and was able to take a new direction because it was not based on any dogmatic structure. What gave it energy was ideals, and they did not restrain initiative.[17] This was a perfect framework to undertake new creations, and it may be that this spirit and example was what triggered Gurvich's fledgling creative forces.

O rinnovarsi o perire

Another key trait in the artist was his openness to contributions from the masters in the history of art. He was always nourishing himself from many sources to feed his creativity, to increase his range of fantasy and to develop a new iconography. He wrote, "There is no birth without father and mother... one must have parents... and break free."[18] One of his students, the artist Lilian Lipchitz, has this to say, "Once I received a card from Israel in which he told me that I should not worry if I saw his influence in my painting. Every composition has a father and a mother."[19]

To set his fantasy free, Gurvich based himself on the work of figures that had already attracted him in books, but that now on his travels he had the chance to see in European museums, masters like Klee, Miró, Chagall, Brueghel, Bosch, Cúneo, Solari and Bezem, to mention just the most important. He gradually moved into collage with simple materials using pieces of hessian, newspapers, small shells collected at the seaside, wood, curtain fabric, wire gauze from packed cold meat and all kinds of *objets trouvé*, and this, together with a random stick-on technique, allowed him to be even more imaginative on his eventful journeys.

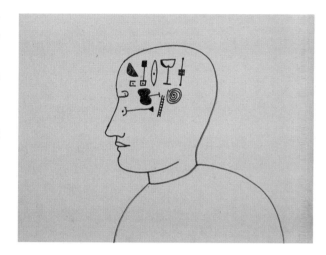

Fables II
n.d.
felt-tip pen on paper
27.5 x 35.5 cm

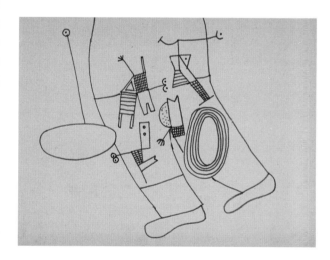

Fables
n.d.
felt-tip pen on paper
27.5 x 35.5 cm

Composition with ladder
and symbols
c. 1965
mixed technique on wood
39 x 24 x 11.5 cm

His reading of Machado caused him to reflect and doubt and move away from rigidity. Machado rejected coverings, blew away the cobwebs, attacked dogmatism and focused on achieving authenticity, on seeking a personal stamp. He delved into the labyrinths of the soul to seek what was not known. In one of his poems, he says that between living and dreaming there is a third thing, and you have to guess at it: it involves starting to discover the unknown. The poet wrote, "*O rinnovarsi o perire...*" The subjects found along this path, the path that Machado trod, the path of leaping into discoveries, of letting oneself be led and just seeing what happens, are significant in his work, and Gurvich found this fascinating. On one of his sketches he wrote a gloss to the famous poem by Machado, "I do not have a road, I make the path by walking, only Watch out! I do not look for things, I just listen attentively in case something sounds wherever..."[20] The path, the river, the smooth flow, to walk and to retrace one's steps, these things reveal a disposition to value innovation. Gurvich had a Heraclitean view of life, a view also implicit in Machado, the idea that reality is a process of becoming, that the cosmos is changing, that change is the universal constant. The fact that everything flows.

Montevideo in the 1960s was a significant factor in the changes in Gurvich and in his development of new creative freedom. The atmosphere favoured change and the search for new languages of expression. During the 1960s, Uruguay went through a period of peculiar ferment with the so-called "*Generación del 60*" (The Sixties Generation), and there was innovation and exploration in the world of the visual arts, theatre, literature and cinema, which played a leading role. These were key contributions in configuration as much as in abstraction. The expression of inner worlds developed and there was a focus on what was interior, secret, subjective and irrational. There were visual texts that encouraged communication at deeper psychic levels, and the oneiric, inner drives, the irrational and the subjective come to the fore. New artistic forms appeared, like happenings and *Arte Correo*.[21] There were exhibitions by the Uruguayan and international avant-garde.[22]

Difference and freedom

The fact that Gurvich was Jewish may have something to do with his capacity to change. To be Jewish is to be in a constant state of change. To be able to survive, the Jews had to rely on openness, amiability, flexibility, elasticity and the ability to adapt and to mutate because with their history so scarred with emigration, journeys, Diasporas, flight and persecution they often had to adjust to new contexts. They also developed the aptitude to fight against the *status quo*. And their ambiguous role of being aloof but at the same time belonging, of being both out and in, spurred them on to seek alternative ways of thinking and to generate new interpretations.

The Jews have always been insular, they lived in the margins, on the edges of cultures, in the space between cultures, and this means they have assimilated elements from many cultures, they have been in and out of many cultures, they have crossed worlds, they have been at the crossroads and they have met different challenges, they have processed new ideas and

Project: leg and arms
c. 1972
ink, watercolour on paper
26 x 19 cm

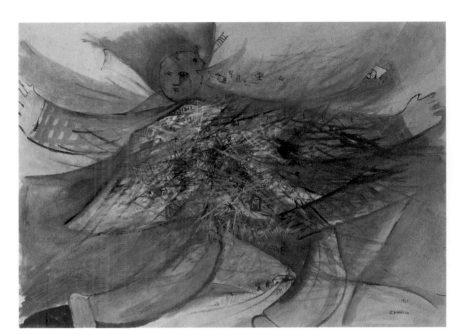

Man song
1965
tempera on paper
35 x 48 cm

incorporated new realities. They are different, in many ways this is like freedom, and this freedom is unleashed in times of change.

Another element to consider is disagreement. This is a fundamental part of teaching and reading religious texts, a discipline that has gone on for centuries, and it has left its mark on Jewish secular thinking. The methods employed in text analysis are to discuss, analyse and expand on the interpretations of the great thinkers, nothing is taken for granted and the reward is the joy of discovery. There is a need to question oneself. This tradition of polemics and openness to different answers generated a life attitude that was crucial to the ability to make changes and to challenge traditional thought.

The *Torah* and the *Talmud* change over time with new interpretations that are accepted and welcomed. Each generation should write its own commentaries on the *Torah*. Thinking is prismatic, it has an infinite variety of perspectives and is multi-dimensional.[23] Each new interpretation reshuffles the order of priorities. Some people think that, to a certain extent, to be Jewish is to search unceasingly for what is unknown and that we should try to learn all the time.

In 1926[24] Sigmund Freud wrote to the *B'nai B'rith* about his Judaism, and he said that the fact that he was Jewish was a crucial factor in the development of his research, "... it did not take long for me to realise ... that it is only to my Jewish nature that I owe the two qualities that have become indispensable to me in the difficult path of my existence. It is precisely because I am Jewish that I found myself free from many prejudices that limit others in the use of their intellect, and being a Jew I was

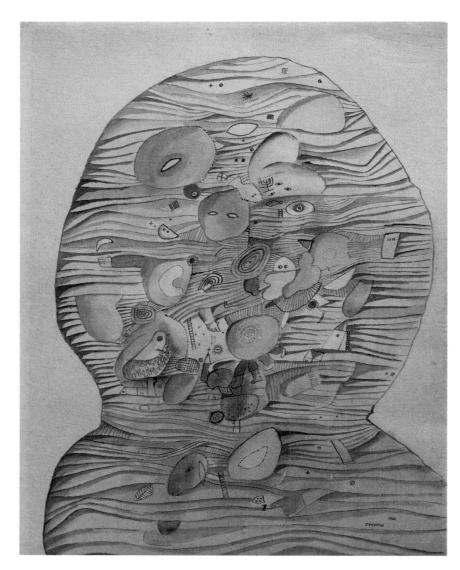

The Golem
1966
watercolour on paper
39.5 x 31.5 cm

prepared to enter into opposition against and to renounce agreement with the solid majority."

Irving Louis Horowitz[25] says, "To be marginalised is a condition that has enabled me to confront problems with the greatest objectivity." The Norwegian-US sociologist and economist Thorstein Veblen said that Jews were iconoclastic and for that reason they were very good at looking for new paths and were always pioneers in change. Raymond Aron expresses it thus, "Jews are a prolific and creative minority, largely because they are a minority. Among the best of them, the status of being in a minority is accompanied by the self-questioning that might be called restlessness." Like foreigners who have been forced to move between two worlds, the Jews have always had to consider questions and problems, and they often ended up analysing society in general. They have had to go beyond themselves, to transcend social conformism and to question the world and open it up for change.

Construction
c. 1961
oil on cardboard
41 x 51 cm

Spiral construction
1960
oil on cardboard
42 x 54 cm

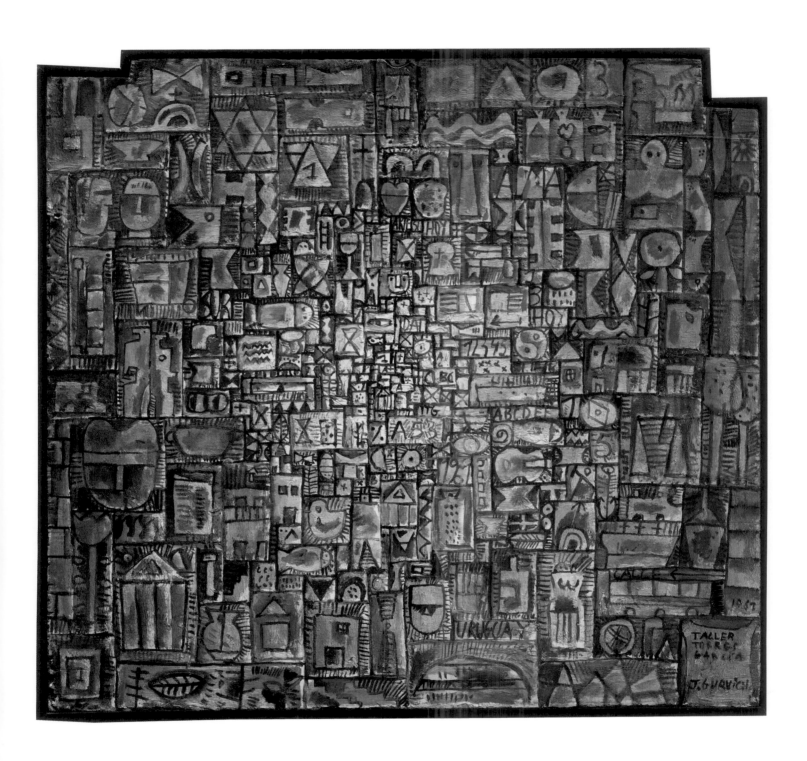

Construction
1961
oil on wood
40 x 42 cm

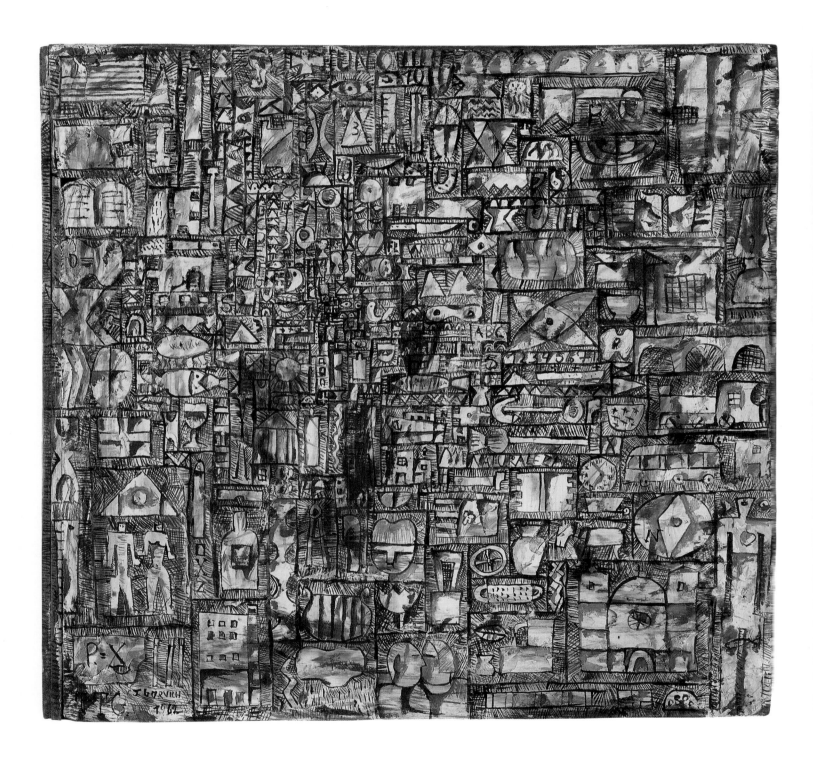

Rhythm
1962
enamel on incised wood
35.5 x 38.5 cm

Composition with circle
1961
oil on cardboard
39 x 50 cm

474

Forms, symbols and images
1967
oil on canvas
61 x 80 cm

Kibbutz rhythms
c. 1967
oil on cardboard
38 x 50 cm

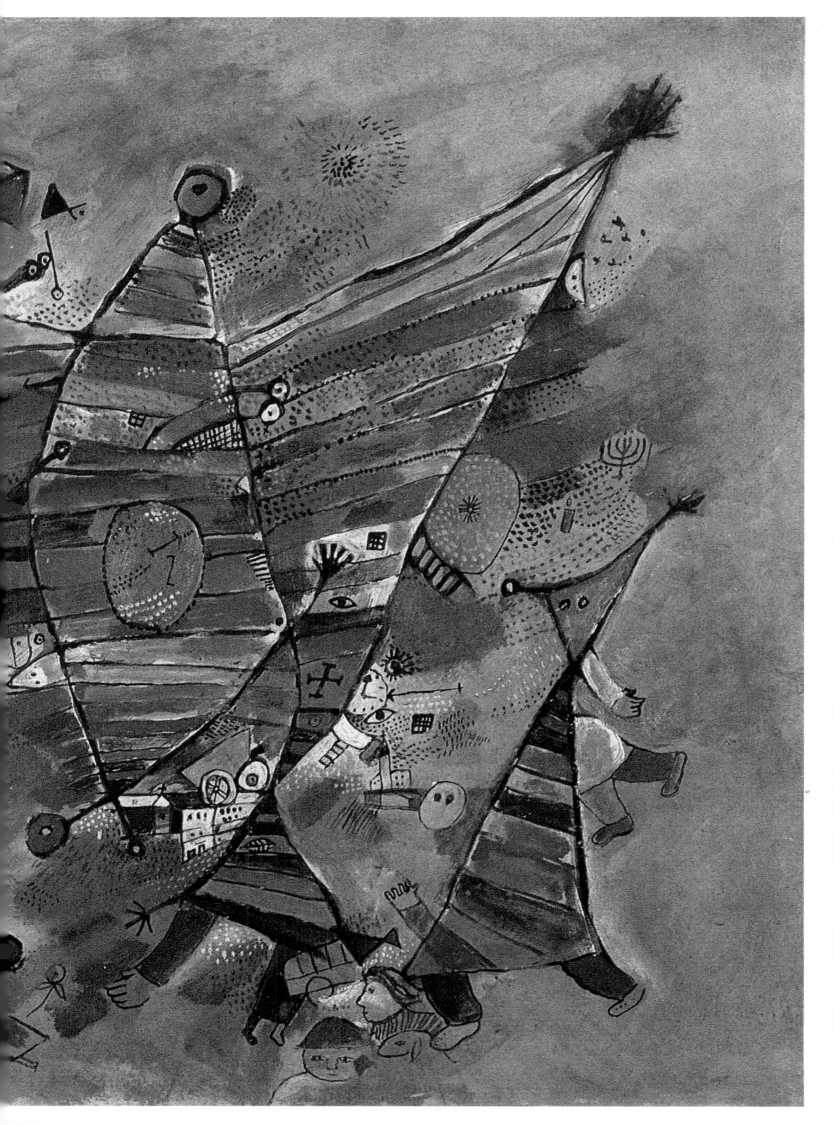

478

(on following pages)
World of forms, symbols and images
1968
tempera on paper
35 x 51 cm

Kibbutz heritage in fantasy world
(with celestial sphere *of Bereshit*, Genesis)
1968
oil on canvas
80 x 99 cm

Forms with perspective
1967
tempera on paper
50.5 x 35 cm

Peasant in his dream world
1967
collage on plaster
40 x 31 x 3.5 cm

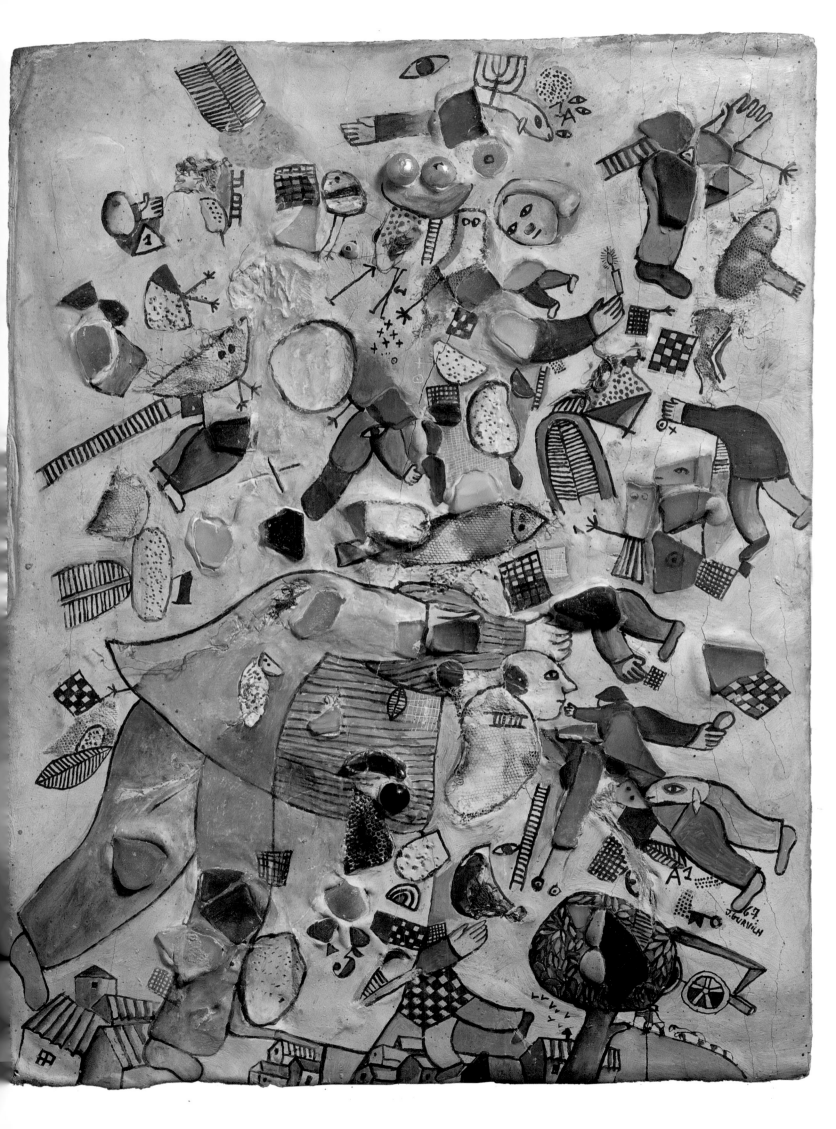

Faith and city
1971
tempera or paper
49 × 61 cm

The world of New York I
1971
oil on canvas
79 x 100 cm

Cosmos with perspective (with menorah)
1966
ink, watercolour on paper
33 x 47.5 cm

N.Y.
1971
watercolour, ink on paper
21 x 13.5 cm

Project for monument iv with bridge

1972

tempera on card

36 x 44 cm

Collage with hand
1972
collage on wood
35.5 x 35.5 cm

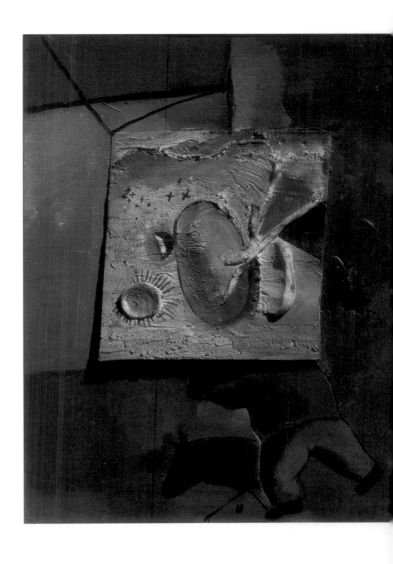

Triptych
1972
mixed technique on wood
27 x 63 cm

End notes

1   Alicia Haber, El mundo íntimo del artista, op. cit.

2   Artist's writing , undated, Gurvich family files.

3   Interview with ulia Morga (Totó), September 199 .

4   Interview with Guillermo Fernández, September 199 . Interview with Guillermo Fernández by Santiago Tavella, 2003, in a book by Alicia Haber and Cecilia de Torres, op. cit.

5   Ernesto Vila was his student and got to know him closely between 1959 and 1964. He has turned out to be an excellent source to better understand the singularities of Gurvich's personality. Numerous interviews conducted by the author with Vila.

6   Ibidem.

7   Ibidem.

8   Ibidem.

9   Text sent to Alicia Haber by Argentine artist Adolfo Nigro, June 2003. Nigro wrote this text, along with others, in 1983. In *Página 12*, in an article entitled "José Gurvich: un espacio imaginario" Nigro also tells of his first meeting with Gurvich in 1966, and how he saw him conceive and paint pieces between that year and 1969. Adolfo Nigro, "José Gurvich: un espacio imaginario", Buenos Aires, *Página 12*, p. 7. He wrote Allá en el Cerro, 1983.

10 Adolfo Nigro, Allá en el Cerro.

11 Ibidem.

12 Ibidem.

13 Artist's writings, undated, Gurvich family files.

14 Ibidem.

15 Ibidem.

16 José Gurvich. Text written by the artist for the Catalogue fo his exhibition at the National Fine Arts Commission, Solis Theatre, Montevideo, May 1969. Quoted in the brochure of the Gustavo Tejeria Loppacher Gallery, Punta del Este, Uruguay.

17 Ernest Krausz (editor), Sociology of the kibbutz, op. cit.

18 Artist's writings, undated, Gurvich family files.

19 E-mail interview, November 21, 2009.

20 Alicia Haber, El mundo íntimo del artista, op. cit.

21 Some of the creators of that period were Germán Cabrera, Manuel Espínola Gómez, Luis Solari, Jorge Damiani, Clarel Neme, Nelson Ramos, Américo Spósito, Jorge Páez, Lino Dinetto, Leopoldo Novoa, Juan Ventayol, Hilda López, José Cuneo, José Gamarra, Washington Barcala, Raúl Pavlotzky, Teresa Vila, Clemente Padín, and the members of the so-called "El Dibujazo" (The Grand Drawing): Eugenio Darnet, Hugo Alíes, Nelson Avdalov, Álvaro Armesto, Marta Restuccia, Jorge Satut, Jorge Páez, Hermenegildo Sábat, Agustín Alamán, to mention just a few key figures.

22 Organized by the El País Centre of Arts and Letters (1959-1966), the 2nd Fair of the El País Centre of Arts and Letters and the exhibitions of the General Electric Institute (1963-1969).

23 Daniel J. Elazar, Bereshith: "A Political Commentary, Introduction: Why Another Commentary? ", Jerusalem, Centre for Public Affairs. http://www.jcpa.org/dje/articles2/bereshithpolcom.htm

24 Paul Mendes-Flohr (editor), Jehuda Reinharz (editor), The Jew in the Modern World: A Documentary History, Oxford, Oxford University Press, 1995.

25 Edited by Howard Wettstein, Diasporas and Exiles, Varieties of Jewish Identity, California, University of California Press, 2002.

7. Uruguay, Israel: identities

Uruguay, Israel: identities

Gurvich was very Uruguayan and very Jewish. He was a real Uruguayan with his roots deep in the country, his intense love for this land (especially for Montevideo and Cerro), his integration into the community in a variety of spheres, his work and his contribution to Uruguayan culture, his commitment to Uruguayan art, his friends in many circles, his devotion to his teaching and the fact that he adopted many of the ways of being Uruguayan.

He had a very intense bond with Joaquin Torres García, he was one of the master's favourite students and one of his most notable followers. He had a key role in the Torres García Workshop and his compositions in the Torres García style are quite outstanding. Besides this, he has bequeathed a rich legacy to Uruguayan and Latin American art, a vast and diverse inheritance that extends its boundaries.

Gurvich, like all Jews who migrated to Uruguay, inserted successfully into the Uruguayan identity. But he jealously guarded his Jewish identity too, and he became an excellent representative of Uruguayan-Jewish culture. He found various answers to aspects of the ambiguous structure of his identity and he passed them on in numerous ways. He made his choices. He always defined and identified himself as Jewish, and in his own unique way he dug into the traditions of his people.[1] He was Jewish and he followed his own personal path, like many Jews have done in the modern age.

There are many options and many ways to be a Jew. The historian Irwin Wall[2] says there is not only one correct form of the Jewish identity. Throughout history, a whole range of varieties have blossomed, and each of these ways to live life has changed and is still changing. According to the sociologist Sergio Della Pergola,[3] even in more traditionalist times the Jews were never monolithic. And this variety is more evident than ever in our modern age. There is no meta-narrative that encompasses the notion of being Jewish; it depends on historical contexts and numerous factors.

The basic definition would be that a Jew is someone whose mother is Jewish or who has converted to Judaism, but beyond that there are many different ways to be a Jew. Judaism is polyphonic. The Uruguayan sociologist Rafael Porzecanski[4] explains, "As much in the past as now, there have been remarkable variations in the specific forms to develop that identity, depending on different social and biographical configurations."[5] Porzecanski also notes that "Jewish history itself teaches us that we are in the presence of a dynamic identity and a human group,

Constructed mural in bas-relief
c. 1963
plaster
150 x 200 cm

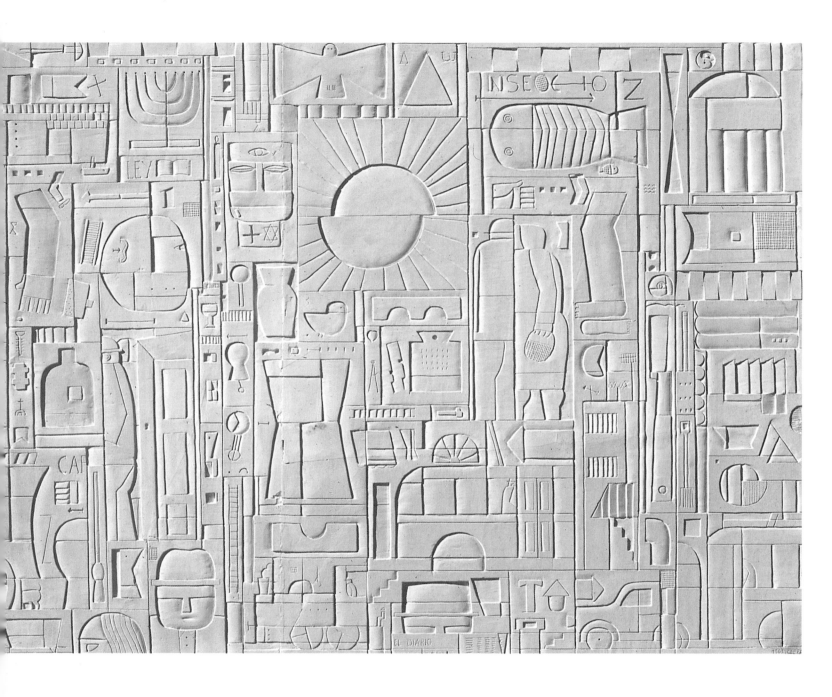

Construction with menorah
n.d.
plaster bas-relief
30 x 24 cm

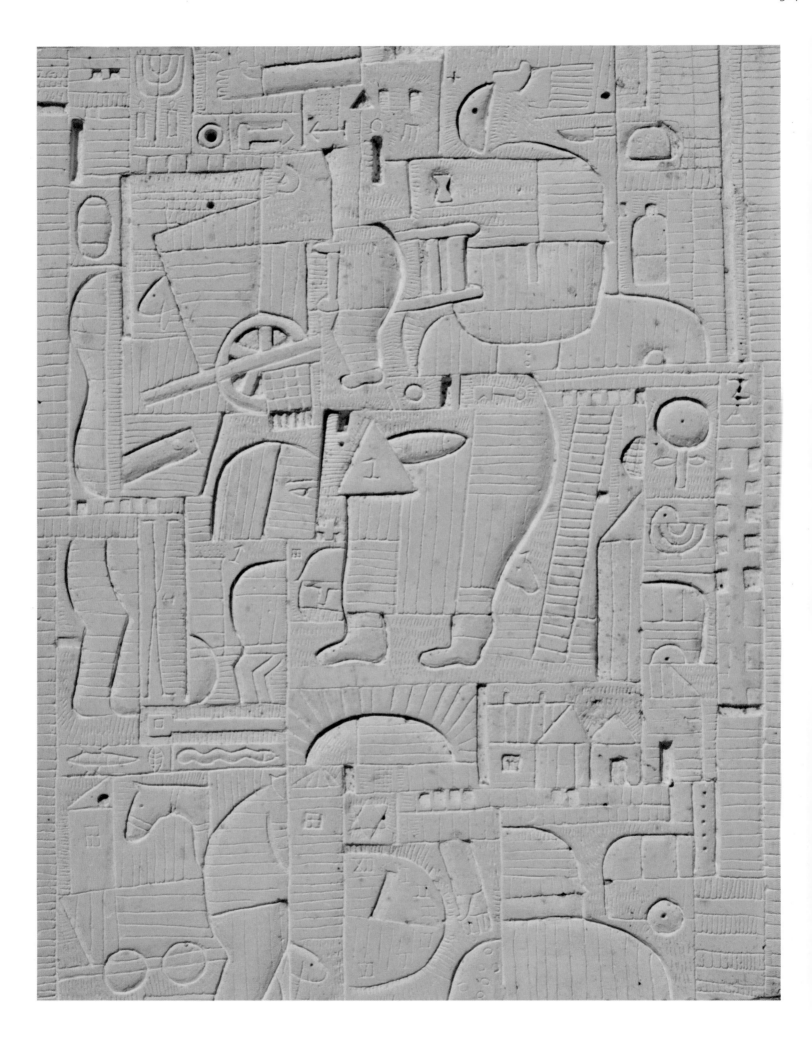

that is to say there is a process of constant transformation in accordance with a whole range of circumstances and historical contingencies." F. Ringelheim says that Jewish identity "Now less than ever can be locked up in a definition."[6] Régine Azria thinks that Judaism has recently revitalised its legacy "...with a new and privileged field of work in the exhumation of everything that makes up Jewish memory."[7] Norbert Elías reflects on the fact that individuals are never finished, they are permanently under construction.

Gurvich grasped many aspects of his Jewishness while in Montevideo and uncovered many others when he went to Israel. He lived at a time when Judaism first became a matter of personal decision, it began to flow freely, and since then it has come into the realm of the so-called culture of choice. He chose to remain in the bosom of his people. US sociologist Norman Linzer[8] maintains that in a culture of options, the Jewish identity has been in constant flux over time and down through the generations, and it can be considered as an interface between religion, ethnicity, politics and nationality, in the context of social change. If one wishes to maintain one's Jewishness there are a variety of options, one can be religious, or work in the local community, or establish links with Israel, or devote oneself to culture, or join groups that nurture their belongingness through shared interests, customs, rites or artistic languages. People can express their Jewishness in art, in essays or in literature, and they can preserve, deepen and communicate knowledge through teaching and research. It is possible to go different ways, or all ways at the same time. And Gurvich decided to take some of these paths.

If you ask a Jew about his identity he will surely have a whole miscellany of answers. The subject of Jewish identity is complex and many different definitions have been proposed. US psychologist David Arnow thinks there is more than one way to approach the question, there is no one single analytical framework.[9] He says that Jewish identity has never been definitively fixed, it is always subject to change from the inside as well as from the outside. Jewish identity is made up of a series of choices, it is fluid.[10] Gurvich's life is an excellent example of this characteristic.

According to the French sociologist Dominique Schnapper,[11] the Jewish identity has always been unfinished and in the process being reformulated, and this is a constant process of construction that is still going on today. It has many levels or dimensions: individual and collective, private and public, national and transnational, legal, religious and cultural, and each reflects the priorities and concerns of a different situation or period in history. She sees it as a variable that it is built up in response to historical conditions. There are so many origins, practices, reference points and connections with Judaism that it is difficult

to give a single definition. Schnapper emphasises the will of each individual to continue asserting themselves, the wish to recognise each other as sharing a common history, to be included among the Jews of the world and of history, and to declare themselves as belonging to this people. In Della Pergola's opinion, "Someone that recognizes himself as a Jew is Jewish. It is a feeling that turns into attitude and action in a thousand and one different ways."[12] The basic element is to choose to be Jewish, to feel Jewish, this is the determining factor. It is essential to look for your roots. And Gurvich did just that.

The Argentine writer, essayist and educator Jaime Barylko expresses it in the following way, "A Jewish person –the minimal definition– is someone who perpetuates the past, who preserves certain messages that have come down through the generations, who carries a pledge that their parents tacitly entrusted to them when identifying them as

Composition with menorah, symbols and chaverim
at Ramot Menashé
1964
watercolour w/Indian ink on paper
16 x 21 cm

Jewish. A Jew is not someone who is but someone who continues to be. That is what the man is, the successor of the man."[13]

Religious Jews believe that it is essential to profess the faith and practice its precepts, but others believe in a religiosity and spirituality that is independent of doctrine or religious rules. For many Jews today faith is an option, they may be practicing or not, so to be religious is not a defining characteristic. There are many lay Jews all over the world who are intensely committed to being Jewish but are not religious, as is very common in Uruguay, for example. And this is what Gurvich was, a secular Jew.

In the modern age the Western world is becoming increasingly secular, religion has been declining among vast swathes of the human race, and the link between religion and ethnicity has to a large extent been severed. Rafael Porzecanski[14] points out that in today's world there are many secular Jews who still respect the customs and observe the festivals, who reinterpret rituals of religious origin by practicing some basic identifying rites like circumcision, *Bar Mitzvah* (a boy's thirteenth birthday) and who have their weddings and funerals in the traditional way. Some people doubt the value of this religious heritage, but during these rites and celebrations, and even when just entering a synagogue, a secular person is moved with a feeling of belonging and of sharing a common past.

People can adopt different stances, like those of Emmanuel Lévinas, André Neher, Léon Ashkenazi, Eliane Amado Levy-Valensi. And people can become involved in speculative dialogue between modern thinking and the wealth of traditional texts, and thus help to restore interest in universal Judaism in its philosophical dimensions, to emphasize identity. Universalism and particularism converse with each other.

The philosopher Emmanuel Lévinas[15] puts his faith in the study of several disciplines including history and above all ethics and the *Talmud*. In this way, he looks for contributions passed on to us in the high moral lessons of traditional Judaism, such as the need to be responsible and the messages of social justice, and these can be shared with people in the modern world and serve to renew a sense of Judaism.

André Neher says. "The Jews are constantly eluding a definition of Jewish identity, whatever that may be, and this definition can never apply to all Jews without exception... there are so many divisions and contrasts that it is difficult to find a universal definition of Jewish identity."[16] Neher leans towards the religious path linked to universal thinking and Zionism. He thinks a Jew is the being seen by God. He asserts that to live the life of a Jewish person is not a disgrace but a privilege, a harsh kind of happiness. When he re-reads the Bible he finds the reflection of his life in a mirror, and he eventually stops having the distressful feeling of being alone: he has a companion. Neher brings biblical texts into modern life and he supports Zionism and the belief in the return to the land of Israel. The State of Israel represents the Jew's hope. With the birth of Israel "... death, which was so real in the genocide, was transmuted into life, absurdity became hope, catastrophe became redemption, and suffering became action." Neher's ultimate response to the question of identity is *Aliyah*: to live in Israel.

Since 1948 a new form of Jewish identity has come to the fore; politicisation through Zionism and support for Israel from a secular as well as a religious perspective. According to the Israeli sociologist Shmuel Noah Eisenstadt,[17] the creation of the State of Israel affected the consciousness of Jewish communities throughout the world and wrought a change in the definition of Judaism, which had hitherto been strictly religious. The political ingredient in identity has now acquired fundamental importance, as have the bonds between all the communities and their bonds with Israel.

Before World War II, the French intellectual Raymond Aron was not interested in himself as a Jew. It was Hitler that made him realize he was Jewish. And then he really understood the pride of being Jewish and he leaned towards Judaism because of the powerful impact the foundation of the State of Israel, and above all the Six-Day War, had on him. "The possibility that the State of Israel might eventually be destroyed hurts me deep down in my soul... Even if he has lost his faith, a Jew should not be unconcerned about the destiny of Israel." Thus Aron analyzed and felt all the paradoxical facets of Judaism.

Outstanding analysts including the French sociologists Régine Azria[18] and Shmuel Trigano[19] and their US colleague Irving Louis Horowitz[20] have stressed the importance of the State of Israel in the definition of Jewish identity. And the French rabbi Yéhouda Léon Ashkenazi, better known as Manitou,[21] agrees. He thinks it is a mistake to define Judaism as a religion and that Jewish identity is defined as a people, a people that have a religion, the Jewish religion. In his opinion, the most important thing is the identity of the people and the land that houses them, Israel, where the teachings of the *Torah* can be revived. This dimension of identity is tied to their Hebrew past, their valiant history that is so rich and is related to the Hebrew future. Israel the Jew has found a shelter, he is at home. A history that has yet to come to pass starts there: the identity of the Hebraic nation. In that context he devoted himself to the study and teaching of the Bible on an academic level, with a modern conception and universal scope, combining contemporary culture and orthodox tradition.

Other figures in French thinking such as Vladimir Jankélévitch, Robert Misrahi, Albert Memmi and Vladimir Rabi identify with Judaism and its symbols but not with the religion: their approach to understanding Jewish existence is intellectual.

The Tunisian writer Albert Memmi thinks that being a Jew constitutes a *raison d'être*, a way to experience the world, a whole complex of relations with others and with oneself. It is not a choice; it is an obligation, a feeling towards other Jews. The Jew's fate, whether he is lauded or humiliated, depends on the behaviour of all Jews. When he hears that the Jews in Iran are threatened with death, he too trembles at the thought of death; he is concerned about the fate of all the Jews in the world. He says that the fate of any Jew is inextricably connected with the State of Israel, and even if he doubts and condemns some of its acts he cannot question its existence.[22] Memmi is not against religious rites, he thinks they contribute to group unity and mark the rhythms of time. But he does condemn their sacralisation, the fact that rabbis present themselves as being the spokesmen of God. He rejects clerical answers, he does not think "That a God can give him peace and soothe his worries." He sees the Bible as an excellent book, but when it comes to being a Jew other things are more important, and these include the bond with the State of Israel.[23]

Besides these views there are many others from a whole range of very diverse thinkers.[24] Porzecanski is of the opinion that Jews have one memory, one consciousness and one belief in a common origin. They have developed practices and symbols of their own that are related to their distinct faith, they have institutions and religious rituals, they acquire identity through procedures based on ethnicity, and they defend their right to have political independence in a specific territory, which is Israel. These religious, ethnic, and national aspects are distinctive, but Porzecanski makes it clear that the above-mentioned definition is a matter of historical contingency.[25]

It is clear there is a varied spectrum of possibilities and ways to comprehend and live being Jewish, and this enhances our understanding of the choices Gurvich made. To be Jewish in today's world means to be porous, as Gurvich was, and also like him to be full of tension about the ambiguities, to be involved in complicated situations and to live a life full of subtle nuances. Gurvich did not need to profess faith, practice religion or speak about Judaism like so many of his co-religionists. He harboured his Judaism in his being and he expressed it throughout his life in numerous ways. His art, after he first went to Israel and for the rest of his life, is excellent proof of this intrinsic condition. His genuine and all-embracing Jewish feeling is concentrated in his art, he carried it within him and it came out very strongly in Israel where the whole accumulation of his experiences fused together. There was the Lithuanian *shtetl*, the immigrant neighbourhood in Montevideo, friends in the Jewish community, *chaverim* on the kibbutz and the powerful emotional bond with his mother. His feelings of loyalty and love for his mother, and the whole package of Jewish identity that he

Forms, symbols and images, detail

inherited from her and treasured in that relation that lit up both their lives, had enormous weight in him as a man and in his art. His early years in the family greatly influenced how he constructed his Jewish identity. This was the inter-generational transmission of experiences, the implanting of experiences that were to be reinforced later in his life. It is the value of these experiences that Norbert Elías emphasizes so much.

Arnow,[26] on the other hand, emphasises the psychodynamic model: Gurvich's life experiences in his early childhood and his precocious interaction with his parents. Other factors Arnow thinks were important are Gurvich's earliest memories of the rituals, the feeling in his family and group that they were vulnerable, members to a minority, suffering discrimination and living in an anti-Semitic environment.

Gurvich had a wealth of experiences to feed his ethnic belongingness. Jews usually find the meanings of their identity in the family, and Gurvich benefited from that situation from his childhood and learned the various codes from his mother, his father and his sister. He treasured the memories of his home where religious precepts were observed and the traditional Jewish festivals were celebrated. According to Judaism experts Steven M. Cohen and Arnold M. E sen,[27] "These memories can be seen as repositories of nostalgia and idealization that served to anchor the identity." They leave strong imprints that are difficult to erase because unforgettable smells, flavours, and sounds bring them back. The food associated with celebrations plays a crucial role in Jewishness. There are studies about this, and also a rich folklore, and empirical tests that show how much ethnic food and the flavours of our past are associated with warmth and affection in our childhood homes, and this affects out thinking when the time comes to define our identity. Ethnic food is particularly important in Jewish homes be-

Couple in room with symbols
1966
oil on canvas
55 x 75 cm

cause there are so many festivals and each involves a wide variety of special dishes. Sociologists and anthropologists have verified this, and those of us who were in that situation know it from experience. Gurvich felt this and he delighted in it because of what his home was like and the kind of person his mother was.

The anthropologist Joël Candau[28] emphasises how crucial the nexus between diet and the notion of personal and family identity is, since there is an extremely strong connection between sensorial experience and memory. He asserts that in fact "Memory is where the perception of our identity lies. Customs at family meals are very important, they build a memory of tastes and smells that often last more than twenty years. I believe they are the most tenacious and persistent preferences we have." This happens mainly when the food is home-cooked and everything is prepared in accordance with traditional methods, with plenty of time, and this is the way it was decades ago, in the times of our mothers and grandmothers. During Gurvich's childhood, adolescence and youth, for example, what was special was not only what his mother cooked, it was that there was always the smell of food in the house because everything was cooked at home and those aromas were peculiar to *Ashkenazi* kosher dishes. There was what Candau calls a "smell environment", and that atmosphere stimulated identity and later on helped to reinforce sensory memories.[29]

Candau lays great emphasis on family memory as the organizing principle of identity, a notion he bases on studies by Anne Muxel and Joëlle Bahloul.[30] The repetition of certain rituals, meals, and celebrations, and preserving knowledge, references, memories, smells and recipes are intangible inheritances, essential dimensions of the feeling of belonging and of fidelity to a heritage. Candau believes these things mobilise the functions of "...reviving and reflecting..." and that through family memory there is a "...learning of alterity. And it is not possible to leave this inheritance behind."[31] This explains why Gurvich always clung to his roots.

Candau[32] asserts that in order to develop a feeling of belonging it is necessary to have the capacity to "...propose sufficiently explicit and comprehensible *memorizable structures*." Many peoples have done this. The Jewish tradition of story-telling (which has been studied by Joëlle Bahloul), with its wealth of tales, legends and memories transmitted and elaborated at length, channels persistent representations, beliefs and opinions, and shapes "...narrative models for the reconstruction of experience through memory." Gurvich was a repository of these *memorizable structures*.

And there are other elements as well.[33] According to Freud there are dimensions of Jewish identity that are beyond the reach of analysis. In 1926 he wrote for B'nai B'rith,[34] "I must confess that what bound me to Judaism was not belief and not national pride. I have always been a non-believer; I was brought up without any religion, though not without respect for what is called the ethical standards of human civilization... Yet, this was still enough to make the attraction of Jewry irresistible for me. There were powerful emotional forces, obscure powers, so strong they could not be expressed in words, the clear consciousness of an intimate identity, the secret familiarity that goes with having the same mental architecture..." What is at work here is the shared thing that is sometimes indefinable but which so many of Gurvich's friends mention, that Jewish feeling that Freud[35] spoke of which comes from intense, intimate, personal inner forces. Freud described it as "That something in common, a certain miraculous thing that is beyond the grasp of analysis and which is common among Jews."[36]

It was a feeling like this that united Gurvich with the musician Leon Biriotti, for example. As the composer[37] proudly said, "Even though we were both Jews, we never talked about politics or religion. He preserved much of the feeling of being Jewish within him - I'm not talking about religion here - and this shows up in many of his paintings, even in the two which he did especially for me."[38] It is hard to explain this kind of feeling, it has to do with belonging, it is the result of a very profound life experience.

Raymond Aron, who was not a religious person, was another who had these obscure, unfathomable, inexplicable feelings that go beyond reason, and he said he could not and did not want to relinquish his Judaism[39] or his love for Israel, even though he always retained his capacity for independent judgement and criticised Israeli policies when he thought they were wrong.

Gustav Andauer,[40] a secular Jewish-German anarchist, spoke of an inalienable spiritual sensitivity. He felt Judaism in his expressions, in everything he was and everything he did. He believed that Judaism is not an external accident but an internal property that transforms a number of individuals into a community. He liked his Judaism, it was a valuable possession.

Isaiah Berlin said his Jewish roots were so deep that he could not consider, analyse, or identify them; his Jewish identity was part of him. He was a secular person, well integrated into England and with a strong Russian identity, and he roamed freely between all those identities, which were quite separate from political ones. He declared that there were many ways to be Jewish and that nobody had the right to force the "glorious variety of human beings" to choose one from among so many possibilities.

Gurvich also felt the unifying and common elements, the effect of the inter-generational relationships that maintained continuity, and the powerful influence of his identity being so ancient. He was part of

Festival on the kibbutz
c. 1966
tempera on paper
26 x 34 cm

Menorah
c. 1966
gouache on cardboard
33 x 47 cm

Hanukkah
c. 1967
tempera on paper
34 x 48 cm

Couple kissing
1969
oil on canvas
59 x 79 cm

an ethno-cultural community with a strong bond to the past that had endured for thousands of years, and he cultivated this historical group memory, he was conscious of this sense of group belonging and common ancestry, it encouraged him, he shared its symbols and he valued its traditions and culture. He shared in a series of beliefs and values that enabled him and his co-religionists to explain themselves and explain the world. There was an ever-changing tradition within his reach and he knew how to make good use of it. Besides this, he took full advantage of the wealth of knowledge, experiences, feelings, interests, purposes, and ethical and moral aims in this tradition.

Someone who feels Jewish, as Gurvich did, feels that he belongs to a widespread family.[41] There is a *historical family-ism*, as Charles Liebman and Cohen (1990)[42] put it, an indescribable kinship with other Jews in the world. Eliezer Ben-Rafael[43] says that although Jews do not give similar answers to the same questions, they always ask themselves the same questions: here is a "family resemblance".

There were many subtle elements in Gurvich's personality, a kind of sensitivity, a type of humour, something in his expression: not everything was categorical. All the people interviewed for this book emphasise Gurvich's Jewish humour and how much he loved humorous books like those by Shalom Aleichem.

As we have seen from Gurvich's life, identity is a construction, it is not a fixed entity but rather something that modifies and redefines itself. It is not something given, it produces and it reproduces. And when in comes into contact with the identities of other people and interacts with them it changes. It is modified by many influences, what one reads, where one travels, where one lives, and by the complex social, political, cultural, technological and economic contexts along the way. Candau[44] believes that identity is a social construct that is constantly being re-defined within the framework of a particular identity strategy. Individuals make their choices, they have a flexible and open repertoire of resources, representations, myths, stories, beliefs, rites, learning, things inherited, and they always maintain a dialogue with this other side. In Candau's opinion, each human being "...builds his identity in the course of a time frame that alters it in an irreversible way."[45]

Antonio Machado felt that in our essential nature we are multiple beings; there are different *me's* in each human being. He said the ego is formed through interaction with other people and he believed in the "Essential heterogeneity of the being," as he put it in his writings[46].

The Lebanese writer Amin Maalouf[47] believes that identity is neither monolithic nor static, it is built up throughout our lives in a series of changes, it is free flowing, multiple and malleable, and often it is composed of conflicting elements. Rafael Porzecanski[48] agrees and says that "Jewish history itself shows that what we have before us is a dynamic identity and human group, this means it is in a process of constant transformation in response to numerous circumstances and historical situations."[49]

Each person has many affinities and makes alliances with people with different positions and different personal histories. Diana Meyers,[50] asserts that we now talk about identities and not a single identity, and we mean multiple or intersecting identities. Another writer who has interesting things to say on this point is Giddens.[51]

Peter Burke[52] explains that there is no univocal or immutable identity, we have manifold identities, and we go on discovering more throughout our lives. In a certain situation one or more is triggered. He thinks that identities meet and interact when people meet and interact. We have identities that are activated, and those that stand out are those that become active with greater intensity and establish themselves. The most prominent ones, those with a greatest degree of commitment, lead the rest and dictate our behaviour in a certain situation.

In line with this view we can say that an individual like Gurvich found his Jewish identities interacting with the *chaverim* on the kibbutz and his Israeli friends, and this activated his Jewish identities in Israel. His life and work clearly show he had multiple identities and he went on constructing them as time went by and as circumstances changed.

In fact, some people hold that the Jewish world was always more heterogeneous than is commonly thought, and this great range of regional, cultural, religious, and linguistic differences is a feature of Israel even when the ethos of the nation-state was at its peak and the ideal was to have a melting pot and bring about homogeneity.[53] The Israeli sociologist S. N. Eisenstadt[54] observes that individual cultural inheritances from different communities have always resisted homogenization and that today this old goal is no longer valid.

The London-born philosopher Kwame Anthony Appiah,[55] who is of Ghana and British descent, asserts that the interplay between different traditions is important and enriching, and it brings people into contact with others who are completely different. Della Pergola finds positive features in those multiplicities because he believes that closed identities are limited.[56] He emphasizes how individual and local characteristics are coming to the fore and trans-national identities are being formed.

And this question is not only a matter of the Jews. Amin Maalouf[57] is an Arab Christian who lives in Paris, writes in French, feels an affinity for French culture, is in contact with Muslims and has a great cultural heritage from his country of origin. He decided to live his life from a position of multiple identities and accept his two countries, his three languages and his various cultural traditions. Maalouf[58] says he has not made a choice; he lives like a Lebanese and a Frenchman, he is both the one and the other, he freely accepts the fact that he belongs to both worlds, he is many things simultaneously, and the complexity and wonder of his myriad belongings are of great value for him. He defines identity as the egalitarian multiplicity of several states of belonging. Maalouf thinks that belonging to a country or nation is important, but at the same time it is possible to join and to feel part of several different groups.

Gustav Landauer wrote that he was a Jew and a German at the same time and this double nature was good for him. There was a weird, close unity in this duality, and he never felt he had to simplify his being or create an artificial unity, he accepted his complexity. Jean-Cristophe Attias, a thinker, writer and lecturer at the Paris Sorbonne, believes that to be Jewish is "...to be Jewish and something else as well."[59] Jewish identity is one dimension among the many dimensions of personal identity.

Albert Memmi had a wide variety of experiences in his native Tunisia and in France when he was politically militant, and he then decided to accept that he really was someone different and to make a virtue of it. He was so many things at once: a Sephardic Jew different from the Ashkenazi, a person in colonised French Tunisia, a Tunisian nationalist Arab who fought for the independence of the countries occupied by the imperialist powers, a Jew rejected by those same societies he supported, a Tunisian in Paris who had to make his way in a circle where he was an Arab amidst Europeans and had to manage the contradictions of the Diaspora existence.

Yéhouda Léon Ashkenazi, who was compelled to emigrate from Algeria, lived in France and then undertook *Aliyah* to Israel, has this to say, "I have always felt like a Jew born in Algeria, and that dimension of Algerian identity does not desert me. I have French culture and citizenship but I am Hebrew by inheritance, by nostalgia, by faithfulness to my inner life, by culture and also by religion."[60]

The heterogeneous, mobile, changeable, multiple identities of a Jew can be far better understood today, from the modern perspective of the age of migrations and Diasporas, and this applies very much to Gurvich. Because in today's world, while a group's identity is set in nation states, groups also have strong ties to their original countries or their families' countries or ethnic groups.

In modern Uruguay there is a clear move to emphasise the contributions of different cultural communities and preserve them from homogenization, from the effort to integrate and amalgamate them and diminish the differences, which was the model the country pursued at the time of Batlle y Ordóñez.[1] Today the trend is to allow

I José Battle y Ordóñez (1856-1929). He was President of Uruguay twice (1903-1907 and 1911-1915). He

immigrants and ethnic minorities to preserve their individual characteristics.

The Uruguayan sociologists Felipe Arocena and Sebastian Aguiar in *Multiculturalismo en Uruguay*[61] demonstrate that despite the myths Uruguay is not culturally homogeneous; it is much more diverse than is commonly thought. They think that to have a clear vision of the country we should recognize the varied forms of existence of the different minorities, recognize and value diversity, broaden our imagery, appreciate the rich contribution of different communities and value this diversity of traditions. And what is more, individuals who are the repositories of these traditions maintain a dialogue with the heirs to these legacies, so it is easy to see how Gurvich would reach out and embrace his Jewishness.

Gurvich belonged to Uruguay, a country in which, according to Rafael Porzecanski,[62] there is a successful ongoing process of inter-generational transmission of the Jewish identity as a main structural component of individual personality. It is a community that strongly identifies itself as Jewish. Uruguayan Jews, even if they are not religious, practice the rituals and celebrate the main festivals as vehicles to express their communal belonging, and the inevitable mainstay of their adherence is their connection with the State of Israel.

According to Porzecanski,[63] the Jews in Uruguay are thoroughly Uruguayan. There is normal social interaction between Jews and gentiles and Uruguayan society looks favourably on the Jewish community, there is an atmosphere of tolerance and of successful social integration, and the Jews identify strongly with Uruguay.[64]

Gurvich was a good example of this. He rejected the limits of a single inheritance, he was motivated by the complexities that enrich and generate a wide and complicated dimension. He shared his difference, he showed the value of the cultural specificities of a minority in Uruguay, he fostered exchange and collaboration and he opened up dialogues to strengthen inter-cultural ties and develop greater understanding between cultures. He promoted diversity through communication, and he contributed to this with pluralism. The existence of different peoples features in his work and is transmitted, it is visually narrated, because he accepted differences and otherness.

In order to live as equals in democratic societies, the Jews of the Diaspora do not have to reject the fact that they are different or renounce their identity. Quite the contrary, they can stress the difference, as Gurvich did, and integrate their uniqueness into a many-faceted identity, and thus, in this case, they can be Jewish and Uruguayan to the full.

founded the Batllismo movement in the Colorado Party. He is credited with making Uruguay the most stable, democratic welfare state in Latin America. During his government he fought for a range of civil rights including unemployment benefits, the eight-hour day and universal suffrage.

New York composition II
1971
watercolour, ink on paper
21 x 13.5 cm

End notes

1   For further information about this polemic stance on the Diaspora, see "Diaspora: Generation and the Ground of Jewish Identity", Daniel Boyarin and Jonathan Boyarin, Critical Inquiry, vol. 19, No. 4, Chicago, The University of Chicago Press, summer 1993, pp. 693-725.

2   Simon N. Herman, Jewish Identity: A Social Psychological Perspective, New Brunswick, Transaction Publishers, 1988.

3   Sergio Della Pergola, Azure, Jerusalem, No. 6, 5759, winter 1999. http://www.azure.org.il/article.php?id=365

4   Rafael Porzecanski, El Uruguay judío, demografía e identidad, Montevideo, Ediciones Trilce, 2006, p. 61.

5   Ibidem, p. 62.

6   Quoted by Joël Candau, p. 16.

7   Ibidem.

8   Norman Linzer, "Comparing American Jewish Identity with Israeli Jewish Identity", Journal of Jewish Communal Service, 77:1, New York, Jewish Communal Service Association of North America, Berman Jewish Policy Archive, 2000, pp. 36-44.

9   David Arnow, "Towards a Psychology of Jewish Identity", Journal of Jewish Communal Service, New York, autumn 1994, pp. 29-36.

10 Judit Bokser Liwerant, "Jewish Civilization Today: A world of Identities", Park City, Utah, The Samuel Bronfman Foundation, July 2008. http://www.thesbf.org/pdf/bokserliwerantpaper.pdf

11 Dominique Schnapper, "Les juifs et la nation" in Pierre Birnbaum, ed., Histoire politique des juifs de France, Paris, Presses de la Fondation Nationale des Sciences Politiques, 1990, p. 298.

12 Interview with Sergio Della Pergola, Catalunya, Catalunya –Israel, Fòrum d'agermanament entre Israel i els Països Catalans April 19, 2008.
http://cat-israel.frbb.net/micellania-f4/entrevista-a-sergio-della-pergola-t565.htm

13 Jaime Barylko, Judío, el ser en crisis, Buenos Aires, Planeta, 1995.

14 Rafael Porzecanski, op. cit.

15 Emmanuel Lévinas, Difficile Liberté, op. cit.

16 André Neher, "El judío moderno ha redescubierto su identidad", Cuadernos de esclarecimiento, Montevideo, published by Nativ, undated. www.nativ.org.uy/menu/identidad.pdf

17 Shmuel Noah Eisendstadt, "Raymond Aron, Israël et les juifs", Le Figaro poursuit ses réflexions sur l'héritage de Raymond Aron. Aujourd'hui, l'analyse du sociologue israélien Shmuel Noah Eisenstadt, Paris, Le Figaro, March 14, 2005, http://www.mafhoum.com/press7/231C40.htm

18 Régine Azria, "Le judaïsme, contours et limites de la reconnaissance", Archives de sciences sociales des religions, 129, 2005 - La République ne reconnaît aucun culte, uploaded on January 9, 2008. URL: http://assr.revues.org/index1117.html

19 Shmuel Trigano, "Le judaïsme français: la fin d'un modèle d'identité", Covenant - Global Jewish Magazine, Interdisciplinary Center (IDC) Herzliya, April 2007.
http://www.covenant.idc.ac.il/fr/vol1/issue2/trigano.html

20 Irving Louis Horowitz, "Minimalism or Maximalism: Jewish Survival at the Millennium", editors Ernest Krausz and Gitta Tulea, Jewish Survival, The identity problem at the close of the Twentieth Century, New Brunswick, Transaction Publishers, 1988, pp. 1-17.

21 Yéhouda Léon Ashkenazi, L'identité d'un peuple, Propos recueillis par Victor Malka et publiés dans "Aujourd'hui être juif", Cerf editions, 1984, pp. 65-75. Extracts chosen by Dr Pierre Cain (from a text by Meir Ben-Hayoun). Ashkenazi (1922-1996) was a rabbi and Kabbalist, philosopher who revived modern Jewish thought.

22 Albert Memmi, Portrait of a Jew, New York, A Viking Compass Book, 1971.

23 Ibidem.

24 Among the French, Robert Misrahi, André Chouraqui, George Perec, Sarah Kofman, Éliane Amado Levy-Valensi, Richard Marienstras, Benno Gross, Théo Dreyfuss and Régine Azria. In other parts of the world figures such as Charles S. Liebman, Steven M. Cohen, David Theo Goldberg, Michael Krausz, Simon N. Herman, Howard Wettstein, Eliezer Ben-Rafael, Yossi Gorny, Raanan Rein, Sergio Della Pergola, Raanan Rein, Zvi Gitelman, Eva Hetzioni Halevy, Irving Louis Horowitz, Solomon Poll, Gitta Tulea, David Graham, Michael Meyer, Anthony Smith, Raanan Rein and Jeffrey Lesser. And in Latin America analysts such as Judit Bokser Liwerant, Leonardo Senkman, Liz Hamui de Halabe, Sonia Bloomfield Ramagem, Adrián Krupnik, Isaac Caro, among many others, including many in Uruguay.

25 Ibidem, p. 66. It is interesting to study the diverse stances of renowned scholars on identity and the issue of current Judaism at the congress organized by the Bronfman Foundation, Park City, Utah, 2008. Why be Jewish? Judaism as Civilizations. It can be consulted on-line at The Samuel Bronfman Foundation
http://www.thesbf.org/, July 1, 2008, Park City, Utah. Well-known university professors, authors, politicians, writers, journalists, philosophers, historians, sociologists, political scientists: Ruth

526

Bevan, Avraham Burg, Patricia Cohen, Esther Dischere t, Arnold Eisen, Wayne Firestone Jonathan Freedland, Konstanty Gebert, Beatrice Godlewicz, Rebecca Goldstein Gidi Grinstein, Enrique Krauze, Benny Lau, Deborah Lipstadt, Judith Liwerant, Yehudah Mirsky, David Myers, Esther Pe el, Daniel Septimus, Gábor T. Szántó, Viviane Teitelbaum, Shmuel Trigano and Leon Wiese tier. Many experts have analysed the challenges of building the Jewish identity in the 21st century: Isaac Caro, "Comunidades judías y surgimiento de nuevas identidades: el caso argentino", Persona y Sociedad, Santiago, Universidad Alberto Hurtado, vol. XX, No. 3, pp 43-72, 2006. Raanan Rein and Jeffrey Lesser, "Nuevas aproximaciones a los conceptos de etnicidad y diáspora en América Latina: la perspectiva judía", Buenos Aires, Estudios Sociales, , No. 32, 2007, pp. 11-30. Jeffrey Lesser and Raanan Rein (eds.), Rethinking Jewish-Latin Americans, New Mexico, University of New Mexico Press, 2008. Judit Bokser Liwerant, Eliezer Ben-Rafael, Yossi Gorny and Raanan Rein (eds.), Identities in an Era of Globalization and Multiculturalism: Latin America in the Jewish World, Leiden and Boston, Brill, 2008. David Arnow, "Towards a Psychology of Jewish Identity: A Multidimensional Approach", New York ,Journal of Jewish Communal Service, 71, 1994, pp. 29-36. Dominique Schnapper, La condition juive en France: la tentation de l'entre-soi, Paris, PUF, 2009 Norman Linzer, "Comparing American Jewish Identity", New York, Jewish Communal Service Association of North America, autumn 2000, pp. 36-40. Norman Linzer, "The Changing Nature of Jewish Identity", New York ,Journal of Jewish Communal Service 72-3, March 1996. Steven M. Cohen and Arnold M. Eisen, The Jew Within: Self, Family, and Community in America, Indiana Indiana University Press, 2000.
26 Arnow, op. cit.
27 Steven M. Cohen and Arnold M. Eisen, The Jew Within Self, Family, and Community in America, op. cit.
28 Joël Candau, anthropologist specialized in sensory science, Hay una uniformización del gusto a causa de la industrialización de los alimentos más comunes, Vizcaya, España , Consumer Eroski, Fundación Eroski, July 15, 2004,.http://www.consumer.es/seguridad-alimentaria/sociedad-y-consumo/2004/07/15/13399.php
29 Ibidem
3C Candau, Joel , Memoria e Identidad, Serie Antropológ ca, Buenos Aires, Ediciones del Sol, 2008, pp. 138-139.
31 Candau, Memoria e Identidad, op. cit., pp. 139.
32 Candau, op. cit.
33 On identity: J. Chaitin, "My story, my life, my identity", Alberta, International Journal of Qualitative Methods, 3 (4), Article 1, 2004. http://www.ualberta.ca/~iiqm/backissues/3_4/pdf/chaitin.pdf
34 Paul Mendes-Flohr (editor), Jehuda Reinharz (editor), The Jew in the Modern World, op. cit.
35 In a B'nai B'rith conference, Vienna 1926.
36 Letter he wrote in 1936 to the sister-in-law of a colleague who died. Dual Allegiance: Freud as a Modern Jew, Moshe Gresser (June 1994), New York, State University of New York Press. This is one of the many pieces of evidence of Freud's Jewish pride and belonging. The Jew in the Modern World, op. cit.
37 "Leon Biriotti: La relación entre las artes", Daniel Rovira Alhers, Proximidades, op. cit., p. 86.
38 Ibidem.
39 Aron, Raymond, Essai sur la condition juive contemporaine, Paris, Editorial Tallandier, 2007.
40 Literary critic, novelist (1870-1919), he expressed these ideas in 1913. Paul Mendes-Flohr (editor), Jehuda Reinharz (editor), The Jew in the Modern World: A Documentary History, op. cit.
41 Charles S. Liebman, Steven M. Cohen, Two Worlds of Judaism: The Israeli and American Experiences, New Haven, Yale University Press, 1990, p. 13.
42 Charles Liebman and Cohen, op. cit.
43 Eliezer Ben-Rafael, PhD (1974). Sociology professor in Weinberg, President of the International Sociology Institute and member of the Israeli Association for the Study of Language. He has published about ethnicity and language in Israel, the transformation of the kibbutz and Jewish identities. He is editor of a publication on identity, culture and globalization.
44 Candau, op. cit.
45 Candau, op. cit., p. 58.
46 Machado, Prosas dispersas (1893-1936), Madrid, Páginas de Espuma, 2001.
47 Amin Maalouf, In the Name of Identity: Violence and the Need to Belong, New York, Arcade Publishing, 2000, p. 164.
48 Rafael Porzecanski, El Uruguay judío, demografía e identidad, op cit. p. 61.
49 Ibidem, p. 62.
50 Theo Goldberg and Michael Krausz, editors, Jewish Identity, Philadelphia, Temple University Press, 1993, p. 5.
51 Anthony Giddens, "Debating the Social Model: Thoughts and Suggestions" pp. 95 -150, The Hampton Court Agenda: a Social

Model for Europe, London, Policy Network, 2006, pdf
www.policy-network.net/publications_download.aspx?ID=142

52 Peter J. Burke and Jan E. Stets, Identity Theory, New York, Oxford University Press, 2009.

53 Sergio Della Pergola, Collective Azure No. 6, 5759, winter 1999,http://www.azure.org.il/include/print.php?id=365

54 S. N. Eisenstadt, "Collective Identities, Public Spheres, Civil Society and Citizenship in the Contemporary Era", Margurer Forum,The Department of Sociology and Anthropology, The Hebrew University of Jerusalem and The Van Leer Jerusalem Institute, January 7, 2006. http://www.philosophia-online.de/mafo/heft2006-5/Ei_Col.htm
Shmuel Noah Eisenstadt is an Israeli sociologist. In 1959 he was assigned as emeritus professor to teach at the Department of Sociology at the Hebrew University of Jerusalem.

55 Kwame Anthony Appiah, The Ethics of Identity, Princeton, Princeton University Press, 2004.

56 Esther Benbassa and Jean-Christophe Attias, Les juifs ont-ils un avenir?, Jean-Claude Lattès, 2001. Hachette-Pluriel, 2002. Benbassa is a specialist in Jewish history and director of the École practique des Hautes Études de la Sorbonne.

57 Maalouf, op. cit.

58 Ibidem.

59 Attias, director of the École practique des Hautes Études de la Sorbonne.
Sergio Della Pergola, Azure, op. cit.
http://www.azure.org.il/include/print.php?id=365

60 Yéhouda Léon Ashkenazi, L'identité d'un peuple, op. cit.

61 Arocena and Sebastián Aguiar (editors), Multiculturalismo en Uruguay. Ensayo y entrevistas a once comunidades culturales, Montevideo, Trilce, 2007.

62 Porzecanski, op. cit.

63 Porzecanski, op. cit.

64 Porzecanski, op. cit.
Regarding Judaism in Uruguay:
Felipe Arocena and Sebastián Aguiar (editors), Multiculturalismo en Uruguay, op. cit.
Clara Aldrighi and others, Antisemitismo en Uruguay, Raíces, discursos, imágenes, 1870-1940, Montevideo, Trilce, 2000. Daniela Bouret and others, Entre la matzá y el mate, Montevideo, Banda Oriental, 1997.
R.P Raicher, "Judíos sefaradíes en el Uruguay", Montevideo, Hoy es Historia, No. 8. 1985
R.F. Raicher, Uruguay, la comunidad israelita y el pueblo judío, Montevideo, Universidad de la República, 1985.
Bronstein and others, Vida y muerte en Comunidad, Ensayos sobre Judaísmo en el Uruguay, Montevideo, Kehila, Israeli Community of Uruguay, 1990.
Rafael Porzecanski, El Uruguay judío, demografía e identidad, Montevideo, Ediciones Trilce, 2006
Teresa Porzecanski, Vida privada y construcción de la identidad: inmigrantes judios al Uruguay, Montevideo, Trilce, 2002.
Teresa Porzecanski, Historias de la vida privada en el Uruguay, under the direction of José Pedro Barrán, Gerardo Caetano, Teresa Porzecanski, Montevideo, Taurus, 1998.
Teresa Porzecanski, Historias de vida de los inmigrantes judíos en el Uruguay, Montevideo, Kehila, Israeli Community of Uruguay, 1986.

Dialogues

Gurvich, a creative Jew, his people and the kibbutz

Nisso Acher

Looking at Gurvich's work from a Jewish, Zionist and kibbutz perspective is a fascinating exercise full of discoveries and symbols. He was a man of his time, a notable visual artist, and he was part of Uruguay's artistic, intellectual and spiritual history. He was in the *avant garde* movement and was linked with the best representations of the country's spirit and culture. In a symbiosis of extraordinary richness, he linked his Jewishness, his Lithuanian origins, and his experiences on a kibbutz with the cultural and artistic education he acquired in Uruguay. However, the Jewish facet is the underlying structure where his identity came to settle. Culture, the Bible, history, and the difficulties of being Jewish in a hostile world are experiential constructions that featured in his pictorial work.

In Eastern Europe the Jews were excluded and persecuted, and for centuries they waged a tenacious fight for survival. Their conditions of life were extremely difficult, the majority was poor and their existence was tied to their religion and their faith. At the end of the 19th century, in response to these very tough conditions, the Zionist movement came up with a possible solution; it offered hope for a normal existence by returning to the Land of Israel, which Theodore Herzl called the "Old New Motherland". The idea was to build a new modern society in which the elements of historical, cultural and traditional Hebrew heritage would be combined. At that time the most important Jewish intellectual centre was Lithuania, especially the capital city, Vilna, and this was one of the hubs of the Zionist movement. People from that region were most likely to be influenced by these currents of thought and action.

Zionism, like many other Jewish conceptions, is composed of different political, philosophical, religious and spiritual visions and orientations, and one of these was the Zionist Socialist Movement. This was inspired by thinkers such as Sirkin and Borojov, and there were men of action such as Katzenelson and Ben-Gurion, and they overcame their differences and worked together to achieve the dream of founding a Jewish State in the land of Israel. When that country was finally brought into being, the next step was to construct a just society with a collective heritage, where no group would predominate or control the others, in an environment of absolute freedom and complete willing participation. It was from this intellectual, ideological and spiritual source that the kibbutz movement was born.

The basic conception was to return to the land, and this was built on three underlying premises: that this was the land where the Jewish people were born and developed, that a return to nature and to physical and manual labour could be achieved there, and that a productive economy could be constructed.

The kibbutz ideology gave rise to the concept of *Chalutziut*, a term that might be loosely translated as *pioneerism*. It was the drive to achieve, to be in the vanguard, to be the first to colonize the most barren land, to set up home in the most remote regions, in the most difficult and dangerous places, to carry out the most strenuous tasks, to dedicate themselves to putting their ideas into practice. But the idea was not to build rural units isolated from progress and urban life, on the contrary, it was to become more involved with people and there were many cultural activities like shows, music, theatre and art. The kibbutz pioneers discussed ideology all the time and analysed events in Israel and the world. Individuals who showed ability or inclination in a particular field could pursue their studies in higher education at universities and schools.

The kibbutz idea was to produce a renewed man, a complete man, a human being geared to culture and progress, and in practice, the social organization of the kibbutz offered the newcomer novel and stimulating situations. Money was not used, all needs were met by the community, people worked for the benefit of everyone and community assets were common property. Meals were prepared collectively, everyone shared the kitchen and the laundry room, and there was a medical centre and dental clinic. It was a completely democratic system; on Saturday afternoons there was a weekly meeting and the *chaverim* (group members) discussed everything about the kibbutz and their work. This project was unique in the history of the human race, and in the early years of the State of Israel a large part of the population and a fair proportion of the country's production was involved in it. This scenario and these basic ideals were what Gurvich encountered when he first went to a kibbutz.

Gurvich and Jewishness, Zionism and the kibbutz

Gurvich's iconography is expressed in a wide variety of symbols and messages, and it makes a strong impression. He had a rich, sensitive personality and a very fluid style, and he took elements from his environment and blended them with his own experiences to produce exceptional works of art.

When he arrived at the Ramot Menashé kibbutz his sister was already there, she was one of the community founders, and there were many Uruguayans from the *Hashomer Hatzair* Socialist Zionist movement as well. There was a lot of idealism and utopian thinking in the air, a sort of applied anarchy, and drawing on the rich background he had acquired in Lithuania Gurvich started to put signs of his Jewish identity into his work.

El sueño de Jacobo

(Jacob's Dream) 1969, tempera on paper, 34 x 50 cm

This is a picture of an episode in the Bible, in Genesis 28.11. The patriarch Isaac summons his son Jacob and tells him to take as his wife a woman from his original family, from the Laban tribe. Out in the country, on the way to that place, Jacob lies down with his head on a stone and falls asleep and dreams. He sees a ladder that reaches up to the heavens and there are angels on it ascending and descending. Yahweh says to Jacob, "I am your God, the God of Abraham, and the land upon which you lie I shall give to you and your descendants... I shall protect you, and you will return to this land."

In Gurvich's painting this biblical text is reproduced exactly, all the elements from the story in Genesis are there, and from that time on they appear as regular features in the artist's work. There is a scroll above Jacob's head with the message from God in a prominent position and it is easy to read the text. There is a large-scale ladder, a recurrent element in Gurvich's work, and angels with wide white wings. There are small simple houses and a flock of sheep, which show how God's promise was fulfilled and connects with the idea of

the settlement of Israel in modern times. Along the lower edge of the painting there are Jewish symbols such as the candelabra, the *Maguen David* (Star of David), the *Shabbat* candles and the Jewish mother at the Sabbath blessing, all of which show that Jacob's dream will come true. These images are part of Gurvich's traditional heritage.

There is another version on the same theme that dates from one year later. It seems that the first painting is of the promise *Yahweh* made and in the second these things have come to pass: Jacob is wrapped in numerous signs, all related to intense agricultural work and life in the countryside. The dominant colour is ochre, in one area the land is barren and in another we can see it has been farmed. The elements in these two pictures are a combination of typical expressions of Jewish tradition blended with fragments of modern life in these rural colonies. It is a timeless symbiosis of the Biblical chronicle with a new world in which the work of construction is well under way. The ladder is smaller and at a ninety-degree angle to the sky, as if it were a path providing direct access to the realization of what was promised in God's message.

Gurvich gives a new dimension to Jacob's dream. Jacob's face is calm and pleasant and conveys the idea that he has no doubt he will carry out his father's command and find a wife. He ignores the difficulties he will have to face on the way to finding the true love

that he seeks. But there is a parallel dream, the reborn State of
Israel and life on the kibbutz, and
this too is reflected in the images.

Pogrom

1969, oil on canvas, 38 x 50 cm

Part of Gurvich's cultural legacy
was the experience of the Jews in
Europe with their difficult lives full
of adversity, and this is reflected
in the predominant colour, which
is gloomy and suggests mourning.
We are in the *shtetl*, the Jewish
ghetto in Lithuania, amid extreme
poverty, very basic rural life and
continuous persecution and abu-
ses. We are told, "A pogrom has
taken place". The terrible event is
now past and we see the reactions
of the bereaved survivors: anguish,
renewed faith or docile acceptance
of what has happened. Again there
are many typical Jewish symbols:
the candelabra that have been lit
in spite of what has happened, or
perhaps because of it, the fiddler
crying as he plays his bitter melody, the husband consoling his
wife, and the man who is embra-
cing his most important support:
the *Torah*. There is a mother protecting her child, a disabled man
with his crutch, and a mother
blessing the candles. And last but
not least there is the omnipresent
lamb, which evokes transgression
and atonement: transgression
has to do with when the Hebrews
adored a craven image in the Sinai
desert while Moses was receiving the Ten Commandments and

atonement because the animal
was used in sacrificial rites. These
elements, which are more or less
prominent in the composition, are
things that the Hebrews and Jews
have reiterated and emphasized in
all their artistic work.

Es difícil ser judío

(It is hard to be a Jew)
(Shwer tzu zain a iydt)

Gurvich did many compositions
with this title. It is an old and
oft-repeated Yiddish saying that
encapsulates the idea of dramatic
anger, self-pity, a touch of humour
and resignation in the face of the
Jewish people's harsh and sometimes terrible fate.

We shall analyse three compositions from different periods.

In the first, there are dispro-
portionately large figures wearing
enormous boots, and these dimensions could very well reflect
the idea of Jewish fortitude, of the
fact that they survived in spite of
persecution. Perhaps this oversi-
zed footwear could be interpreted
as the Jew's obstinate attachment
to the land, to the present world,
and also to the fact that he has
life, the feeling of joy at just being
alive.

In the 1970 version the main
figure's face is fearful and irate,
and a hand points to the sky as
if questioning and appealing for
answers that may not come. There
is a walking house with legs and
boots, which might suggest the
eternal wandering of the Jewish
people. There is a ladder interlaced

with the scroll of the *Torah* that the figure in holding tight, a *Shabbat* table with the candles barely upright and a glass, which must have contained the celebration wine, has been knocked over. The traditional Sabbath fish is there but it is hard to see. The table seems to be escaping from the man's powerful arm and his small hand seems to be unable to hold on to it. The picture is almost all in ochre with a few hints of white, and we have the impression of anger, incomprehension, anguish and confusion.

In a 1974 version of this theme the scenario is different. The figures are the couple, an icon that features repeatedly in many of the artist's works. Marriage and family were highly esteemed in the Jewish social structure, and this is probably why Gurvich is so fond of using this image. There is a hand rising towards the sky and another, a counterpart, directed towards the Earth. The ladder is only leaning at a sixty-degree angle and it would seem that access to the firmament is easier. We can see satisfaction on the woman's face. The artist has also included the Tree of Life (*Etz Jaim*) from the Book of Proverbs, which is considered similar to the *Torah*. In the mystical language of the *Kabbalah* it is possible to comprehend the nature of God and how the world was created in six days. In this version, unlike in the painting discussed above, Gurvich puts his signature on a plate held by a hand that emerges from undernea-

th the old man's coat, which was the typical attire of the *chasidim* (the devout) of the *shtetl*.

In another work from 1974 with the same title the predominant colour is reddish ochre with a few spots. As in the scene described above, there is an angel flying over the figure, which is clearly Jewish. All the traditional elements are there: a man superimposed on the image of his wife, who is blessing the lighted candles with a serene expression on her face. The ladder is no longer in the top part of the painting but on the lower edge, the man's foot rests on a rung (again, his boots are excessively large) yet it still supports him as he leans on it. The tree of life grows out of the figure's hip or perhaps kidney, passes through his wife's belly (her womb?) and breaks out into space covered in thick foliage. On the right there is a Jew about to carry out the Sabbath blessing, almost in balance with the *Shabbat* table. There is another tree of life, also full of foliage, and in it the traditional fiddler plays his instrument on a sort of rooftop.

There are people, there is activity, there is construction, it is a world in action, full of life, much like the tree itself. The main figure has a terrible expression on his face, he has his right hand to his brow, a smiling angel seems to be protecting him, his left arm holds the *Torah*, and another limb that appears from behind holds the *Menorah* (candelabra) on his chest.

It is interesting to judge how the three pieces with the same

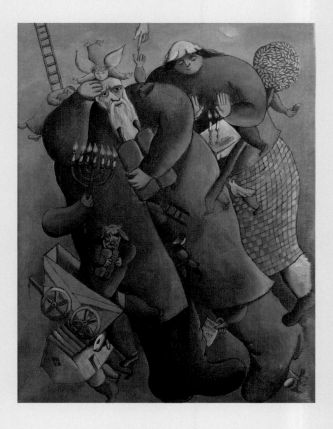

subject reveal how Gurvich's feelings and his interpretation of himself as a Jew changed over time. He witnessed the rebirth of Israel and he felt very strongly that he was participating in the epic journey of a people that have redeemed themselves with their work and through their tremendous faith in their task. This contrasts with the older idea, "It is hard to be a Jew", which was subsumed when the new State of Israel came into being. This can be seen in Gurvich's work: the shift from a resigned acceptance of his bitter Lithuanian past to a positive affirmation of the Jews' vigorous present and promising future in Israel.

Gurvich is very closely connected to his origins and his identity as a Jew. The elements that he extracted from these sources and showed in his work are exceptionally rich in Jewish imagery. All this was in him, as part of his being, and it came out very strongly when he came into contact with and was immersed in the modern manifestation of that culture. It was a Zionist mystique energized by idealism after two millennia of oppressed existence, and this created the stunning phenomenon of a new, modern country that must have mesmerized Gurvich.

Images of the kibbutz

He painted a lot on the kibbutz. There is an important mural that is still there, I have seen a portrait he did of a friend we had in com-

mon, and there was much more, scenes and people from daily life that he turned into visual art because that unique way of life made such an impact on him.

Panorama del kibutz con huevos

(Panorama of the Kibbutz with eggs), 1960, oil on canvas

This painting is done in uniform ochre with touches of white in some places. It is a town with people going about their business and there are typical elements from kibbutz life like a man sowing seeds, and there is water – such a scarce resource in that country – flowing from a tap and being collected in containers similar to those in the Bible, as we know from archaeology. The centre of attention is the builders; this was a very important activity in modern Israel, especially on the kibbutz, because the land had been abandoned and there were hundreds of thousands of new immigrants to absorb so it was vitally necessary to build houses. A man is walking across a rooftop carrying a ladder horizontally, and here the ladder is no longer a symbol of access to heaven, it is a work tool. Practical considerations have priority over the mystical dimension, the concrete balanced against the mythical. In one corner, a man and a woman are whispering together - the gossip so typical of a closed and isolated society, especially a small one.

There are symbols of rural life, a dominating tree that crosses the image from north to south. It is not in flower, it looks more like a tree in winter with few leaves, and there is a man in one of the forks. He head is covered with a hat and he seems to be reading. The Jews were always the People of the Book, on a kibbutz or up a tree, reading cannot be denied.

The most important elements are two eggs, which are in the top right-hand part of the scene. One of them is open and the other is whole and is held by a man. The broken shell is a metaphor for something newly-created, something newborn, it is the new Jewish life and the new egalitarian society that has broken out of its shell and emerged into the world. And the other egg is the unfinished evolutionary process, a world that is evolving, not yet consolidated. So we have on the one hand a chick being born and on the other something that is still gestating.

Composición del kibutz

(Composition of the Kibbutz) 1966, oil on canvas

Kibutz, composición con pareja

(Kibbutz, composition with couple), oil on canvas

These two compositions are from the same period, six years after the painting discussed above. Both have a predominant colour, they show us a mass of humanity engaged in hectic and demanding activities, and they contain many symbolic images that allude to the

past and the present. There are people in a torchlight procession like at a Jewish festival, others playing various musical instruments, memories of the old *shtetl* in Lithuania, Sabbath tables, etc. There are two clocks both with Roman numerals, and they are showing nearly but not exactly the same time. The whole piece is reminiscent of the Uruguayan pictorial school. There is a scroll that reads, "Homenaje al hombre de carne y hueso... que mue...y nace al...". (Homage to the man of flesh and bone... that di... and is born to..."). In one of the pictures there is a couple, two figures hugging each other. One aspect that comes over clearly is that the painter was very impressed with the wide variety of intense activities on the kibbutz.

Years later, Gurvich did *El Mundo del Kibutz* (The world of the Kibbutz) 1970, tempera on cardboard. He was in New York at that time, shortly before his father died of a heart attack, and although he was not on the kibbutz it remained strong in his memory. The colours are bright, the elements are clearer, they are not all stuck to each other, many of them can be separately distinguished and they are more individual and meaningful. The kibbutz seems to be established, the couples are consolidated, and a biblical patriarch presides over the scene from above. The Sabbath table is there, and there is one ladder leaning against a wall that is built up and solid, and another that is clearly a work tool propped against a cart.

In this painting Gurvich again combines modern rural life with tradition. The *Torah* can be seen in the arms of a wise man who is protecting it, there is a cart loaded with straw, a fish and an egg from which a chick seems to be emerging, and these are symbols that represent abundance (fish) and fertility (egg). These are two of the elements of the *Passover* (Jewish Easter) and they represent the blessings that are emphasised in the festival.

After Gurvich left the kibbutz, the impression that it made on him lasted a long time and matured. In his work in New York the image is more stylised, the outlines are more ideal, but all the features of that life experience are still present.

Gurvich the shepherd

The normal system on the kibbutz was that all the members were assigned tasks in line with their capabilities and interests, and Gurvich's job was to take care of a flock of sheep. He was a shepherd. Our first reaction might be that this is rather unusual but not particularly significant, but there is another level on which the symbolism of what he was doing is very striking indeed.

The first inhabitants of the land of Israel had flocks of sheep, that was where their wealth lay, and many of the main figures in the Bible were shepherds. Moses lived a life of affluence at the Pharaoh's court but then he killed an Egyptian who was flogging a Hebrew and he fled to the Midian desert and took refuge with his father-in-law, Jethro, and he minded the sheep. And when he was very old he asked Yahweh who would be his peoples' shepherd after he passed away. And later on, King Saul and King David were shepherds, as were the prophets Elijah and Amos. When the pioneers came to settle in the Land of Israel, Bible stories loomed large in their minds and they wanted to re-connect themselves with that historic past and recreate it with the same labour and in the same land.

Gurvich was no stranger to this tradition, and his work as a shepherd could be seen as a personal return to that common past he was attempting to recover. There is also a link in that the shepherd's crook, with its distinctive shape at the top representing creative force, was like the painter's brush that Gurvich used.

In all of these paintings there is an undeniable connection between the painter and his Judaism. His European roots and his New World experiences led him into artistic expression, and the kibbutz with its very distinctive characteristics stimulated his art still more. In all of this we can perceive his quest to communicate his deep feelings on subjects close to his very being. Those of us who have had similar experiences in our lives as regards the State of Israel and the kibbutz quickly recognize and share the creative spark that Gurvich acquired. He was like the thousands of others who participated in the rebirth and reconstruction of a nation and had the experience of living in a collective system based on equality.

These events and experiences have had a long-lasting impact on all of us, regardless of time.

Nisso Acher
Co-founder and director of the Chair in Judaism of the Catholic University. He held several posts in the communal life, as president of the Israelite Central Committee, Avodá Zionist Party, and coordinator for the Commission of Fight against Anti-Semitism, among others. He carries out research works, among which are: *Una visión Marrana de La Celestina* (A Marrana view on La Celestina), *La Comunidad judía de Amsterdam en el siglo XVII* (The Jewish Community of Amsterdam in the 17th century), *Mesianismo y Falsos Mesías* (Messianism and False Messiahs).

Testimony

Joséphine Balken

> We live to tell who we are...
> JOSÉ SARAMAGO

My meeting with G.

When I first met Gurvich I was a young university student preparing myself professionally in an area apparently quite foreign to the arts, but I already had a strong inclination and need for contact with different forms of artistic expression. This has remained with me throughout my life and it has expanded my knowledge and my range of experiences.

The first time I met G, in my socio-cultural environment at that time, it was a real culture shock, and I had the same reaction each time we saw each other and chatted. We talked about art and other aspects of life, and G always had very personal and original points of view, which led me towards other interesting and different perspectives on the world and made me reflect because he was not repeating the usual intellectual paradigms of the time.

His observations were very natural and spontaneous, intuitive and accurate, and they were not contaminated with fashionable attitudes or clichés. He asserted himself without pretensions, and what came across in a totally natural and spontaneous way was his powerful individuality.

Our conversations took me very far from the usual ways of thinking, away from rational, scientific limitations, they expanded my horizons, they intensified even more my natural curiosity, my searching, and of course they caused me to question the certainties I had more or less explicitly inherited.

I would describe G as a fascinating personality. I was able to appreciate and value more and more the total congruence and coherence in his personality, and this made him very authentic as a person and as an artist. This is also revealed in his paintings, in their richness and imaginative diversity, in their frank originality that broke away from normal patterns and in particular from Uruguayan painting at that time (the Torres García Workshop). I think that those that knew G closely would say the same, that his conversations always gave one a starting point for reflection. I always admired G's courage in constantly asserting his individuality, in expressing himself in all environments in a completely genuine way without making concessions or compromises to obtain benefits or advantages. I was fascinated and I always admired these life values that are so inseparable and so rare.

Figures
1959
carved wood
100 x 58 cm

Mi first contact with G the painter was at the 1957 Fine Arts Exhibition, which had a big impact on me. I was thrilled, and I went over to talk to him because his work had stirred up such strong feelings in me. Then, on numerous visits to Cerro,[1] we got to know each other better and I developed a very friendly relationship with him. This later extended to his wife and his son, and I have been friends with them ever since.

When I first met G he was an artist living alone in the back part of Cerro in Montevideo in quite simple conditions in an old small house with a lovely non-urban view of part of the bay, and he was quite happy. This landscape is reflected in many of his paintings from that time.

His lifestyle could be described as bohemian, but this was completely authentic as it faithfully reflected his life choices. He had no need to present himself as a character or to show off or pose as someone important; there was no challenge and no denial. Just by being himself G was a character, his very essence was authenticity; he was what he appeared to be.

He was vivacious, he had small shining eyes that were perceptive, always ready, and he was cheerful and ironic and he had a mischievous expression that had a certain childish charm. He had loose curly hair that stood up on his head whenever he got excited about painting or just in conversation, and this

was something about him that his friends knew very well and laughed about.

G fully lived out his natural constant curiosity and he fully enjoyed the small things of daily life. He was always searching for self-fulfilment as a human being and experimenting in all possible directions. I suppose I could say that he enjoyed being himself and being able to express that, and he transmitted it too, which was a solid base for stimulating conversation.

He was a person of tremendous vitality, he was amazed at being able to paint what he was experiencing, and when he painted he was astonished at what he discovered. This was part of his never-ending quest to comprehend the world to better understand himself, or to comprehend himself to better understand the world. And this was the essence of G, as it is in every real artist.

When he was living in Cerro he was giving classes, and he enjoyed being able to communicate and transmit his personal observations about life and art. He was very integrated into the community in Cerro —I remember he showed me a mural he had done in a social club there. He was naturally drawn to communal life on the kibbutz in Israel, where he was able to feel part of a cooperative group labour system that was based on a common ideology and rooted in the land. He thoroughly enjoyed his work as a shepherd every morning and being free to paint in the afternoons. What more could he ask for?

---

1   A neighbourhood in western Montevideo home to Eastern Europe immigrants and where Gurvich spent part of his adult life.

I think that the aspect of kibbutz life that attracted him most, apart from being part of an organized community, which in a certain way reflected an adolescent Jewish ideal before the State of Israel was set up, was the "return to the land", a principle that Jewish youth had at that time. Previously he had fully integrated into the community at the Torres García Workshop in Montevideo; he was a very social and communicative being.

Another positive factor was that on the kibbutz he knew that his wife and son were well integrated and comfortable in the community and took part in the friendly social life of the group, and that too gave him the freedom to paint. It is no surprise that most of his paintings of Jewish subjects, traditions, festivals and kibbutz life, date from his various stays in Israel.

From an overview of his work as a whole it is clear that G, like any artist, worked on themes related to his life and his environment at any particular time, and he transmitted his experiences, as can be seen from his paintings of the port of Montevideo, Cerro, Israel, the kibbutz and New York.

Later on I saw G when he was married, when he was a father, and this was in line with his own perspective on life, this completed his position as an "upright man", as a human being in the world. He often said that he felt a man should *leave his mark* when he passed through the world (and he made a gesture with his fingers) like planting a tree, having a child or leaving a body of artistic work. This is why his family, his social relationships and in particular his marriage were so important to him, and it is clear from different situations in his life and in many of his paintings that this was a core element in him, it represented life itself.

The man and the artist: the problem of perception

G was a passionate being, passionate about art and about life in general, he was constantly trying to go beyond his human or rational limits, he was in a constant state of expansion. Sometimes, much later in his personal evolution, he even fasted so as to further increase his intensity and perceptive alertness to paint, and I suppose he was also urged on by his innate curiosity to try different experiences, but always in a natural way.

When G was an adult he was still in many ways a child, full of curiosity, always on the move, absorbing and harmonizing influences from the past, the present and the future he imagined, always trying to break on through to what was universal. We can see this incessant flight of the imagination in all his work, although like that other universal Jew, Chagall, he always based it the real world around him.

I remember something the writer Henry Miller once said - Miller also painted, and he said he would like to reach old age doing what children do without realising it. What was he after? Freshness? Communicative spontaneity?

G's work is very diverse; as well as paintings he did murals, ceramics and paintings on wood, and this reflects his intense spontaneous need to experiment, to seek adventure with that natural curiosity that children have when they try to find how to integrate themselves into their surroundings, and what possibilities they have to go beyond the limits and assert themselves in the world.

Once when G was talking about some of his paintings like *Carta al hombre* (Letter to man) he told me he was trying to capture immediate perception, because he thought we only perceive loose elements of reality in an immediate manner, and later we organize them in our minds into a more or less coherent and significant whole. Each person does this in his own way, but the mental construction comes later, and what G was pursuing was what he called "simultaneous perception".

How to handle perception is one of the basic problems that painters have pondered since Classical times in their search to capture their own personal perceptive construction of reality in their work (Fra Angelico, Rembrandt, Monet, Picasso, Dalí), and this quest has come down through impressionism, cubism and all the way to abstract art.

In this sense, what Matisse said about how he saw a tomato is very interesting: the way he saw a tomato when he was going to eat it was completely different to how he saw it when he was going to paint it. Perceptions are not the same, because they are closely linked to the act, to the aim of perception, and

this is partly defined by the existential context of the moment.

G's ideas on perception coincide perfectly with the constructivism of Torres García, which embodied certain plastic principles that G was able to absorb quite easily. He subsequently added intense energy and that constituted his style - his paintings reflect simultaneous perceptions - but there is also an influence, in perception or ideas perhaps, from Brueghel and Bosch. G felt strongly about these two old masters and he shared their view of the world around them.

In those early days G's intuition about the mechanism of perception was very accurate insofar as it was in line with theories of perception that only emerged much later. According to these, the perceptive process is a personal construction based on elemental information in our consciousness, and it is later organized as our personal reality (Watzlawick, Von Foerster, Von Glasersfeld, Mahoney). In addition, G said explicitly that his paintings should be "read", that they could stimulate the viewer to construct reality and reflect images or ideas about it.

G used scattered elements from simultaneous perception in an essentially rhythmic organization, which was different from the rhythmic organization of Torres García, and at the same time G showed his strong sense of musical rhythm – in fact, at a younger age he had begun learning the violin. He told me that when he was about 14 years old he had wavered between choosing the visual arts or music.

In the end he chose the visual arts as his path to self-fulfilment, but his musical inclinations are evidently reflected in his work, as another root or core element along with his Jewish heritage. Is musicality a Jewish trait? The Jewish people have always been more inclined towards music than the visual arts; their synagogues have never had images, which are forbidden in their religion, but they do have singers. The combination of musical inclination and the constructive principles of the TTG[II] gave G's work a very personal character, and this immediately made him stand out at the TTG.

Besides this, G must have been very responsive to the strongly supportive communal organization of the TTG, which was much like the painters' workshops of the Renaissance in which numerous pieces were actually done collectively by the students. Many paintings by Workshop painters were signed with their name and on the back they put the reference, TTG. G felt very comfortable as part of that community, as he did in the kibbutz community, and this was because of the emotional and relational aspect of the TTG, which was a tremendously important cultural focus in society at that time.

G and imagination

One could associate G's need for basic spiritual expansion, like the movement from the particular towards the universal, with the myth of flight, which has existed since Classical times. One example is the well-known myth of Icarus, which represents the "flight of the soul" that goes beyond earthly limits towards the heavens. And there are angels, hybrid beings of human form but with wings so they are earthly and ethereal at the same time.

Is there another symbol that expresses the bond between the earthly and the aerial as a metaphor for spiritual ascent towards the divine? There is indeed, the ladder, which features in the well-known Jacob's dream and represents the aim of mystical elevation to ascend to other spheres of higher knowledge, knowledge of what lies beyond, that which is superior, that which is metaphysical. When dealing with biblical or traditional Jewish scenes, Chagall and G both used mythical references to space, to flight and especially to the dynamics of ascending, and this gave their work a spiritual and more universal significance. It is also interesting to note that "flight of the imagination" is commonly described as the force –is this solely human?– whereby one leaves behind what is earthly or concrete and gains access to other dimensions of experience.

Imagination is at the very foundations of all creative processes precisely because it is the impulse to rise above everyday reality. Yet in the creative process a certain connection with concrete reality must remain for it to be viable. This means that imagination needs a

II   Torres García Workshop, for its initials in Spanish – Taller Torres García.

certain degree of rational control, although the proportions in the dynamic balance are completely individual. This is the great challenge that many artists face, and G experienced it to the full and wrestled with it, sometimes as a very vivid internal struggle as he attempted to discipline his imagination which broke out of everywhere, and achieve that subtle and elusive balance in his paintings.

The evolutionary spiral

Each human being's origins are the starting point of their personal history, and they are conditioned by the history of their ancestors and the biological laws of phylogenetics and ontogeny. Right from birth a person absorbs the characteristics of his unique social context, he lays the foundations on which very varied experiences will be based, and this goes on throughout his life as more elements are superimposed, reinforcing and transforming personal evolution in a constant expansion of successive existential contexts. In a sense this corresponds to the physical expansion of the Universe.

Since Classical times, the symbol of the spiral has been used in many cultures to represent the force of growth and the development of living organisms, because evolution constantly harks back to earlier stages and characteristics that are useful and come to the fore, and these are integrated into the dynamism of the constant evolutionary swing between past and future, between deep and shallow, between what is below and what is above. This double movement, this to and fro, strengthens the evolutionary force between upwards and downwards; the roots go deeper and at the same time the organism expands, grows and develops.

According to Purce, who has made an in-depth study of the spiral in mythologies since Classical times, it is a representation or metaphor for evolution in time and space, and in it we intuitively recognise the evolutionary dynamics of living matter. The spiral's constant organized movement towards the future represents the movement of constant universal expansion, which is effected through the continual incorporation of certain elements from previous evolutionary stages, but always geared to the whole, to an organized form. The spiral can be found in the most primitive life forms, on fossils, in snail shells, in certain plants and so on.

G had this same intuition and he captured that idea in many paintings in which a spiral movement is a clear feature. This is even apparent in his references to the energy and rhythm of the universe, to the original explosion, the Big Bang, which were subjects that also interested him at a certain time. In this sense, G was aware that he wanted in some way to capture and reflect the intense, evolutionary impulse of life, which was the source of his tireless and insatiable curiosity, the strong inner need that took him beyond his roots to go further and further, and very often swimming against the current. And this is why he is so authentic.

Thus the act of artistic creation could be understood as the attempt to introduce a certain order into the Universe, an order that corresponds to the evolutionary force inherent in living matter.

The life impulse

It is the continuous evolutionary movement inherent in all living matter, the individual as well as the species, which pushes life towards the future in a process of constant expansion. This was defined by the French philosopher Henri Bergson as *élan vital*, the life force that acts in the evolution of the species, the creative drive, and the emergence of increasingly complex forms that are unforeseeable. The expansion of the being manifests itself as an impulse that humans have to break through the limits that define and enclose them, as a need to go beyond, to go further, like the urge to explore the earth, space and the cosmos.

The life impulse manifests itself in curiosity, which is so strong and instinctive in children, it is the thirst for experience of any kind, and this is necessary for development in any environment in a process of constant evolutionary enrichment. G had tremendous curiosity. We might almost say he was always lying in wait, alert, ready to grasp everything he could from life in all its aspects, and he continued evolving and enriching himself. And throughout his life he was continuously integrating his Jewish roots into his experiences.

G's Jewishness

When I looked at some of G's paintings that I was familiar with so as to consider them from the point of view of his relationship with Jewishness and Judaism, I realised my own perception process had changed because I was now looking at them with a pre-established idea, which in this case was his connection with Jewish culture.

I had not focused on this aspect before because I was always attracted by the visual qualities and the aesthetic values of his work, not by the theme, which I believe to be secondary. My usual perceptive method can be called intuitive global apprehension, which means I pay attention to the impact the work has on me and to its emotional significance. This is what could be described as empathetic comprehension, since I enter into direct dialogue with the paintings, I want my spontaneous emotional reaction, I want to simply enjoy the pleasure of feeling I am in a dialogue, in a kind of communication, which is perhaps spiritual.

However, when I fixed my attention on the Jewish aspects of G's work I did so with an analytical perspective that took me towards more rational comprehension in line with a pre-established scheme and certain principles, and this was expansive and reductive at the same time.

When I paid more attention to the Jewish themes in G's art I realized I had seen them before but I had not considered them very important. I then went on to discover Jewish details and references, and I realised that apart from paintings with explicit Jewish themes there many Jewish details and references in other works, when he tackles other subjects that reflect various situations throughout his life not just on the kibbutz in Israel but in Montevideo, the Old City, Cerro and New York.

I had never looked at G's paintings in that way before, although of course I had seen them. Indeed, these two modes of perception, the immediate impact and the analytic eye, complement each other in various ways, depending on the viewer and his individual purpose in contemplating works of art.

Each human being's work will inevitably show an intertwined collection of aspects of their personal history. This was expressed very well by Saramago when he said, "We live to tell who we are..." and added that when we tell it, we understand it. Quite possibly, this self-understanding is what we are seeking when we create a work of art, as the artist Alberto Giacometti said in a short text entitled, "I only know what I see when I do". This in itself is a clear statement of the artist's stance, and it means that sculptures, for example, must represent something other than themselves. "It is the medium I have for fulfilling my vision of the world... or better still, it is the method I have for knowing that vision".

In fact, what matters most in a work of art is not so much the explicit theme but *how* the artist resolves the plastic problems of personal perceptive organization when he tries to capture that subject. The question is *how*, that is to say using what resources, he can express what he feels and thinks, his own vision of the world resulting from his life experiences. A work of art is inevitably a reflection of the artist's personality and the vision resulting from his varied experience throughout the course of his life, starting from his very roots. What is important is how the theme is handled. Is this imposed by circumstances or is it freely chosen by the artist in any given moment of his existence, depending on the conditions of the moment?

When we look at G's work as a whole we notice that a theme directly related to his life context, to his circumstances, to the moment, is always of paramount importance. He shows us Montevideo, the Old City, Cerro, the kibbutz, New York or whatever.

During the Renaissance, themes were generally imposed by heads of state or patrons like the Church, the king or the nobles that ordered the piece, but many artists produced work of universal import that has remained valid in other space-time contexts. And to this day we still admire these works with the same enthusiasm for their aesthetic worth, as is the case with Leonardo, Rafael or Michelangelo.

Artists at that time did not sell what they produced, they worked on a commission basis, and it would seem that having a theme proposed or imposed did not inhibit their creative forces because the subject matter was nothing more than the basic framework within which the artist constructed his own personal vision. This allowed him to escape from the theme and achieve some kind of universal impact by transcending it, an impact stemming from the plastic and aesthetic worth he achieved. In G's case this would be his paintings of the universal and cosmic man. This is what remains in a work of art when it stands the test of space and time.

Is this the magic of art?

The film director Andrei Tarkovsky clearly expresses how he experiences art and the image that can be defined as artistic, "An artistic image is that which intrinsically possesses the ability to develop on its own and has its unique historic perspective. This image is a seed, a living organism that continues to evolve". It is true that every work of art reflects the socio-cultural context of the time and personality of the artist, but the piece does not survive because of its subject matter, it endures because of how it is executed, and this has come to be called its visual, aesthetic value.

This has to do with the direct experience of a work of art, which is different from subsequent analysis because analysis seeks to relate it to its original socio-cultural context or seeks interpretations as to its possible meanings. Or conjectures about the possible intentions of the artist that created it, although in fact nobody can legitimately assert anything about them, not even the artist himself. At all times, the challenge lies in how the artist has been able to overcome his personal qualities and individual references, which are his inevitable starting point, to achieve a more universal impact. That is to say, how he can arouse feelings that differ from his own. Rafael or Goya, for example, not only reflected their own space-time context, but were also able to transcend it.

This is also what happened to G in his paintings of the port, Cerro, the kibbutz and New York. (In fact his stay in New York was short because he succumbed to a heart attack brought on by a health problem he never thought was very serious.)

Usually, but not always, there is a connecting thread of Jewish references that are completely integrated into the painting's subject, and this reflects the fact that this element was so deeply rooted it amounted to G's very being. Yet Jewish references can also be found in Rembrandt, who lived in a Jewish neighbourhood in Amsterdam but was not Jewish. Needless to say, the fact that G's work contains Jewish subject matter was never a factor in my enthusiasm and admiration for it even though I myself am of Jewish European descent and I came to Uruguay because of World War II. In no sense am I moved by his work because it makes my Jewish core resonate; what moves me is what I feel to be transcendental and universal about it.

Thus, what matters, as a fundamental value in all art seems to be the possibility to transcend everyday reality while remaining in everyday reality and this is manifested in visual and aesthetic values that are universal. The quality of a work of art, whether it is a picture, music or literature, lies in its capacity to project what is universal, what is timeless, so it continues to arouse emotions and thoughts even when the times have changed, and when people too have changed.

A Greek tragedy, a Shakespearean drama, a Machado poem, a Brancusi sculpture or a Dostoyevsky novel can move us so much, even today, as much as some modern work. Perhaps we seek out works of art that are not modern precisely because they transcend everyday reality. Or is it that our concrete aspirations to immortality are manifested in art? In any case, it seems clear that this was one of G's aspirations.

I think that G was very aware of the need to overcome the space-time limits of the many contexts of his life, as this was his only chance of victory in the face of his inevitable death. When he said explicitly that he wanted to leave his mark in the world he made the traditional *Talmudic* gesture with his thumb as if leaving his thumbprint in the air. And he added that to achieve this, every man had to plant a tree (in the land, in Israel), have a son (he had one) and leave a life's work. And

he achieved his goal, even though he passed away too soon. Did he sense that that would happen?

Once again I quote the words of Andrei Tarkovsky, which I feel to be very pertinent, "The (artistic) image is a symbol of life, but it differs from life because life includes death while the image of life excludes it, or could be considered the only possibility of asserting life... it is a scream of hope and faith... creation in itself is a negation of death."

G's Jewish roots constituted a connecting thread throughout the course of his life, in Montevideo, in Israel, on the kibbutz and at the end in New York, and they were always subtly manifest in his individuality and in his cosmic projection, as can be seen from his paintings of *Hombres cosmicos* (Cosmic men).

In some of G's paintings there are numerous Jewish references that remind us of the imaginative-lyrical Jewish elements in Chagall, like the sacrifice of Isaac and some aspects of *Carta al hombre* (Letter to man). This picture also contains references to Brueghel and Bosch, painters who, like G, were sensitive and overflowing with imagination, and who presented an almost surreal vision of everyday reality. However, G. differs from these old masters in that he attempted to capture the immediate perception of reality, which he felt to be a superior mental construction. And we know that in this approach personal elements including imagination, which is always present to some degree, and immediate circumstances come into play. This position reflects his notion of the Torres García style of constructivism.

G felt he had a lot in common with Chagall because they both had Jewish roots and they both let their lyricism take flight. Both painters used these roots and universalized them, possibly in a more of less conscious attempt to contribute to the effort to maintain traditional Jewish culture as part of universal culture.

G spent his early childhood, his first four years, in a small Lithuanian *shtetl*, and he was immersed in Yiddish tradition and culture. When his family moved to Uruguay he quickly absorbed Uruguayan cultural references as well. This second culture was superimposed on his Jewish-Lithuanian background and the two strains mutually enriched each other in a balanced and harmonious way. These influences can be seen in his work either as central themes or as details in other paintings, and in this way he projected them universally.

Later on he assimilated the teachings of the Torres García Workshop (TTG), which in a way echoed the workshops of the Renaissance painters. The TTG gave the Uruguayan artistic movement of the time a great boost as it brought native Uruguayan and South American elements into constructivist universalism.

The Jewish people have been dispersed in the Diaspora for many centuries, they have assimilated many cultures, eastern as well as western, and they have contributed to and enriched various cultures in the world. A lot of this took place before globalization, before international movement became easy and commonplace, and the Jews have inherited a kind of mobile mentality; even before the global circulation of information they were assimilating other cultures and making their own contributions to them.

For example, when there was interest in Spain in examining the sources of a collection of Spanish ballads the experts had to turn to the rich Sephardic tradition, which maintained and transmitted these songs in their original language, Ladino.

Let us take one of G's works that I feel is a key example of the fusion of personal (Jewish) and contextual (Torres García style symbols) references, and which creates an aura of universal significance: the painted and carved wooden board with two indistinguishable and separate geometric figures that are wonderfully intertwined in such a way that they form one single shape. This piece was executed in line with the constructive universalism norms of the Torres García Workshop.

I was lucky enough to be able to witness how it was produced when I made a long series of visits to Cerro. G completed it 1959 after more than a year of exacting work on the fine details, and it is full of marvellous dynamic rhythmic combinations and meticulous detail. The geometric construction of the board is very well executed because the two figures are interrelated in a way that creates the sensation of harmony and balance as they are separate but united in space, which is the background that at the same time shapes and sustains them. The figures are not individualized because their form is overlapping, they are not differentiated, not even sexually, and as far as I know, and G did not even the board a name.

What is outstanding is the formal construction, which is so well-achieved in its harmonic balance that it seems to reflect the basic non-differentiation of the living matter represented by the couple, which perhaps harks back to original man and original woman. And the figures are united by a force of attraction that supports both of them in the space area of the board, almost like planets.

At certain times G was interested in the enigma of the origin of matter and he produced paintings with the dynamic movement of universal rhythm like the origins of life itself. He did paintings that express the explosion of matter, particles in space, sometimes like a kind of maelstrom that calls to mind to the original genesis of the world.

G tackled the theme of the creation of the universe in a very particular way, with lovely metaphorical images from Jewish mysticism that connect with the description of the second stage of the biblical Genesis and with the term *Chavirah*, which refers to the breaking of the jars where the divine primal light was trapped. God had to take these jars out of the Universe to make the room for the creation, and this was the first stage of creation, known as *Tzimtzum*. But the jars exploded because of the tremendous force of the sparks trapped inside them, and these fell and scattered chaotically throughout space. This lovely 16th century metaphor, from Isaac Luria's *kabbalah of safed*, also indicates falling from the primal divine order without bringing in the notion of sin. What this expresses, above all, is that everything that constitutes the Universe has a divine spark, and that the task of man, who has some spark(s) of divinity, is to attempt to re-establish a measure of order in the Universe.

What better metaphor could there be for the act of creation inherent in every human being? As the German philosopher Nietzsche, who was an atheist and even agnostic) said, "Man is creature and creator".

I remember G telling me that he needed to have disorder around him, in his environment, in his workshop, since that gave him the impulse to paint as a means to impose order. In other words, he painted to introduce his own personal order. He used to say that if everything was perfectly tidy, he would not have been able to paint.

The two figures seem to be symbols of individuality but they are related to each other and make up one particular form which is defined by the relation between them as part of an undifferentiated whole and not by their differentiation. What is important is the relation between them.

They are a couple: is this G's vision of Adam and Eve? The two forms are inter-related without being stuck to each other or superimposed, they are delineated by the space that results from the outline of the two forms, they look like humanoids, and it is this same space that sustains and maintains them. Incredible, isn't it?

Is G transmitting in some way, more or less consciously, his conception of the strength of the couple? They are *Juntos y separados* (Together and Separate), and there is enough space between them. The subject of couples and human relationships was crucially important for G and it features in many of his paintings and ceramics. On the other hand, I know that the board was commissioned for a wedding, in other words, the couple's new life, and this clearly demonstrates the influence of the work's context as having to do with human relationships.

Let me tell you a short personal anecdote about G making the board, a memory that has remained within me (and there must be a reason). I went to Cerro one day and saw the board and it seemed to me that it was finished, but G was not satisfied and he said he had to let it "rest", so that he could "see". I remember the two figures were placed on a uniform grey background, and the board looked finished to me. A few days later I went to Cerro and when I saw the board the background had been changed, he had added the green strokes and the grey was underneath like an undertone, and this adds a whole other dimension, it reinforces the energy of the two shapes, which are apparently quite static in their geometric construction.

I understood why he was dissatisfied and needed to add energy, so as to diminish the frigidness of total *planism*.

Communication

Art is a form of communication in a language that is both consensual and individual in human society, since art has been inherent to the human condition from prehistoric times. There are paintings of hands and animals in caves in North America, South America and Europe that may even precede spoken language. They are very moving to see.

G often said he wanted people to go deeper into a painting with the same intensity as if they were reading a good book, which is a source of various feelings and thoughts, of diverse images. We discussed this during our friendly chats. G was attempting to attract people's attention, he wanted people to stop and look, to see the numerous details in the painting, to enter into the piece to establish an inspiring dialogue, like a book that one reads and re-reads and each time discovers some new and enriching perceptions.

So is a painting a significant book?
In some way, G was like modern art in that he wanted to set up an authentic and stimulating interaction (like the forms on the board) to achieve a co-elaboration with what he offered in his painting, to take the viewer out of his passive role. In fact all art is an encounter, a form of dialogue, and not a monologue by the artist who creates it or by

the eventual viewer. And to achieve that, one must start by *stopping to look and see*. Is this the cause or the effect of G's meticulous style of painting, his idea of simultaneous perceptions that need to be organized by each viewer himself?

It is possible for any art to establish a flow of emotional vibration or resonance between the artist-creator and the viewer-participant. A work of art is fundamentally a stimulation of emotional experiences that enrich the individuals that come into contact with it. Anyone who had any kind of a lasting relationship with G would agree that he was a communicative and stimulating being who found pleasure in dialogue with all kinds of people. And in a way, his paintings converse and will continue to converse with those who take the time to really look at them.

However, while G wanted his art be "read", he also did not want his work to be merely decorative, and that is why he constantly attempted to add another dimension with his use of geometric *planism* from Torres García universalism, which was his personal mark. He kept repeating, "It must be read," with the idea, I suppose, that the reading was more than ideographic perception and was ultimately aesthetic, as is the case with some written script such as Chinese, Hebrew and Arab writing, and that a level of empathy and rational comprehension could be reached. In this sense, the painters and sculptors that we usually call great have achieved this dimension. It is very difficult to hu-

rry past a painting by Fra Angelico, Leonardo, Klee, Soulages or Rothko, all with such different styles, or a sculpture by Michelangelo or Brancusi, or a photograph by Man Ray, and not stop to look.

I think that right from the beginning I instinctively sensed all these qualities in G's art, and now that I have lived with several of his works for more than fifty years I have enough distance of interpretation when I look at them, and I look at them with renewed pleasure.

And right from the beginning I felt I was in the presence of an exceptional being, someone I admired, and I have continued to admire throughout my own personal evolution. He was someone rooted in his own history, yet he did not feel tied down by it. This is what I consider to be an authentically free being, someone who did not have to renounce anything in order to continue "walking", as Machado put it so well.

G's authenticity, which was so natural and spontaneous, was the externalization of that inner freedom that made him independent of the outside world. And this was not due to any reflection or philosophical decision whatsoever, he simply "was that way because he was that way" and that was it. His force came from within.

Just to be in his presence had a great impact on me, he was so genuinely free of all commitments and ties even while he was living with them, and that is true freedom. It is not the freedom of the hermit who withdraws to give himself the impression that he is free. In his own way, G was immersed in daily life, in what was taking place around him, and he felt he was an integrated part of his socio-cultural movement. He felt free *within* his family ties, and his Jewish, Uruguayan and Torres García ties, he accepted them as the basic groundwork for his evolution, he did not reject or shy away from them. On the contrary, he continually integrated them into his own socio-cultural framework of references in a constant evolutionary spiral that projected itself towards the universal in a different sense to Torres García.

G was one of the few painters that because of his personality quickly stood out at the Torres García Workshop, and he later overcame the ideological limitations of the Workshop, as well as other limitations, and achieved a very personal style using his own references and incorporating his own personal doubts and quests to give his work a personal mark, without ever becoming a renegade or an outsider.

Inner, subjective freedom is also an evolutionary spiral.

Joséphine Balken
Philosophy graduate from the Faculty of Humanities and Sciences of the Universidad de la República, Uruguay. Linked with artists of the Torres García Workshop, she attended courses with J. Romero Brest, Celina Rolleri, and cultivated a close friendship with José Gurvich and his family. She specialized in psychology psychotherapy in Switzerland. She is a psychologist, and author of books and many articles in specialized magazines.

Sacrifice of Isaac
1970
tempera on paper
60 x 48 cm

Biblical and Talmudic sources in the work of Gurvich

Isaac Margulies

"We Uruguayans are descended from boats'

"Shifs Brider"

In 1933, a year that is remembered for the rise of Nazism in Germany and Terra's coup d'état in Uruguay, the five-year-old Zusmanas Gurvicius arrived at the port of Montevideo. He was with his sister Miriam (who they called Merke) and his mother Jaie, and they had come to join the father of the family, Iankl (Jacobo), who had gone on ahead, which was common practice in those times.

On the same boat there was a couple named Moishe and Ite Lea Furman, they all got to know each other and became what was called in Yiddish, *shifsbrider* (boat brothers). The immigrants had left family and friends behind in Europe, and they had to cope with a new life in a country that was strange to them and an unfamiliar language, and they clung to the new friends they had made on the ship. The Gurvichs and the Furmans stayed in contact and lived near each other. The Furmans rented rooms in a building on Isla de Flores and Rio Branco streets that was known as "The Kremlin" because it was entirely occupied by Jews, who were often called "Russians". The Gurvichs were only a few blocks away at Durazno and Julio Herrera y Obes streets. Both families established their homes in the Barrio Sur area, a neighbourhood that has its own peculiar mystique: the singer Jaime Roos[1] made it popular and with his song "Durazno y Convencion".

The young José Gurvich divided his time between his family home and the Furmans' house. They were all practising Jews and José's mother kept to the traditional rites, and in this environment he naturally absorbed Jewish traditions. He had Jewish friends like Mauricio Muller, who came from a family with strong orthodox roots and had a rich Jewish culture. There is no doubt that when Gurvich went to Israel it must have been a great life experience and an opportunity to rediscover his roots. And later on, in New York, he was in contact with one of the Furmans' sons, José, a religious man who studied the *Talmud*.

All this clearly shows that from a very early age Gurvich was familiar with the Bible and *Talmudic* stories that we can identify in his work.

Shabbat

This is an emblematic painting Gurvich did in 1974 and it has Jewish subject matter. It shows the extent

---

1   Jaime Roos (b. 1953, Montevideo), Uruguayan musician and composer.

to which the traditions in his home and the environment he grew up in had impregnated his memories and his sensitivity. There are many versions of this painting. The central figure is a woman blessing the candles on the eve of *Shabbat*, and it does not take too much imagination to see her as a reference to Gurvich's mother. The child watching her so attentively is the painter himself. There are two candles; these evoke the two different constraints concerning the *Shabbat* that appear in the texts of the first tablets with the Ten Commandments that Moses brought down from Mount Sinai, and on the second tablets that replaced the first after these were broken.

On the first tablets, the text of the fourth commandment reads "Remember the day of the *Shabbat* to sanctify it...", and on the second tablets this commandment reads "Keep the day of the *Shabbat* to sanctify it...". And it is because we have two versions, "Remember" (*Zajor*) and "Keep" (*Shamor*) that two candles are blessed.

The following is from Rabbi Yosef ben Yehuda, quoting the *Talmud*, "When on the eve of *Shabbat* a Jew leaves the synagogue to go home two angels accompany him: one good and one evil. If when he gets home he finds the candles lit, the table prepared and the bed made, the good angel exclaims, "Thy will be done that the next *Shabbat* in this house shall be like this one!" And the evil angel reluctantly answers, "Amen!" If this is not the case, the evil angel exclaims, "Thy will be done that the next *Shabbat* in this house

shall be like this one!" And the good angel reluctantly answers, "Amen!" In Gurvich's painting, the good angel is watching over the mother as she blesses the candles. Like in the *Talmudic* story, the candles are lit, the table is prepared, and on it we can see the traditional braided bread: the *challah*.

The home itself is protected, it is covered by the mother's skirt, and there is a Jew playing a fiddle and another holding a *Sefer Torah* (Pentateuch Scrolls). An image Gurvich often repeated is there too: the ladder from Jacob's dream that unites the earth and the heavens.

El sueño de Jacob (Jacob's Dream)

This 1970 oil painting on wood recreates the famous story in the Bible. There are many Bible stories that have to do with dreams, and the elements that make up those dreams reveal what the dreamer is concerned about. The Pharaoh of Egypt dreamed only of earthly, tangible, material things, and this showed his concerns were economic, "Cows of full meat and of beautiful appearance" that were devoured by "thin and ugly cows", and "full and beautiful shoots" that were devoured by "meagre and withered shoots".

Joseph was Jacob's son. His brothers called him "the dreamer". He had two dreams, one with earthly elements and the other with heavenly ones, the first with "bundles of shoots" and the second with "the sun, the moon and the stars". Jacob's second dream represents the link between the earthly and the heavenly,[8] "A ladder rested on the earth, its top was touching the heavens, and angels of God were going up and down." Gurvich represents this "earth-heaven" symbiosis by painting the sky, the earth and Jacob's own body with the same colours and strokes.

The *Talmud* teaches, "Know that above you there is an eye that sees, an ear that hears and a book that records all your acts."[9] In this painting there are eyes that look down from the heavens and an eye that looks up to the heavens. And also in the heavens there are loose hands, unattached to any body, which are holding a book and writing in it. On the other side, coming down from above, there are hands holding a scroll from the *Torah*. In the heavens there is a *Menorah*, the seven-branch candelabra that Moses ordered to be made and that were one of the elements of the Tabernacle in the desert and later in the Temple of Jerusalem.[10] This image often features in Gurvich's paintings, and he may well have felt it to be the most emblematic of all the Jewish symbols.

The most dramatic element in the painting is the arms reaching up to the heavens. One of these arms comes from the "tree-man", which denotes the biblical expression "Man is a tree from the field."[11] The ladder represents the union between earth and heaven, and winged angels ascend and descend. The representation of angels as winged beings arises from the description of a vision the prophet Isaiah had.[12] And Gurvich's memories are displayed on Jacob's body: the Sabbath table with the two candles and the hands blessing them. At Jacob's feet the two candles appear again, this time beside a half-eaten loaf of bread.

The repeated image of the sheep is an echo of Gurvich's time as a shepherd in Israel.

Gurvich, the "ro'eh"

The Hebrew word *Roe* means shepherd and Gurvich was a shepherd in Israel. There is a *Midrash*[13] that mentions a biblical text, "The Eternal shall test the just",[14] and it says that this applied to David when he was a shepherd. It is explained in the following way: when David was a shepherd he organised his flock by age. He would let the older sheep, whose teeth were more fragile, graze first, so they could eat the top part of the grass which was softer. He then set the middle-aged sheep to graze so they could feed off the next part, which was not as soft, and lastly he would send the youngest sheep, whose teeth were the strongest, to eat the hardest parts. The Eternal One then said, "He who knows how to graze his sheep shall know how to feed my people," and this occurs in the following verse, "And he chose David, his serf, and he took him from the flocks of sheep."[15]

This commentary about the art of shepherding came up when Gurvich was interviewed by Maria Esther Gilio.[16] "What does a shepherd currently do? Does he sit and observe nature? Not in Israel. That was in Garcilaso's poetry. In Israel the sun burns, the sheep seek shelter and they gather in a circle forming a sort of braid, and the shepherd must separate them and force them to walk so they can eat."

Being a shepherd in the land of the patriarchs and kings of the Jewish people must have had a very special mystique for Gurvich, and this comes across in his work. In the above-mentioned interview he said, "I felt I was living intensely and fully."

Of Joseph and Joseph[II]

The first Joseph in history, Yosef, the son of Jacob the patriarch, told his brothers that when they left Egypt they should take his bones and bury them in the land of Israel[17]. And Moses carried out that command.

José Gurvich, the son of Jacobo and Jaie, died in New York. His re-

---

II   An allusion to José Gurvich. José is the translation of Joseph.

mains were taken to the Ramot Menashé kibbutz, where he rests alongside his parents, in the land of the shepherds of Israel.

End notes

1   Exodus 20:8
2   Deuteronomy 5:12
3   Talmud-Shabbat Treatment 119b
4   Genesis 28:11/15
5   Genesis 41:17/24
6   Genesis 37:19
7   Genesis 37:6/9
8   Genesis 28:12
9   Talmud-Avot II-1 Treatment
10   Exodus 25:31/40
11   Deuteronomy 20:19
12   Isaiah 6:2
13   Midrash is the literature that has co-existed with the Talmud since the 1st century. It is made up of explanations of the underlying meaning in Biblical texts.
14   Psalms 11:5
15   Psalms 78:70
16   Quoted in Angel Kalenberg, Jose Gurvich, p.152
17   Genesis 50:25

Isaac Margules

Talmud expert. Lecturer of classes on "Talmud and Law" in the Postgraduate Centre of the Faculty of Law of the Public Accountancy, permanent professor of "State Financial Management" in the Faculty of Economics and Administration of the Universidad de la República, and "Public Accounting" in the Faculty of Business Science of the Catholic University. Author of the book, *Public Accounting*, and co-author of the book *Financial Administration and Accounting in the Public Sector in Uruguay*.

Gurvich the Jew

Manuel Tenenbaum

Alicia Haber asked me for my reflections as a Jew on the work of
the famous Uruguayan painter José
Gurvich, and although I usually
leave art to others I happily agreed.
I first got to know Alicia when she
was a talented and intellectually
restless student on a course called
History of the Jewish People.

The impression I get from contemplating Gurvich's paintings
of Jewish themes and from his
work that has elements that could
be classified as such, is that the
painter's roots are purely Jewish;
they are memories of his Lithuanian childhood and the powerful
experience of his three stays on a
kibbutz in Israel. He is not the sort
of Jew who stands out for his contributions to culture or in universal
arts in general and then one day
rediscovers himself as Hebrew. The
"pintele Yid" (*ner tamid*) (the Jewish
flame) burned inside him from the
very beginning and derived from
the grandmother who blessed the
sabbatical candles, and from the
ancient traditions and festivals of
his people.

It is true that in all periods of
history there are Jews that stand
out in general society who are dis-
tanced from their origins or even
willing to abandon them to adopt
another religion. In some cases the
individual will take spiritual fright
when he is on the verge of conver-
sion and return to the flock. One of

the great thinkers who experienced
this was Franz Rosenzweig; he was
going to become a Protestant but
one day he was passing a small
synagogue and he heard the sound
of Jewish prayers and suddenly
he did a complete about-turn and
wrote the notable philosophical
opus *The Star of Redemption.* Another
example was Henri Bergson, who
was acclaimed in France for his
intellectual stature. He was on the
way to converting to Catholicism
but he relented at the time of the
Nazi occupation and fully assumed
his Jewish identity even though
the collaborationist Vichy regime
wanted to spare him the indigni-
ties the Jews were suffering. But in
Gurvich's case there was no "fright",
and if we accept the idea that the
work of a painter is completed in
the eyes of the viewer, it seems to
me that he was a Jew from the very
beginning, and this transcended
his art.

One cannot separate Gurvich
and his Jewish themes from his life
as an immigrant in Uruguay. He
was poor, and in the early years
things were difficult. Newly-arri-
ved Jews were crowded together
in squalid dwellings in the Barrio
Sur. Isla de Flores street was typical
of those places, and in the Yiddish
of the newcomers it mutated into
"Isla de *Tzores*" (Island of Sorrow).
Gurvich absorbed this experience,
although today it is almost forgot-

ten. Like many who lived that way, he must have been attracted to universalisms - an attraction that should not be confused with forsaking one's original heritage. I think these Jews were secular and religious at the same time, secular because of their way of life, and religious because of the weight of Judaism they brought with them.

The tremendous strength of Gurvich's painting entitled *shavuot* has to do with the very quintessence of Judaism and with the founding principles of the Hebrew people. The artist shows the Tablets of the Law and there are people receiving this great gift under the intense brightness of the heavens. *Janucá* (*Hanukkah*) is not a severe or grave painting, the people there are happy and it expresses the triumph of freedom. In another picture of

Hanukkah the celebration is set in the framework of a kibbutz. *El Embarazo de Sara* (Sarah's pregnancy) is impressive; there is strong biblical content and the representation of the pastoral group is striking.

The Jewish symbols and *Tanakh* elements that occur throughout his work reveal Gurvich's deep-rooted Jewish core and his intense open and underlying Judaism. His pictorial homage to the kibbutz combines a fondness for that type of community with esteem for its members. The omnipresent sheep represent him personally, since he divided his time between being a shepherd and working as an artist.

So my answer is Yes, I believe that quite apart from the twists and turns of his life, Gurvich was a Jewish painter, a Jewish soul.

Manuel Tenenbaum
Professor in History of the Jewish People, author of educational works and lecturer in almost all the Latin American countries, in United States, Spain, and Israel. He was director of the Latin American Jewish Congress, being awarded many times for his administration. He received the Centre of the Iberian and Latin American Communities in Israel (CICLA) 2004 award *ex aequo* with Mordechai Arbell, from Israel, and Pilar Rahola from Spain.

Shavuot, detail

Documents

PULGAR DERECHO
RIGHT THUMB

FIRMA DEL TITULAR
SIGNATURE OF BEARER

Kaišiadorių
Žydų Metrikacijos Punktas
1942 Balandžio mėn. 12 d.
№ 16

גֶעבּורט־שֵיין

Gimimo pažymėjimas

Sūnus ar dukta _Sūnų_ gimimo vardas _Zusmanas_
Tėvo vardas ir pavardė _Jankelis Burgačius_
Motinos vardas ir pavardė prieš ištekant _Chajė Galperaitė_
Tėvo užsiėmimas _Kirpėjas_
Tėvų gyvenamoji vieta _Žiežmariuų miest. Trakų apsr._
Tautybė _Žydų_ Pilietybė _Lietuvos_
Tūkstantis devyni...
devyniolikt septintais metais Sausmen
šešto dienų
Gimimo vieta _sąp kute_
Šoul pažymėjimas įneša į žydų išrašytas iš _Kaišiadorių_
Metrikac Punkt. gimimų metrikų knygoj 1927 m.
gakovžės mėn. 20 d. kurią tas įrašytas 6 numeriu ir turi galios
skaip patrui patas knygom

A. Jofanas

Kaišiadorių, Metr. Punkto Raštinė

José Gurvich (1927 - 1974)

Chronology

by Martín Gurvich

Lithuania

1927

January 5th: José Gurvich was born in a snowstorm in Yezna (Jieznas) in the district of Trakai in Lithuania. His parents, Jacobo Gurvich and Jaie Galperas, lived in poverty in this small village. Before the Second World War Lithuania was in social, political and economic turmoil. Gurvich's memories of his homeland were vague, but he recalls them in his writings and they appear in his pictures.

1928

May 30th: His only sister,
Myriam, was born.

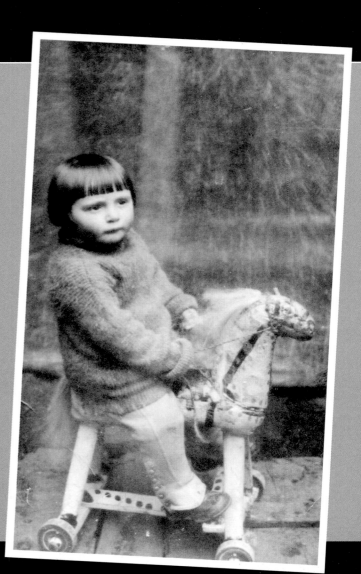

Montevideo

1931

1932

1933

Jacobo Gurvich emigrated to Uruguay with some friends for the same reason as millions of other Europeans: to seek a better world and to escape from religious persecution.

Jacobo Gurvich sent for his wife and children, and they arrived in Montevideo at the end of 1932. The family settled in a neighborhood called *Barrio Sur*, an area with many Jewish immigrants, most of whom lived in very humble circumstances. Jacobo worked as a barber and he eventually owned several barber shops. They lived on Durazno, Isla de Flores and Río Branco streets.

José Gurvich adapted quickly to his new country. He went to the "Chile" school, and he later remembered this is a wonderful time in his life and fondly recalled his teachers, his friends (such as Basilio Bernat and Martín Muller), his copy-books, his school drawings. His father, who did not speak Spanish very well, registered him at the school as José Gurvich instead of Zusmanas Gurvicius, which was his legal Lithuanian name. The child quickly showed his talent for drawing and he drew not only in his own copybooks but in those of his sister and her friends.

1940

1942

1943

1944

When he finished school, to help the family financially he got a job at a factory called Montag, which manufactured raincoats and rubber articles. At home he did sculptures and reliefs in plaster, but this was dirty work and in their confined living space it irritated his mother. By now he had completely adapted to his new country, and in a way he was a divided person with two separate lives, one in the outside world and the other in the microcosm of the family, which adhered to traditional Jewish ways.

He started to study painting at the National Art School under the direction of José Cúneo.

He studied music and had violin lessons with professor Julber and he got to know Horacio Torres, who was also taking violin lessons. As a result of this contact his life was to take an abrupt turn.

Julber got him an interview with the famous painter Joaquín Torres García, and Gurvich later studied under him. The interview strengthened his desire to pursue painting. When he had to choose between music and fine art he chose painting and he immersed himself completely in the world of shapes and colours. In his later teenage years his life was dominated by the iron routine of his work schedule at the factory, and he kept on working there for years while in his spare time he practised the violin, painted and had interminable conversations with his friends in the Sorocabana café. He got used to an eight-hour working day, and in later life he applied himself to his art with the same discipline. He always considered himself an "art worker".

1945

1946

He was invited by Torres García to join the master's workshop, and what he learned there was to have an extraordinarily powerful influence on his life. From the moment he joined the Torres-García Workshop (TTG) until it officially closed down, he took part in all its activities including publications, exhibitions, doing murals and teaching.

January: Some of his work was featured in the 20th Torres-García Workshop (TTG) exhibition, at the South American Federation of the YMCA in Piriápolis.

January 25th: The magazine *Removedor* was launched. This was to serve as the mouthpiece and organ of the TTG, and it went on to become one of the most important modern art publications in Latin America. It came out every two months, it ran to twenty-three issues (until May 1950), and subsequently there were two special issues, in December 1950 and July-August 1953 (with illustrations by Gurvich on the cover).

October 2nd: He contributed material to the 23rd TTG exhibition, at its new exhibition venue.

October: He contributed works to the 24th TTG exhibition at a school, the Liceo Departamental de Artigas. This was organised by the Artigas city council.

November 6th: His work appeared in the 25th TTG exhibition, at its permanent exhibition venue at a bookshop, the Librería Salamanca in Montevideo.

March: He contributed material to the 27th TTG exhibition, at another bookshop, the Librería El Yelmo de Mambrino in Punta del Este.

May: His work was featured in the Autumn Exhibition in the IMM (Montevideo City Council).

June 15th: The book *Nueva Escuela de Arte del Uruguay* (New Uruguayan Art School) was published. It contained a summary of TTG activities and photographs of TTG art including ceramics, tapestries, toys, murals and pictures.

July 1st: He contributed works to the 28th TTG exhibition, at the Municipal Culture Commission in the city of Minas.

July: His work was featured in the 29th TTG exhibition, at the YMCA in Montevideo.

September 21st: He contributed material to the 34th TTG exhibition, at the Social Club and Public Library in the city of Artigas.

November 28th: His work appeared in the 35th TTG exhibition, "Painting and New Art of Uruguay", at the Ateneo in Montevideo. He also had his first individual exhibition, in the city of Melo.

1947

1948

1949

1950

July 28th: He contributed works to the 38th TTG exhibition, "Painting and Constructive Art" at the Ateneo in Montevideo, and he was involved in a joint exhibition at the Museo Juan Manuel Blanes (art gallery), which acquired some of his compositions. December 4th: He contributed works to the 41st TTG exhibition, at the Ateneo in Montevideo.

July 28th: His work was shown at the 45th TTG exhibition, at the Ateneo in Montevideo, and also in a joint exhibition "Plastic Arts", organized by the El Galpón theatre in Montevideo. His sister Myriam emigrated to Israel with other members of the Hatzomer Hatzair to set up the Ramot Menasche kibbutz near Haifa.

August 8th: Joaquín Torres-García died in Montevideo at the age of seventy-five. October 11th: Gurvich compositions were shown in the 49th TTG exhibition, which was in honour of his mentor, at the Ateneo in Montevideo

February 2nd: He contributed material to the "Torres-García and his Workshop" exhibition at the Pan American Union of the OAS, in Washington DC. June 12th: His work was featured in the 51st TTG exhibition, at the Ateneo in Montevideo. July 28th: He contributed works to the 52nd TTG exhibition, "Painting and Constructive Art", at the Ateneo in Montevideo. November 8th: His work appeared at the 53rd TTG exhibition, at the Ateneo in Montevideo.

1951

1952

March 20th: His work appeared at the 54th TTG exhibition, at the Liga de Fomento de Punta del Este in that city.

August: His work featured in the 55th TTG exhibition, at the University of Chile in Santiago de Chile.

October 2nd: He contributed to the 56th TTG exhibition, "Amigos del Arte" in Montevideo.

December: Gurvich took the place of Alpuy (who was travelling to the Far East and Europe with Gonzalo Fonseca) as a teacher at the TTG, and he worked in that capacity until Alpuy's return in 1953. He moved to Fonseca's room-workshop near the port, in 25 de Agosto Street, while Fonseca was away. He worked there intensively until 1954, when he went on a trip to Europe and Israel.

June 30th: The TTG published a limited edition of 400 books with thirty reproductions of constructive drawings.

August 19th: Gurvich's work appeared in the 59th TTG exhibition, at the Ateneo in Montevideo.

September 7th: There was a performance in aid of the TTG, at the Cine Central in Montevideo.

November 22nd: His work was featured in the 61st TTG exhibition, at the Club Tacuarembó and the Club Municipal de Arte y Cultura in Montevideo.

November: His work appeared at the 62nd TTG exhibition, at the Ateneo in Montevideo. Together with Fonseca and Alpuy

he painted a mural (which has since been destroyed) at the El Temerario bar in the Old City (Ciudad Vieja).

1953

March: He began to do illustrations for the programmes of the Cinema Club, jointly with other members of the TTG, and he continued with this until 1957. He also did scenography for various theatres: Teatro del Pueblo, Club del Teatro, El Galpón, El Tinglado, La Máscara, (Los Intereses Creados, Minnie la Cándida), for the Sodre Ballet and for the Hashomer Hatzair in Montevideo, and thus he forged a link with the world of theatre and cinema. Together with other painters, writers and journalists, he formed a group called Artes y Letras (Art and Letters), whose aim was to undertake a study trip to Europe.

October 20th: His work was shown at the 66th and 67th TTG exhibitions, at the Ateneo in Montevideo.

Ramot Menashé

1954

1955

1956

He travelled to Europe with Manuel Aguiar and Antonio Pezzino, and when he was there he met up with other members of the TTG including Horacio Torres, and visited art galleries in Spain, France and Italy. In Madrid he met other Latin American artists and became friendly with the critic Moreno Galván.

June 1st: He held an exhibition at the San Marcos Gallery in Rome. His sister, who was living in Israel, invited him to the Ramot Menasche kibbutz to paint a mural for their communal dining room, and he made his first trip to that country. He settled on the kibbutz for a while and joined in its everyday life. And it was there that he gradually started to draw deeply on the cultural wealth of his ancestors' religious traditions –his mother had always had kept him in contact with this heritage– and he become immersed in the great project of helping the newborn Jewish State of Israel to grow. On the kibbutz he worked as a shepherd (which in Hebrew is *Roe* or "he who looks") and he painted what he saw, the world of the kibbutz he was living in.

April 19th: He had an exhibition at the Katz gallery in Tel Aviv. He returned to Europe, and in Spain he studied the Spanish masters Goya and Velázquez, but the masters that really fascinated him were El Bosco and Pieter Brueghel. June: His work appeared in the 99th TTG exhibition, at the Ministry of Public Instruction and Social Security at the Salón Nacional de Bellas Artes of Montevideo. August 28th: His work was included in the 100th TTG exhibition, at the Municipal Underground of Montevideo.

El Cerro

1956

1957

1958

December 21st: His work was featured in the "Jonge Schilders uit Uruguay" exhibition at the Stedelijk Museum of Amsterdam, and it was well received by the Dutch press. In December he returned to Montevideo and to his parents, and he went back to his work at the TTG and to giving painting classes.

Gurvich replaced Julio Alpuy (who was moving to Colombia) as a teacher at the TTG. Artists studying at the TTG when he was teaching there included Pepe Montes, Guillermo Fernández, Yuyo Goitiño, Sara Capurro and Eva Díaz Yepes. When Fonseca left Uruguay Gurvich moved into his house, Polonia Street 3166, in the Cerro neighbourhood in Montevideo.

December 26th: He contributed material to the 109th TTG exhibition, at the Ateneo in Montevideo.

September: He had his own exhibition in the Arte Bella Gallery in Montevideo.

October: The TTG published the first issue of the magazine *Escuela del Sur*.

Uruguay

1959

1960

1961

He organized the exhibition "Amigos del Arte" in Montevideo. The second issue of *Escuela del Sur* came out.

February: His work was featured in another TTG exhibition, at the National Fine Arts Commission in Punta del Este.

March: Some of his works were included in the 125th TTG exhibition, at the Municipal Culture Commission and the Laurenzo Gallery, in Paysandú.

August 18th: He married Julia Helena Añorga.

December 1st: His work was featured in the 136th TTG exhibition, at the Americana gallery.

December 12th: He contributed material to an exhibition entitled "The New School Presents: The Torres-García Workshop", at the New School Arts Center in New York. He was invited by the University of Chile to contribute material to the "Arte y Espacio" (Art and Space) exhibition in Santiago.

January: The TTG published the third and last issue of the magazine *Escuela del Sur*, which had a reproduction of a Gurvich composition on wood on the cover.

July: He contributed material to the 143rd TTG exhibition, at the Comisión Nacional de Bellas Artes (National Fine Arts Commission) in Montevideo.

August: His work was featured in the "Premio Blanes" exhibition, which was organized by the Banco de la República Oriental del Uruguay, in Montevideo.

December: His work was featured in a mobile exhibition, organized at the Amsterdam Museum, that visited Baden-Baden and Staalich Kunsthalle.

1962

1963

He painted a number of murals - one was for the Caja de Pensiones del Frigorífico del Cerro (Cerro Meat Processing Plant Pension Fund) at the request of the architect Vaia. This mural is 17 metres long, it has been restored by Mr Barra with materials provided by the painter's widow and the engineer Eduardo Irisarri, and it is now in perfect condition. There is talk of moving it to the passage between the Palacio Legislativo (Parliament building) and an annex. Gurvich did another mural at Malhos' house in Punta del Este, and another in the Reims building on Sarmiento Street, which was designed by the architect

Luis San Vicente and was auctioned at Castells and Castells on 11 June 1997. Gurvich material was also on view in the "Salón de Arte" exhibition, which was organized by General Electric of Montevideo. April: The TTG closed down. The news was announced in an article in the *El País* newspaper in Montevideo .
December: Gurvich's mother went on a trip to Israel to visit her daughter and she decided to stay in that country.

January 25th: José Gurvich's son, Martín José, was born.
July 28th: Gurvich work was included in the "Homage to Torres García" exhibition.
October: Gurvich's father emigrated to Israel, to live on the Ramot Menasche kibbutz with his wife and daughter.
José Gurvich moved to his house in the Cerro, which was very near his old house on Polonia Street, and converted the place into living quarters and two workshops, one for ceramics and one for painting. Over the years many young artists went there for classes and thus the Taller Montevideo (Monte-

video Workshop) was born. Gurvich's students included Eva Olivetti, Celeste Núñez, Blanca Minelli, Gloria Franchi, Clara Scremini, Dorita Mandirola, Linda Kohen, Lilian Lipschitz, Adolfo Nigro, Ernesto Vila, Ernesto Drangosh, Rafael Lorente, Gorki Bollar, Héctor Vilche and Armando Bergalo.

1964

1965

May: He contributed material to an exhibition organized by the National Fine Arts Commission. He made his second trip to Europe and Israel, this time with his wife and son. They first went to France (Le Havre, Paris and Marseilles) and then on to Israel where they lived on the Ramot Menasche kibbutz. Gurvich worked as a shepherd and he painted.

May 1st: He had his second exhibition at the Katz gallery in Tel Aviv. He went on a trip to Greece and stayed for three months, and later he visited Rome and Naples. At the end of that year he returned to Montevideo.

El Cerro

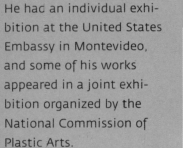

1967

May: He had his own exhibition at the National Fine Arts Commission with over 200 paintings, drawings, and ceramics, and it was well received by the public and the press. Some of his work was included in the "One Hundred Years of Uruguayan Painting" exhibition at the Corcoran Gallery in Washington DC.

1968

He had an individual exhibition at the United States Embassy in Montevideo, and some of his works appeared in a joint exhibition organized by the National Commission of Plastic Arts.

Israel

1969

1970

April 24th: He contributed material to the "Homage to J. Torres García" exhibition organized by the Culture Department of the Banco La Caja Obrera, in Montevideo.

November 22nd: He made his third trip to Europe and Israel with his family, and visited Madrid, Barcelona, France, Greece and Israel.

December: Some of his work appeared in the "Homage of the City of Montevideo to the Artist Joaquín Torres-García" exhibition at the IMM (City Council) Exhibition Hall.

April 4th: Gurvich's father Jacobo died of a heart attack in his son's arms on the way to hospital. .

May: His work was featured in the "Constructive Universalism" exhibition, organized by the Museo Nacional de Bellas Artes (National Fine Arts Museum) in Buenos Aires.

July 18th: He had his third exhibition at the Katz gallery in Tel Aviv, and it was a great success.

New York

1970 1971 1972 1973

September 18th: He went to New York and stayed for a few months with relatives of Lithuanian origin who were concentration camp survivors. Some time later he joined a group of artists from the TTG and other Latin Americans who lived in New York including Julio Alpuy, Gonzalo Fonseca, Horacio Torres, Marcelo Bonevardi, Abularach and Elba Damast. He had a small workshop in the basement of the apartment block where he was living with his wife and son.

Some of his compositions were shown in joint exhibitions entitled "Select Works from Latin America", at the New York Greenwich Library and at the Couturier Gallery in Stanford, Connecticut.

Some of his material was shown in joint exhibitions entitled "Fair of Latin American Opinion", at the San Clemente Church in New York and at the Iramar Gallery of the University of Columbia, New York.
June: He had an exhibition at the Lerner-Misrachi Gallery in New York, and it was favourably received by the public and the press. He contributed material to the Third Coltejer Bicentennial exhibition in Medellín, Colombia.
December 24th: His mother Jaie died after a long illness.

He was invited by the Jewish Museum of New York to hold a retrospective exhibition.

1974

February 2nd: He contributed works to the "Sculpture by Painters" exhibition at the Humanist Center in New York.

April 27th: He contributed works to the "Masters of Today and Tomorrow" exhibition at the Israel Temple in Great Neck, New York.

June 24th: On a grey, stormy evening he passed away, abruptly, the victim of a coronary. He was only 47. When he was taken from us he was in the middle of many projects, many quests, he left many friends and he left many pictures unfinished. Curiously, or perhaps inevitably, the painting he was working on when he died was of a Jewish festival, Succot (the Harvest).

Bibliography on José Gurvich
Books

(alphabetical order)

Agosín, Marjorie
Entremundos: Jewish Artists of Latin America
Singer Gallery, Denver, 2001.

Álvarez, Tulia
Fermentos de Vida del Arte Uruguayo
Instituto Jung, Buenos Aires, 1983.

Argul, José Pedro
Las Artes Plásticas del Uruguay
Ed. Barreiro y Ramos. Montevideo, 1966.

Battegazore, Miguel
J. Torres García: La Trama y los Signos
Edición Intendencia Municipal de Maldonado, 1999.

Bayón, Damián
La Peinture de l'Amérique latine au XXe siècle
Éditions Mengès, París, 1990.

Bazzano Nelson, Florencia
Latin American Artists of the Twentieth Century
New York, 1993.

García Puig, María Jesús
Joaquín Torres García y el Universalismo Constructivo
Ediciones de Cultura Hispánica, Madrid, 1990.

González, Mercedes; Rubio, Rosina; Zorrilla, Carmen
Rescate de la memoria cerámica en el Uruguay
Edición Ministerio de Educación y Cultura / Fondos Concursables. 2009.

Haber, Alicia
José Gurvich Un Canto a la Vida
Museo José Luis Cuevas, México, 2000.
José Gurvich: El Mundo Íntimo de un Artista
Fundación José Gurvich / Fundación Buquebus, Montevideo, 1999.
Latin American Art in the Twentieth Century
Phaidon Press, London, 1996.

Kalenberg, Ángel
Arte dell'Uruguay nel Novencento
Instituto Ítalo-Latinoamericano, Roma, 1989.
Arte Uruguayo y Otros
Ediciones Latina, Montevideo, 1990.
Voces de Ultra Mar - Arte en América Latina y Canarias
Centro Atlántico de Arte Moderno de las Palmas, 1992.
I Bienal de Artes Visuales del Mercosur
Porto Alegre, 1997.
José Gurvich: Pero Yo voy a Pintar
Edición Arteaga-Tejería, Montevideo, 1998.
Artes Visuales del Uruguay
Edición Testoni, Montevideo, 2001.

Maslach, Adolfo
Joaquín Torres García, Sol y Luna del Arcano
Unesco, Caracas, 1999.

Pacheco, Marcelo
Colección Constantini
Museo MALBA, Buenos Aires, 2001.

Peluffo Linari, Gabriel
El Paisaje a través del Arte en el Uruguay
Edición Galería Latina, Montevideo, 1995.
Historia de la Pintura Uruguaya
Ediciones de la Banda Oriental, Montevideo, 1999.
Pintura del Uruguay
Ediciones del Banco Velox, Buenos Aires, 1999.
Pintura del Mercosur
Ediciones del Banco Velox, Buenos Aires, 2000.
Pintura Uruguaya
Ediciones del Banco Velox, Buenos Aires, 2001.

Ramírez, Mari Carmen
La Escuela del Sur: El Taller Torres García y su Legado
Universidad de Texas en Austin, 1991.

Rovira Alhers, Daniel
Proximidades. Testimonios sobre José Gurvich
Fundación José Gurvich, 2003.

Sullivan, Edward
Latin American Still Life; reflections of Time and Place
Katonah Museum of Art Wechester, 1999.

Torres, Cecilia de
El Universalismo Constructivo y la Escuela del Sur
O.E.A., Washington D.C., 1996.

Torres, Cecilia; Haber, Alicia
José Gurvich. Murales, esculturas y objetos
Edición de Fundación José Gurvich, Montevideo, 2003.

Traba, Marta
Art of Latin America, BID, Washington D.C., 1995.

Varios
Montevideo y La Plástica
Edición Intendencia Municipal de Montevideo, Montevideo, 1996.

Varios
J. Gurvich N. York, N. York
Fundación José Gurvich, Montevideo, 2007.

Catalogues

Los universos judíos de José Gurvich
Museo Gurvich. Montevideo, 2010

José Gurvich – Canción de la pintura
Galería Oscar Prato. Montevideo, 2010

José Gurvich – Pinturas – Dibujos – Esculturas
Galería de Arte Isabel Aninat. Santiago de Chile, 2010

The fantastic World of José Gurvich
Frost Art Museum. Miami, 2010

José Gurvich
Galería Palatina. BsAs, 2008

Murales TTG
Museo Gurvich. Montevideo, 2007

José Gurvich Constructive Imagination
Americas Society, 2005

José Gurvich – Pinturas – Dibujos – Esculturas
Galería de Arte Isabel Aninat, Santiago de Chile, 2003

José Gurvich y el retrato
Museo Torres García, Montevideo, 2003

Gurvich
Galería Tejería Loppacher, Punta del Este, 2002

Una Aventura Llamada Gurvich
Galería Guillermo de Osma, Madrid, 2000

José Gurvich en el Museo José Luis Cuevas: Un Canto a la Vida
Museo José Luis Cuevas, México, 2000

Gurvich
Galería Palatina, Buenos Aires, 2000
José Gurvich Paintings and drawings
Cecilia de Torres Ltd., New York, 2000

Unidad y pluralidad en la Escuela del Sur
Galería Gustavo Tejería Loppacher, Punta del Este, 1999

José Gurvich y La Naturaleza Muerta
Museo Torres, Montevideo, 1998

José Gurvich: del Universalismo Constructivo al Hombre Universal
Quinta Galería, Bogotá, 1998

José Gurvich
Galerie Mireille Batut D'Haussy, París, 1998

José Gurvich
Galería Palatina, Buenos Aires, 1998

José Gurvich
Galerie Ruben Forni, Bruxelles, 1997

Gurvich
Centro Cultural Borges, Buenos Aires, 1997

José Gurvich
Galerie Ruben Forni, Bruxelles, 1997

La Colección de Adolfo Maslach: Visión de una Poética Constructiva
Museo de Bellas Artes, Caracas, 1997

Gurvich Un Canto a la Vida
Galería de la Matriz, Punta del Este, 1995

Gurvich
Galería Sur, Punta del Este, 1987

Homenaje a José Gurvich
University of Haifa, 1985

Uruguay: 6 Artistas Plásticos
Museo de Arte Moderno, Buenos Aires, 1983

José Gurvich
Galería Faunas, Madrid, 1978

Gurvich en El Mensaje
Buenos Aires, 1977

Bibliography

ALDRIGHI, CLARA Y OTROS, *Antisemitismo en Uruguay, Raíces, discursos, imágenes*, 1870-1940, Montevideo, Trilce, 2000.

AMISHAI-MAISELS, ZIVA, "The Jewish Jesus", *Journal of Jewish Art* vol. 9, 1982, 84-104, *Depiction and Interpretation: The Influence of the Holocaust on the Visual Arts*, Oxford, Pergamon, 1993, Part 2, Chap. 3, R.I.

APPIAH, KWAME ANTHONY, *La ética de la identidad*, Buenos Aires, Editores Katz, 2007.

ARNOW, DAVID, "Towards a Psychology of Jewish Identity: A Multidimensional Approach", *Journal of Jewish Communal Service*, 71, New York, autumn 1994, pp. 29-36.

AROCENA, FELIPE, "Elogio de la diversidad", ed. Enrique Mazze , *El Uruguay desde la sociología V*, Montevideo, Universidad de la República, 2006.

AROCENA, FELIPE, "La contribución de los inmigrantes en Uruguay", *Papeles de CEIC*, 2009/2, España, Universidad del País Vasco, 2009.

AROCENA, FELIPE, "Dilemas para construir democracias multiculturales", in *Relaciones* nº 301, Montevideo, June 2009.

AROCENA, FELIPE, "How Immigrants Have Shaped Uruguay", in *Culturales*, nº 9, Universidad Autónoma de Baja California, Centro de Investigaciones Culturales-Museo, México, January-June.

AROCENA, FELIPE Y AGUIAR, SEBASTIÁN (editores), *Multiculturalismo en Uruguay. Ensayo y entrevistas a once comunidades culturales*, Montevideo, Trilce, 2007.

ARON, RAYMOND, *Essai sur la condition juive contemporaine*, Par s, Editorial Tallandier, 2007.

ASHKENAZI, YÉHOUDA LÉON, *L'identité d'un peuple, Propos recueillis par Victor Malka et publiés dans "Aujourd'hui être juif"*, éditions du Cerf, 1984, pp. 65-75.

AURON, YAIR, *Les juifs d'extrême gauche en mai 68*, Paris, Michel Albin, 1998.

BAR-LEV, MORDECAI Y DROR, YUVAL, "Education for Work in the Kibbutz as a Means Towards Personal, Social, and Learning Fulfillment", *Journal of Moral Education*, Routledge, New York, vol. 24, nº 3, September 1995, pp. 259-272.

BARYLKO, JAIME, *Judío, el ser en crisis*, Buenos Aires, Planeta, 1995.

BAUER, YEHUDA, "HaShoa: HaMeyuhad VeHaUniversali", "(The Holocaust: the Singular and the Universal"), Jerusalem, *Jinuj LeTarbut BeJevra Rav Tarbutit - Sugviot BeHishtalmuyot Morim (Cultural Education in a multicultural society – Issues for the improvement on teachers)*, Anthology 9, The Hebrew University of Jerusalem, School of Education, Department of Teachers' Improvement , 2000, pp. 161-162.

BENBASSA, ESTHER Y ATTIAS, JEAN-CHRISTOPHE, *Les juifs ont-ils un avenir?*, Jean-Claude Lattès, 2001, Hachette-Pluriel, 2002.

BEN-RAFAEL, ELIEZER, *Crisis and Transformation: The Kibbutz at Century's End* (S U N Y Series in Israeli Studies), New York, State University of New York Press (March 1997).

BEN-RAFAEL, ELIEZER, "Las etnicidades judías en Israel", *Araucaria, Revista Iberoamericana de Filosofía, Política y Humanidades*, Sevilla, vol. 10, nº 19, 2008, pp. 99-111

BEN-RAFAEL, ELIEZER; GORNY, YOSSI Y REIN, RAANAN (eds.), *Identities in an Era of Globalization and Multiculturalism: Latin America in the Jewish World*, Leiden and Boston, Brill, 2008.

BOURET, DANIELA Y OTROS, *Entre la matzá y el mate*, Montevideo, Ediciones de la Banda Oriental, 1997.

BOYARIN, DANIEL Y BOYARIN, JONATHAN, "Diaspora: Generat on and the Ground of Jewish Identity", *Critical Inquiry*, vol. 19, nº 4 (summer of 1993), pp. 693-725, Chicago, The University of Chicago Press.

BRONSTEIN Y OTROS, *Vida y muerte en Comunidad. Ensayos sobre Judaísmo en el Uruguay*, Montevideo, Kehila-Israelite Community of Uruguay, Uruguay, 1990.

BUBER AGASSI, JUDITH, "The Israeli Experience in the Democratization of Work", *Sociology of Work and Occupations*, vol. 1 nº 1, Tel Aviv University, February 1974.

BURKE, PETER J. Y STETS, JAN E., *Identity Theory*, Nueva York, Oxford University Press, 2009.

CANDAU, JOËL, *Memoria e Identidad*, Serie Antropológica, Buenos Aires, Ediciones del Sol, 2008.

Caro, Isaac, "Comunidades judías y surgimiento de nuevas identidades: el caso argentino", *Persona y Sociedad*, Santiago, Universidad Alberto Hurtado, vol. XX, nº 3, pp. 43-72, 2006.

Cohen, Steven M. y Eisen, Arnold M., *The Jew Within: Self, Family, and Community in America*, Indiana, Indiana University Press, 2000.

Ertel, Rachel, *Le shtetl, la bourgade juive de Pologne: de la tradition à la modernité, Le Régard de l'histoire*, Paris, Payot, 1982.

Feldman, Yael S., "The Akedah and the Intellectual Melting Pot of the 1950s", New York University, AIS Association for Israel Studies. Conference, Israel, June 2007.

Feldman, Yael, "Isaac or Oedipus? Jewish Tradition and the Israeli Akedah", en *Biblical Studies/ Cultural Studies*, edited by J. Cherul Exum and Stephen D. Moore, *Journal for the Study of the Old Testament Supplementary Series*, nº 262, pp. 174-184.

Goldberg, David Theo y Krausz, Michael (editors), *Jewish Identity*, Filadelfia, Temple University Press, 1993.

Gouri, Chaim, "Heritage", en T. Carmi, ed., *The Penguin Book of Hebrew Verse*. Penguin Books, 1981, p. 565.

Herman, Simon N., *Jewish Identity: A Social Psychological Perspective*, New Brunswick, Transaction Publishers, 1988.

Heschel, Abraham, *Les bâtisseurs du temps*, Paris, Éditions de Minuit, 1957.

Heschel, Abraham, *The Sabbath: Its Meaning For Modern Man*, New York, Farrar, Straus and Giroux, 1975.

Horowitz, Irving Lou s, "Minimalism or Maximalism: Jewish Survival at the Millenium", in Ernest Krausz and Gitta Tulea, editors, *Jewish Survival*, *The identity problem at the close of the Twentieth Century*, New Brunswick, Transaction Publishers, 1988, pp. 1-17.

Johnson, Paul, *A History of the Jews and A History of Christianity*, New York, Harper Perennial, 1988.

Kierkegaard, Søren, *Temor y temblor*, Madrid, Tecnos, 1987.

Krausz, Ernest (editor), *Sociology of the Kibbutz (Studies of Israeli Society)*, New Jersey, Transaction Publishers, 1983.

Kristeva, Julia, *Historics de Amor*, México, Siglo Veintiuno Editores, 1987.

Leibowitz, Nejama, Parashat Bereshit, *A la imagen de Dios*. From "Reflexiones sobre la Parasha", published by the Department of Education and Religious Culture for the Diaspora, of the World Zionist Organiztion, Jerusalem, 1986, pp. 9-13.

Lesser, Jeffrey y Rein, Raanan (eds.), *Rethinking Jewish-Latin Americans*, New Mexico, University of New Mexico Press, 2008.

Lesser, Jeffrey y Rein, Raanan, "Nuevas aproximaciones a los conceptos de etnicidad y diáspora en América Latina: la perspectiva judía", *Estudios Sociales*, Buenos Aires, nº 32, 2007, pp. 11-30.

Lévinas, Emmanuel, *Difficile Liberté*, LGF - Paris, Livre de Poche, 2003.

Liebman, Charles S. y Cohen, Steven M., *Two Worlds of Judaism: The Israeli and American Experiences*, Yale University Press, 1990, p. 13.

Linzer, Norman, "The Changing Nature of Jewish Identity" *Journal of Jewish Communal Service* 72-3, New York, March 1996.

Linzer, Norman, "Comparing American Jewish Identity with Israeli Jewish Identity", *Journal of Jewish Communal Service*, 77:1, New York, Jewish Communal Service Association of North America, Berman Jewish Policy Archive, 2000, pp. 36-44.

Maalouf, Amin, *In the Name of Identity: Violence and the Need to Belong*, Nueva York, Arcade Publishing, 2000.

Medam, Alain, *Mondes Juifs: L'envers et L'endroit*, Paris, Presses universitaires de France, 1991.

Memmi, Albert, *Portrait of a Jew*, New York, a Viking Compass Book, 1971.

Mendes-Flohr, Paul (editor), Reinharz, Jehuda (editor), *The Jew in the Modern World: A Documentary History*, Oxford University Press, 1995.

Neher, André, *L'existence juive*, Paris, Seuil, 1962; 5th re-edition, 1990, pp. 38-42.

NEHER, ANDRÉ, *Le dur bonheur d'être juif*, Paris, Le Centurion, 1978.

NEHER, ANDRÉ, *Regards sur une tradition*, Paris, Bibliophane, pp. 11-13, 1989.

Pirkei Avot (Words of the Fathers).

PORZECANSKI, RAFAEL, *El Uruguay judío, demografía e identidad*, Montevideo, Ediciones Trilce, 2006, p. 61.

PORZECANSKI, TERESA, *Vida privada y construcción de la identidad: inmigrantes judíos al Uruguay*, Montevideo, Trilce, 2002.

PORZECANSKI, TERESA, *Historias de la vida privada en el Uruguay*, under the direction of José Pedro Barrán, Gerardo Caetano, Teresa Porzecanski, Montevideo, Taurus, 1998.

PORZECANSKI, TERESA, *Historias de vida de los inmigrantes judíos en el Uruguay*, Montevideo, Kehila-Israelite Community of Uruguay, 1986.

RAICHER, R.P., "Judíos sefaradíes en el Uruguay", in *Hoy es Historia*, nº 8, Montevideo.

RAICHER, R.P., *Uruguay, la comunidad israelita y el pueblo judío*, Montevideo, Universidad de la República, 1985.

ROBIN, RÉGINE, *L'amour du yiddish: écriture juive et sentiment de la langue, 1830-1930*, Paris, Le Sorbier, 1982.

SAGI, AVI, "The Meaning of the Akedah in Israeli Culture and Jewish Tradition", *Israel Studies*, 3.1, Indiana University Press. Indiana, spring 1998.

SCHNAPPER, DOMINIQUE, "Les juifs et la nation", in Pierre Birnbaum, ed., *Histoire politique des juifs de France*, Paris, Presses de la Fondation Nationale des Sciences Politiques, 1990, p. 298.

SCHNAPPER, DOMINIQUE, *La condition juive en France: la tentation de l'entre-soi*, Paris, PUF, 2009.

SHOLEM, GERSHOM, *The Curious History of the Six Pointed Star; How the "Magen David" Became the Jewish Symbol*, Commentary, 8, 1949, pp. 243-251.

SIMON, SHERRY, "Mémoires en partage", *Voix et Images*, vol. 34, n° 1, (100) 2008, pp. 33-41. http://id.erudit.org/iderudit/019402ar

SOSIS, RICHARD Y RUFFLE, BRADLEY J., "Life, Ideology, Religion, and the Evolution of Cooperation: Field Experiments on Israeli Kibbutzim", *Socioeconomic Aspects of Human Behavioral Ecology, Research in Economic Anthropology*, Elsevier Ltd., Oxford, Near, H., 1992, edited by Michael Alvard, vol. 23, 2004, pp. 89-117.

TSUR, MUKI, "Pesach in the Land of Israel: Kibbutz Haggadot", *Israel Studies*, Indiana University, Indiana, July 2007, vol. 12, nº 2, pp. 74-103.

TSUR, MUKI AND YUVAL, DANIEL, editors, "Going Forth in the Month of Spring", *The Kibbutz Haggada - Israeli Pesach in the Kibbutz*, Jerusalem, 2004, in Hebrew.

WETTSTEIN, ED HOWARD, *Diasporas and Exiles, Varieties of Jewish Identity*, University of California Press, 2002.

WIESEL, ELI, *Messengers of God: Biblical Portraits and Legends*, Random House, New York, 1976.

 museogurvich

Gurvich Museum

Founder and Advisor
Julia Añorga de Gurvich

Director
Martín Gurvich

Executive director
Silvia Listur

Financial director
Sylvia Barriola

Human Resources
Joaquín Ragni

Archive and library
Ana Guerra

Administration
Marcel Loustau

Gift shop and Reception
Alicia Murillo

Promotion
Josefina Giucci

Security
Daniel Gularte

Maintenance
Eduardo Molina

Honorary members
Aninat, Isabel
Cadenas, Enrique y Teresa
Campos, María Estela
Castillo, Jorge
Castillo, Martín
De Francesco, Hugo
De Torres, Cecilia
Elsztain, Eduardo y Mariana
Grosskopf, Sergio y Raquel
Manhard, Enrique y Viviane
Prato, Oscar
Quarrato, Norma
Stainfeld, Jorge y Miriam
Werthein, Darío
Winter, Jackie

Sponsor:
Ministry of Education and Culture
Culture Board

Under the auspicies of:

with collaboration of: